The Angel and the Beehive

The Angel and the Beehive

The Mormon Struggle with Assimilation

ARMAND L. MAUSS

University of Illinois Press
Urbana and Chicago

Manufactured in the United States of America

C 5 4 3 2 1

This book is printed on acid-free paper.

Library of Congress Cataloging-in-Publication Data

Mauss, Armand L.

The angel and the beehive : the Mormon struggle with assimilation / Armand L. Mauss.

p. cm.

Includes bibliographical references and index.

ISBN 0-252-02071-5 (alk. paper)

1. Mormons—Cultural assimilation—United States. 2. Church of Jesus Christ of Latter-day Saints—United States—History. 3. Mormon Church—United States—History. I. Title.

BX8643.C84M38 1994

289.3′0973—dc20 93-11328

CIP

To my mother, Ethel Louise Lind,

who taught me to love learning

for its own sake

&

to my father, Vinal Grant Mauss,

for whom new ideas, however challenging,

were more to be welcomed than feared

Contents

Preface

History suggests that the overwhelming majority of religious movements fail to survive even one generation, to say nothing of enduring across the centuries. A religious movement that survives for nearly two centuries then, as has Mormonism, may offer the scholarly investigator some clues about what makes for the success and survival of some movements but not others. Not that there is any lack of literature on the religious movements of history, including those which have arisen in North America, although, as Rodney Stark (1987) has pointed out, scholars have tended to give more attention to explaining (or explaining away) the failed religious movements than to understanding the durability of the successful ones.

For the Mormon movement too, we have seen the emergence of a rich historical literature, especially during the past two or three decades. Yet most of that literature has emphasized the first century of Mormonism over the more recent period and historical description over sociological analysis. We have not seen much application of theoretical frameworks from social science that might explain either the development of the Mormon movement itself or how well that development fits with theories about the evolution of new religious movements.[1]

Implicit in much of the extant literature is the theory (such as it is) that the unpopular Mormon movement, having failed in a desperate nineteenth-century struggle for religious and political autonomy, finally achieved success and respectability in North America by abandoning its most offensive practices and deliberately pursuing a policy of assimilation with the surrounding American culture. Such a perspective is, of course, accurate enough in the main, and it certainly accords well with the classical Weber-Troeltsch predictions about the assimilation of new religious movements as they are transformed from "sects" to "churches."

Yet there is much more to the story. Mormons in the United States largely achieved respectability as a church by midcentury, but the assimilation of the Mormon movement has not continued apace as traditional theories have predicted. In many ways the past few decades have witnessed an increasing reaction of the Mormons against their own successful assimilation, as though trying to recover some of the cultural tension and special identity associated with their earlier "sect-like" history. It is this retrenchment mode among Mormons of more recent decades that is the main theme of the present book.

It is important to emphasize, however, that this work is not intended as a systematic modern history of Mormons or Mormonism, but rather as an application of theoretical ideas in an effort to help interpret general historical developments. Many of these developments have already been identified and documented by historians, though here they will be augmented considerably by primary data and evidence original to this specific study.

I have set out these theoretical ideas in part 1 of this book. Chapter 1 offers the reader a general overview and demonstrates the links between these ideas and some more general and abstract concepts in the sociology of religion.

Part 2 focuses on the "Americanization" of the Mormons in North America. Chapter 2 reviews briefly the well-known history of that assimilation process. Chapters 3 and 4 draw upon original survey data to demonstrate just how fully assimilated Mormons had become by the middle of the twentieth century, not only in secular, civil matters but even in most religious beliefs and practices. Chapter 5 considers to what extent, and in what ways, Mormons ought still to be regarded as a people apart, a "peculiar people." Are Mormons really a kind of "ethnic group" (like the Jews), as some observers think, or have they already become too highly assimilated for such a designation?

Part 3 considers the Mormons' reactions to their own successful assimilation. The erosion of Mormon peculiarity, or distinctiveness, during the first half of this century has left a certain feeling of uneasiness or "blurred identity" among the Mormons. The church leaders have reacted to this feeling with various forms of retrenchment, in effect trying to call the Mormons back to their heritage as a truly distinctive people with a unique message. At the grass-roots level, the reaction has not been so clearly focused, but it has included for some Mormons a tendency toward a kind of "fundamentalism," an effort to demonstrate to themselves and to others that Mormons can and ought to exemplify a special posture and life-style of austerity, scriptural literalness, and unquestioning obedience to leaders. Such a reaction, ironically, gives some of today's Mormons a religious style that bears more of a resemblance to that of Protestant fundamentalists than to that of their own nineteenth-century Mormon forebears.

Chapter 6 opens part 3 with a general overview of the retrenchment argument, drawing evidence and illustrations from recent Mormon history. Chapter 7 takes this theme into some depth with two specific case studies of the official press toward retrenchment, namely the changing uses of the King James Version of the Bible and the hardening of the Mormon political posture against certain national trends. Chapter 8 draws upon recent survey data to examine the religious, political, social, and life-style attitudes of contemporary Mormons, with direct and indirect comparisons to what the earlier surveys had revealed. In this chapter we will be able to see to what extent the retrenchment motif in the church leadership has been reflected at the grass roots.

Chapter 9 goes beyond the issue of retrenchment to review contemporary Mormon religiosity more generally, with comparisons again both to the contemporary American religious scene and to the Mormon past. Chapters 10 and 11 examine the emergence of the new Mormon fundamentalism, a religious outlook that attempts to define anew the distinctive Mormon boundaries by resorting to extremes in both the content and the style of being Mormon. Finally, Chapter 12 will summarize my argument and my findings and then offer some prognostications about the future of Mormonism as it approaches the twenty-first century, particularly in light of its continuing struggle for a distinctive American identity, on the one hand, and its increasingly successful penetration of other cultures of the world, on the other hand.

This work is the product of a decade of thinking, research, and writing; and segments of it have already appeared in print. The earliest crystallization of the general idea came during the preparation of an invited lecture under the auspices of the Charles Redd Center for Western Studies at Brigham Young University in November 1982. In many ways, however, the inception of this work is to be found much farther back in my own intellectual and spiritual biography.

I am a third-generation Mormon, born in Salt Lake City and reared in California (both southern and northern), starting in the depression years.

My understanding and my feelings about institutional Mormonism as I grew up were, of course, mediated through the Mormon folk and leaders whom I knew in California. These were unpretentious and unsophisticated folk, largely of farm and working-class origins, but open, adventurous, and upwardly mobile. They had, after all, left the "bosom of the Saints" in Utah to seek their fortunes in cities where there had never before been any Mormons to speak of.

The "outside world" presented both opportunity and temptation to these migrating Saints, so they had to be wary. Yet the social boundary between insiders and outsiders was more often drawn by the non-Mormons than by the Mormons, who were regularly called upon to account for their religious peculiarities. Inside the Mormon community, however, everyone, even the occasional maverick, found acceptance. New ideas seemed welcome, learning and achievement were praised, and the rare intellectual (always self-made) was respected, as long as it was clear that he or she was essentially an insider in sentiment. People felt close to God and often shared stories of spiritual experiences, either personal or vicarious. Church callings or positions in the lay ministry were regarded as sacrifices, not sinecures; burdens, not badges of prestige.

During my visits with friends or relatives back in Utah during those years, the church had a different "feel" there; it felt more powerful and secure, to be sure, but also more smug, complacent, parochial, rigid, and intolerant. In the intervening years, Mormon community life along the West Coast has come increasingly to "feel" more like Utah did then, while Utah itself has perhaps become even more so. The different feel of Mormonism today is partly the subject of the present book. This aspect of my thinking is, of course, very personal, subjective, and autobiographical. It would not necessarily be valid for all other Mormons who grew up on the West Coast, even in my generation, but I suspect that it carries a familiar ring for many other California Mormons of my day.

Yet I have tried very hard not to let my own nostalgia, the idealization of my own past, intrude unduly into my scholarly detachment. In my more analytical moments, I know that organizations have to change, especially as they grow large and complex, and not in all ways for the better. I know too that I have changed much during the past half century, and perhaps not for the better in every respect. Whatever the reasons, the fact remains that I have come to feel increasingly marginal to the Mormon community during my adult life, at least in a social and intellectual sense, despite my continuing and conscientious participation in church activity (including leadership), and despite my own deep personal faith in the religion itself. As much as anything, then, this book is an effort to help me understand my own changing relationship to the Mormon institutions and people. Perhaps it will thus have special meaning to others who have experienced similar migrations to the margins, but I hope it will enhance the understanding of everyone who reads on.

Note

1. Throughout this book the term "Mormon" (or alternatively "LDS") refers to the Church of Jesus Christ of Latter-day Saints or to members thereof.

Acknowledgments

Any scholarly effort is likely to be the synthesis and product of ideas, criticisms, and suggestions gathered from a number of colleagues, collaborators, and assistants. This work is no exception. First and foremost, I am grateful to the University of Illinois Press for accepting this work for publication and to its editorial staff, particularly Elizabeth G. Dulany, for seeing it through the editorial process with such great care. A major consideration in the Press's acceptance of the manuscript was, of course, the favorable reviews it received from two referees, Wade Clark Roof of the University of California, Santa Barbara, and James B. Allen of Brigham Young University. The latter, in particular, subjected the manuscript to two rounds of critical review, and I'm sure that my efforts to accommodate his critiques greatly strengthened the final product. Certain parts of the work, which appeared earlier in published articles, had also been subjected to the review of peers who remain anonymous to me but are nevertheless much appreciated. While the contributions of all these colleagues are greatly valued, I cannot ask them to share any of the responsibility for the weaknesses that inevitably remain in this book.

As the thinking for this project gradually developed over a decade or more, I benefited greatly from fortuitous events that occurred at certain important junctures in my intellectual life. In 1982, I was invited by the Charles Redd Center for Western Studies at Brigham Young University to give a lecture as part of its annual series. The title for this book, as well as its general argument, were originally set forth in that lecture, so I shall always be deeply grateful to the Redd Center for its sponsorship at a strategic moment. In 1985, during a sabbatical leave at the University of California, Santa Barbara, I met M. Gerald Bradford, who was then managing the financial affairs of the Hutchins Center for the Study of Democratic Institutions and teaching in the Department of Religious Studies at UCSB. He provided me with some badly needed office space and other resources at the Hutchins Center. Perhaps even more important, he joined me in a fruitful collaboration that produced a publication on the changing Mormon political posture, parts of which comprise one of the case studies in chapter 7.

Not long thereafter, I came across another stimulating collaborator in Philip L. Barlow, whose extensive research on the changing Mormon uses of the King James Bible made possible another joint publication, parts of which comprise the other case study in chapter 7. Finally, parts of chapter 5 come from a lecture that I was invited to present at a conference of the Canadian Mormon Studies Association at Edmonton, Alberta, in 1987 and that was later published by the University of Alberta Press as part of an edited collection from that conference. Other bits and pieces of my work have been presented before numerous study groups and symposia and have occasionally also appeared in print. All such opportunities to present my ideas contributed greatly to my evolving opus, and I feel much indebted to those responsible for these opportunities. Yet these earlier fragments do not constitute a major portion of the book, the overwhelming majority of which appears here in print for the first time.

The following publishers have graciously given permission for the portions published earlier to be integrated into this more comprehensive work, and I hereby acknowledge their generosity with gratitude:

Paragon House, New York, for permission to include in chapter 7 some excerpts from Armand L. Mauss and M. Gerald Bradford, "Mormon Assimilation and Politics: Toward a Theory of Mormon Church Involvement in National U.S. Politics," pp. 40–66 in *The Politics of Religion and Social Change*, edited by Anson Shupe and Jeffrey K. Hadden, vol. 2 of the Religion and the Political Order Series, © Paragon House Publishers, 1988.

Dialogue: A Journal of Mormon Thought for permission to include in chapters 2, 6, and 8 a few of the paragraphs that appeared in Armand L. Mauss, "Assimilation and Ambivalence: The Mormon Reaction to Americanization," 22 (1): 30–67, © Dialogue Foundation, 1989.

University of Alberta Press, Edmonton, Alberta, for permission to include in chapter 5 some of the material that appeared in Armand L. Mauss, "Mormons as Ethnics: Variable Historical and International Implications of an Appealing Concept," pp. 332–52 in *The Mormon Presence in Canada*, edited by B. Y. Card, H. C. Northcott, J. E. Foster, Howard Palmer, and G. K. Jarvis, © University of Alberta Press, 1990.

Sociological Analysis: A Journal in the Sociology of Religion (recently renamed *Sociology of Religion*) for permission to include in chapter 7 some excerpts from Armand L. Mauss and Philip L. Barlow, "Church, Sect, and Scripture: The Protestant Bible and Mormon Sectarian Retrenchment," 52 (4): 397–414, © Association for the Sociology of Religion, 1991.

Rutgers University Press was kind enough to give permission gratis for the inclusion in chapter 9 of Figures 6–1, 6–2, 6–3, and 6–4 taken from Wade Clark Roof and William McKinney, *American Mainline Religion: Its Changing Shape and Future*, © Rutgers, the State University, 1987; and Charles Y. Glock kindly granted me permission to include in chapters 3 and 4 some of the figures from his unpublished codebook for his and Rodney Stark's 1963 northern California survey. Expert and indispensable assistance in the processing and analysis of my own Mormon survey data from the 1960s was rendered by Julie C. Wolfe Nelson while a former student of mine some years ago at Washington State University.

Last but not least, I am grateful to Manfred Heim for repeated careful and critical readings of the entire manuscript and for the preparation of a rather comprehensive index for the book.

PART I

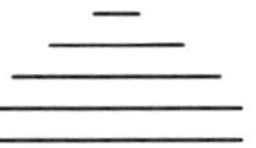

The Mormons as a Religious Movement

CHAPTER ONE

The Mormon Movement in Metaphor and Theory

In the center of Salt Lake City, on either side of Main Street, two important traditional Mormon symbols confront each other: the angel on the temple spire and the beehive atop the roof of the Hotel Utah. In its usage among Mormons, the beehive seems originally to have represented the word *deseret* from the Book of Mormon, but it has since come to be considered primarily as a symbol of worldly enterprise throughout the Mormon heartland. The symbol will be used here in a somewhat expanded sense to represent all aspects of Mormon involvement with the world, cultural as well as economic. Indeed, in its identification with one of the most elegant hotels in the country, the beehive suggests not merely business enterprise but also the aesthetics of the world, and more generally the sense of accommodation and comfort with the ways of the world that one enjoys while sitting in the ornate hotel lobby.[1]

The angel, on the other hand, represents the other-worldly heritage of Mormonism, the spiritual and prophetic elements, the enduring ideals and remarkable doctrines revealed through the Prophet Joseph Smith and passed down as part of a unique and authentic Mormon heritage. To use a term that has gained popularity in recent years, we might say that the angel represents the charismatic element in Mormonism. Ideally there is no conflict between the influences represented by the angel and by the beehive, for Joseph Smith taught that there was no distinction, ultimately, between the spiritual and the temporal or material and that, in any case, it was up to us to subordinate worldly things to spiritual imperatives.[2]

However, the influences of the angel have always had to contend with the influences of the beehive in Mormon history. This is but the Mormon counterpart of the age-old struggle of "Christ against culture" in the rest of Christianity. Indeed, a recurring and depressing theme in both the Bible and the Book of Mormon is the eventual triumph, in all previous ages, of the ways of the world to the final detriment of God's people. Perhaps we are entitled to wonder, then, if there is anything portentous about the diminishing visibility of the angel as Temple Square in Salt Lake City is increasingly surrounded and obscured by modern high-rise office buildings.

The Typical Fate of New Religious Movements

In many ways, the rise of the Mormon movement on the American frontier 170 years ago can serve as a prototype for new religious movements of all kinds, but particularly for those (like "Moonies" or "Hare Krishnas") that begin as conspicuously deviant and unpopular (Beckford, 1985; Hampshire and Beckford, 1983). The appearance of such a new religious or social movement, like an invasive organism, presents a challenge to the normative order of the surrounding host society. This challenge will be the more serious, of course, the more militant and deviant the movement is; and survival itself might of necessity initially preoccupy the new movement. That so many new movements of all kinds fail to survive even one generation testifies clearly enough to their usual fragility. Much interest by sociologists is thus focused on what factors make the difference between those few movements that survive and prosper and the great bulk of the others that disappear rather early (Moore, 1986; Stark, 1987; Wilson, 1987).

If survival is the first task of the movement, the natural and inevitable response of the host society is either to domesticate the movement or to destroy it. In seeking to domesticate or assimilate it, the society will apply various kinds of social control pressures selectively in an effort to force the movement to abandon at least its most unique and threatening features. To the extent that the society succeeds in this domestication effort, the result will be the eventual assimilation of the movement. Failing to achieve sufficient domestication, the host society will eventually resort to the only alternative: persecution and repression.

The logical extreme of either of these two societal responses (assimilation or repression) is, of course, oblivion for the movement. In what might be called the "natural history" of the interaction between radical social movements and their host societies, there seem to be no historical exceptions to the proposition that new movements must either submit to assimilation in important respects or be destroyed.[3] Of course, the process is bilateral, and entire societies themselves often experience profound changes while assimilating powerful social movements; but that is another subject.

Movements which, like Mormonism, survive and prosper are those that succeed in maintaining indefinitely an optimum tension (Stark and Bainbridge, 1985; Stark, 1987) between the two opposing strains: the strain toward greater assimilation and respectability, on the one hand, and that toward greater separateness, peculiarity, and militance, on the other. Along the continuum between total assimilation and total repression or destruction is a narrow segment on either side of the center; and it is within this narrower range of socially tolerable variation that movements must maintain themselves, pendulumlike, to survive.

If, in its quest for acceptance and respectability, a movement allows itself to be pulled too far toward assimilation, it will lose its unique identity altogether. If, on the other hand, in its quest for uniqueness of identity and mission, it allows itself to move too far toward an extreme rejection of the host society, it will lose its very life. Its viability and its separate identity both depend upon a successful and perpetual oscillation within a fairly narrow range along a continuum between two alternative modes of oblivion.

At any given point in time, then, a movement is grappling with either of two predicaments: If it has survived for some time as a "peculiar people" (in the biblical phrase), conspicuously rejecting the surrounding society and flexing the muscles of militancy, then it will begin to face the predicament of disrepute, which invites repression and threatens not only the movement's success but its very existence. In dealing with the predicament of disrepute, the movement typically begins to modify its posture and to adopt selectively those traits from the surrounding culture that will make it more acceptable to the host society. Just which traits are selected will be contingent, in part, on the movement's own ideology, on its own internal political struggles, on its resources, and on other variables, not just on sheer expediency.

After a movement has achieved some success through this strategy of purposeful accommodation, however, it will soon find itself in the opposite plight: the predicament of respectability. Now the movement has taken on so many traits of the surrounding culture that it is not readily distinguishable from the establishment. Accordingly, its very identity as a separate people is in jeopardy. At this point, a different strategy becomes necessary: the movement must begin to invent, or to select from the surrounding social environment, a set of traits that will allow it to lay credible claim once again to uniqueness in identity, values, folkways, or mission.

As the movement succeeds in thus reasserting its peculiarity, it will move back again toward the earlier predicament of disrepute, and the cycle begins again. To complicate matters, every time the movement switches direction, it must contend with the endemic internal tendencies toward schism and defection (apostasy), for different kinds of individual needs among the members are satisfied (or threatened) by different forms and degrees of tension with the surrounding society. Theories of social psychology have taught us that people tend to commit themselves to those causes for which they are required to sacrifice to some degree (Festinger, 1957; Kanter, 1972). A religion that achieves greater comfort or respectability in a society, therefore, does not necessarily enhance thereby the commitment of its members at the individual level.

The Broader Theoretical Picture

Those who are acquainted with classical sociological theory will recognize immediately that the above description of alternative predicaments is a variation of the "sect-to-church" transition explicated by Ernst Troeltsch (1931), a disciple of Max Weber, in his study of the history of Christianity. This scheme has since been elaborated and variously applied by others (e.g. Iannaccone, 1988; Benton Johnson, 1957, 1963, 1971; Niebuhr, 1929; Stark and Bainbridge, 1985; Swatos, 1979; Bryan Wilson, 1990; and Yinger, 1970). In general, this concept is a kind of natural history model which postulates that new religions typically begin as schisms (or "sects") from older ones that have grown worldly and comfortable with the surrounding culture (i.e., have become "churches").

Sect founders and converts tend to be somewhat less successful in worldly terms and more needful of other-worldly demands, hopes, and promises, which their "mother church" has all but eliminated from its preaching as the price of rapprochement with the world. Alas, however, it is only a matter of a few generations before the new sect, with its austere and disciplined life-style, also comes to enjoy a degree of worldly improvement and is thus itself largely assimilated. As it becomes increasingly churchlike, it begins to spawn still other schismatic sects, and the cycle starts again.

A typical element in the assimilation process seems to be the upward social mobility and growing affluence of the later generations of sectarians, who begin to find the religious zeal of their ancestors primitive and unsophisticated. More recently, Stark and Bainbridge (1985) have suggested that "cults" (which they define as imported or spontaneous—like the Mormons—rather than schismatic), if they survive, follow the same general pattern toward gradual assimilation and increased respectability within the surrounding culture. Cults, however, do not necessarily begin with constituencies from the lower socioeconomic strata, as most sects do.

Whether or not they attract the dispossessed and unsophisticated, however, new sects and cults typically begin in a state of high tension with their host societies and cultures; that is, they promote ideologies, requirements, and life-styles among their members that are noticeably deviant from those of the surrounding normative environments. From this point of view, one way of understanding the evolution from sect (or cult) to church is to describe it as a transition from a high-tension religion to a low-tension one within the host society.

Many new sects and cults, of course, simply fail to make this transition, in which case they are likely either to be snuffed out by external hostility or to remain arrested indefinitely in a sectarian posture (Stark, 1987; Bryan Wilson, 1987; Yinger, 1970). If they do survive and develop, however, conventional theory predicts a generally unilinear evolution from sect (or cult) to church as the price for survival. The pace of evolution might be faster or smoother for some movements than for others; there might be zigs and zags (Swatos, 1979); and even reversibility has been allowed for theoretically (Benton Johnson, 1971:131); but the expected pattern has always been unidirectional and, for classical sociology, predictable (but see Harper and LeBeau, 1993, for a recent reformulation).

The Mormon Anomaly

While more than one empirical anomaly to this pattern might be cited, it was Thomas F. O'Dea (1954, 1957) who first recognized an anomaly in the Mormon case. Writing at midcentury, O'Dea argued that the Mormons had retained enough sectlike traits that they could not yet be considered as a "church" in the sociological sense. Yet they had also managed to avoid the "sectarian stagnation" often befalling those "established sects" whose development was arrested short of significant assimilation. O'Dea's observations were somewhat premature: They were based mainly on the Mormonism prior to World War II, barely two generations removed from Utah's acceptance as a state, with a membership concentrated in the Rocky

Mountain area of North America. Even by then, however, the Mormons had moved far from the "incipient nationality" O'Dea had attributed to their turn-of-the-century grandparents, and Mormon "Americanization" was still proceeding apace (Alexander, 1986b; Hansen, 1981; Lyman, 1986; Shipps, 1985). The Mormons would continue assimilating for some time, and the real anomaly was yet to come.

It has now come in the form of a reversal of evolutionary direction, a partial retrenchment, back toward a more sectlike posture accompanied by some increase in tension with the rest of North America. It is as though the Mormons spent the first half of the twentieth century striving to become more like Episcopalians, only to reverse course with the approach of the twenty-first century and begin emulating the Southern Baptists instead. This process, of course, challenges the unilinear and unidirectional predictions of the classical sect-to-church continuum; but it accords with a striving toward optimum tension. Such might seem an anomaly to traditional social science, but it also has much to do with continued Mormon growth; for the implicit contention of the theory advanced here is that a religious movement must strategically reverse course from time to time as a condition of meaningful survival and success.

Much depends, of course, on how one defines "success." It is a paradox in the sociological literature (noted in Mauss, 1993) that most social reform movements are considered "successful" to the extent that their ideologies, reform programs, and membership are embraced by the political and cultural establishment. Yet religious movements are considered successful to the extent that they avoid the assimilative embrace of the surrounding society and maintain a degree of tension with it. In other words, success in the one case involves the loss or erosion of a separate identity through assimilation, while in the other case success requires the maintenance indefinitely of a separate identity (Stark, 1987).

This principle seems to have been recognized, at least implicitly, not only by the Mormon leadership but also by leaders and factions in other denominations now struggling with cultural compromise, on the one hand, and the resurgence of fundamentalism, on the other (e.g., see Ammerman, 1987, 1990, for the Southern Baptists; Poloma and Pendleton, 1989, for the Assemblies of God; Furman, 1987, for the Jews; and—for even the Catholics—Kennedy, 1988; and Seidler and Meyer, 1989).[4] For at least two decades, ever since Dean Kelley's (1972) discovery that the more conservative religions seemed to be growing at the expense of the more mainline (assimilated) ones, sociologists of religion have recognized that the maintenance of optimum tension with the surrounding society is a major determinant of the survival and growth of any religion. To understand why this is so, we must move down from the macrosocial level of discussion to a more social-psychological level.

Sectarian Tension and Religious Commitment

High-tension religions tend to distinguish themselves from the world by drawing moral boundaries against the encroachments of the outside culture. These boundaries are likely to express themselves internally in member discipline entailing various forms of sacrifice, self-denial, and personal investment. Why do people join and remain in religions that make such demands and that evoke ridicule, suspicion, hostility, and stigma from the surrounding society? One explanation is that such a religion's institutional identity is internalized by the individual member in the form of a clear and satisfying personal identity, as in the case of Hassidic Jews (Shaffir, 1978). Without the moral boundaries, the demands for personal investment, and the distinctive (even stigmatizing) traits of a sect or cult, its members do not enjoy a clear and separate identity at the individual level.

In addition, both historical and laboratory data point to a natural human strain toward "cognitive consistency" (Festinger, 1957), or, in other words, a tendency to strive for consistency among cognitions and between cognitions and behavior. Contrary to the conventional wisdom that behavior is simply the concrete expression of ideas, cognitive consistency research has shown that the reverse can also be true: Ideas and values that are discrepant from behavior tend to be changed so as to conform to behavior and to justify it. Thus, people who, through social networks or for other reasons, become involved in new religions will come increasingly to bring their ideas and values into consistency with their newly acquired religious activity and behavior. Indeed, they will come to love what they must sacrifice for. In this process, they will be assisted by a "plausibility structure" consisting of their new coreligionists amongst whom they negotiate their new constructions of reality (Berger and Luckmann, 1966).

More recent theorizing has supplemented this explanation. Rosabeth Moss Kanter (1972), in a comparative study of historical utopian experiments (religious and otherwise), identified several key "commitment mechanisms" successfully employed by those utopian groups that enjoyed the greatest longevity and growth. These consisted simply of various demands made by the communities for individual sacrifice, investment, conformity, and transcendental commitment as conditions for continued membership. Kanter seemed to recognize, but only in passing, the convergence of her organizational functions with the psychological functions identified in cognitive consistency theory. She apparently did not recognize the convergence of all such theorizing with the earlier "exchange theory" of George Homans (e.g., 1974; see also Emerson, 1976). Borrowing ideas and analogues from microeconomics, exchange theorists understand behavior as products of one or another kind of "exchange," in which persons invest commitment, energy, and resources in the expectation of a material or nonmaterial "return."

The most recent explanation of the relation between sectarian tension and individual commitment is to be found in the work of Rodney Stark and his colleagues, which subsumes the ideas developed above into a more comprehensive framework focused particularly upon the sources and maintenance of religious commitment (Finke, 1989; Finke and Stark, 1988, 1989, 1992; Iannaccone, 1988, 1990, 1992; Stark and Bainbridge, 1985; Stark and Iannaccone, 1991). In an explicit appropriation of the "market" concept, this explanation identifies the transcendental values and rewards of the "other world" as the chief "products" of religion. The promise of such products will provide the incentives that must accompany the strong demands typically made upon sect and cult members.

To the extent that the members feel confident in eventually obtaining these products, they will sacrifice much for their faith. Concomitantly, the more they sacrifice, the more dependent they will become upon the rewards offered by their religion. The more "costly" such products, in terms of member sacrifice, investment, and stigmatization, the more "valuable" they become. Of course, religious organizations, like all human institutions, also offer worldly benefits like social acceptance, conviviality, and identity; but it is the other-worldly benefits that are the unique products of religion.

Wherever a religious market is not controlled by the state, varied religious products for various sectors of the market will always be in some demand. Such will be the case especially in modern societies, where secular values have largely displaced the traditional, transcendental ideologies that once offered some meaning for endemic human suffering and failure. To the extent that a religion becomes a church, reduces its other-worldly emphasis, and merely competes with secular institutions in the products it offers (or the "causes" it embraces), it cannot make costly demands on its members; and it cannot compete successfully with those religious sects and movements offering other-worldly rewards and products on the market in exchange for member sacrifice and investment. Secularized and low-demand religions also typically suffer from some proportion of parasitic "free riders," but in more demanding religions these are driven off by the relatively high costs of membership. (A valuable critique of such "economic" explanations for this religious behavior will be found in Bruce, 1993.)

This line of theorizing goes far toward explaining the counterintuitive discovery of social scientists that those religions that emphasize unfalsifiable, transcendental, and other-worldly benefits are also those that attract and retain the most committed members. It also helps to account for religious zeal and commitment without resort to facile and simplistic "explanations" reflecting upon the socioeconomic status or mental health of the believers. From this theoretical framework, we can understand much about the historic appeal and success of Mormonism and of other religions that have taken an unpopular, high-tension posture vis-à-vis the surrounding society and yet have elicited high levels of investment from numerous converts. We can see also why continued Mormon success depends in large part on its recent partial retrenchment and reversal of the evolution toward reduced tension and assimilation with American society.

Locale, Tension, and Assimilation

It is important to remember that locale helps to determine how sectlike or churchlike a religion may seem, both to the outside establishment and to the membership on the inside. The Roman Catholic church is much more "churchly" in Rome (or even Boston, Massachusetts) than it is in Lexington, Kentucky, or in Tokyo, Japan. Similarly, the Mormon church is much more churchly in its far west heartland (especially in Utah) than it is in Mississippi or in Germany. Richard Bushman has informally suggested three historical stages in U.S. Mormon migration and settlement during the twentieth century: the pioneer stage, the settlement stage, and the entrenchment stage. His overview seems useful here not only as a description of historic reality for American Mormons but also as typical, at least in general outline, of the process that can be expected to characterize Mormon growth and settlement in any given locale as the church continues to expand around the world.[5]

In the pioneer stage (starting about World War I for American Mormons outside the Mountain West), a local branch or congregation would consist of a few local converts plus two or three western Mormon families, fairly well educated, who had been attracted to professional positions "out in the mission field." The mixture of the "locals" and the "imports" presented both advantages and disadvantages. On the one hand, the western imports brought experience with church doctrines and procedures (especially important given the Mormon dependence on a lay ministry); their education and professional positions, furthermore, tended to give them a certain amount of influence with the local civic establishment, once they settled in, which they could use to promote Mormon interests. On the other hand, their superior education and western ways made them culturally different from the locals and created a certain amount of strain, especially when (as was often true) they were made church leaders "over the heads" of local converts, some of whom had been stalwarts in the face of adversity for many years.

With or without such a contingent of westerners, the church program in these missions was highly truncated and depended heavily upon the work of missionaries (also sent from the West, of course). The congregations rarely had buildings of their own.[6] With such small numbers, individual persons were important. Everyone's service and contributions were desperately needed, so that eccentrics and mavericks (usually local converts) were tolerated with more or less sincere good nature. Unfortunately, individual personalities could also prove destructive: an interpersonal feud could split and immobilize a small struggling branch.

The settlement stage, for most American Mormons outside the West, began with the World War II (somewhat later for Mormons in Europe and elsewhere). The youthful volunteer missionary corps of the church expanded enormously during the postwar period, with a corresponding harvest of new converts. Also, a great many more western Mormons moved east in search of advanced education and business or professional opportunities. Accordingly, the sheer number, sizes, and stability of local Mormon branches or congregations throughout the country increased greatly, especially in the more urban areas.[7]

Organizationally, mission branches gradually began to be transformed into regular "wards" and clustered into "stakes," the traditional Mormon designations for large, permanent congregations and dioceses, respectively, where the general church program could then be more or less fully implemented. Both growth and transiency made for a lot of turnover in membership from year to year, but such no longer threatened the permanence or viability of the Mormon presence. Financed mostly by the headquarters in Utah, new Mormon churches were built rapidly, symbolizing the new Mormon permanency and permitting the Saints finally to move out of rented halls for Sunday services.

The old tension between western imports and local converts remained but was somewhat mitigated by a shared predicament—namely, the problem of trying to adapt to local circumstances the church policies and programs that had been created in Utah and the sense that local needs and situations were not sufficiently appreciated by the Utah leaders in church headquarters. Local bishops and other leaders found it difficult to keep the lay leadership positions staffed, so many of the Saints had to take more than one calling (church job). Willing individuals, even if not fully orthodox, remained highly valued.

The surviving converts from the pioneer period, often lovable eccentrics, were appreciated as exhibits of devotion and endurance, but they were usually shunted aside from real leadership positions by younger and perhaps better-educated converts and westerners who were not in a position to appreciate the lore and history of the old struggling branches. Yet those who had originated in the West never felt quite at home, and there was (and still is) a tendency for them to return to the West, so that their children could more easily marry within the church or so that they could retire in more familiar surroundings.

Finally, in the entrenchment stage, the local Mormon wards and stakes strongly resemble those of Utah in size, in demographic traits, and in the fullness and complexity of their organization and programs. They are likely also to be quite heterogeneous; that is, those who have migrated in from outside the local area are no more likely to have come from the West than from anywhere else, so the tension between westerners and others, seen in the two earlier stages, has largely disappeared. Church members might think of Utah as the Rome or Mecca of their faith, but they do not identify with it so strongly as in earlier stages, nor do they think of their own wards as being on the periphery of the church. They identify instead with their own local temple, or they aspire to have one if it has not yet been built. They tend to think of their local area as home and are not so likely to move to the West, even for retirement.[8]

In relationships with the outside, Mormons in the entrenchment stage are, of course, much more highly assimilated than in the two previous stages. Not only are Mormon communities as a whole quite visible in the local area, but Mormons are well integrated into the local business, professional, and political establishments (though rarely at the pinnacles). As such, they help to bring a certain respectability to their religious community as a whole, and they can be instrumental in helping the church acquire real estate or in mobilizing support and goodwill of various kinds when needed.[9]

Implications of Locale for Religious Culture

The implications of Bushman's above typology suggest certain hypotheses or theoretical expectations about the varying nature and quality of Mormon religious life in the three situations. First and most obvious is the expectation that the Mormon experience involves decreasing tension with the surrounding society across the three stages. At any given time and place, then, the nature of Mormon religious life is a product partly of the effort by the denomination as a whole to find the optimum tension between the two polar predicaments and partly of the local Mormon community's own stage of development. Some of the conflict in the first two stages between the local congregation and the denominational hierarchy might, indeed, be understood as a consequence of the effort from headquarters to impose churchlike policies upon more sectlike situations.

Second, tolerance for marginality and deviance can be expected to decrease from one stage to the next. By the time a congregation reaches the entrenchment stage, it does not need to strive with its mavericks, and it can afford the luxury of sidelining or even formally excommunicating them. In part, this tendency represents an effort at boundary maintenance, for it is at the third stage (entrenchment) that the Mormon community begins to have trouble defining its unique identity. Enforcing cultural and moral boundaries seems more important. Every case of ostracism thus becomes a statement about boundaries and identity, a less necessary process in the two earlier stages, where the boundaries tend to be maintained as much by the surrounding non-Mormons as by the Mormons themselves.

Third is the implication for the position of women from one stage to the next. Only men and boys are ordained in the Mormon lay priesthood. Yet there are many auxiliary positions, some of considerable importance, that do not require holding the priesthood. Though the male leadership might have equally strong patriarchal proclivities across all three stages, one can expect the value and power of women to diminish from the first to the third stage. In the earlier stages, especially the first one, women are much needed for all kinds of church service. However, in the third stage, the membership is large enough that men can almost always be found for the most important roles. Accordingly, women can be shunted off into the less visible and less powerful auxiliary roles.

Fourth is the implication for the demands accompanying membership and leadership in the church. These can be expected to diminish from the first to the third stage. In the pioneer stage, there are so many church jobs, so few people to hold them, and so much distance to travel to carry them out (or even to get to meetings), that the demands placed upon members and leaders are very time-consuming. Everyone is needed, and that is a major reason for the greater acceptance of women and mavericks in responsible church positions. This also means that members accepting church jobs, especially the most important ones, are likely to accept them more out of religious commitment or obligation than out of a quest for power or prestige in the church community. In social-psychological terms, this means that church service is more "costly" to the individual at the earlier stages, which helps to explain the special zeal that is so often observed among members in areas where church strength is not as great as in Utah.

In the third stage, however, as in Utah, many more members are available for church tasks and leadership, so in a sense these become more "competitive." Yet, most church jobs are apt to require a less total commitment of time and self than in a small struggling branch, so the "cost-benefit ratio" of a church leadership role is more favorable. Accordingly, in the third stage, we can expect aspirations for power and prestige to play a larger part than in earlier stages, relative to religious commitment per se, in the acceptance of church leadership positions. This does not mean, of course, that Mormon bishops, stake presidents, and Relief Society presidents are not still very busy people, but it does mean that they stand to enjoy more prestige for less sacrifice, both in and out of Mormon circles, than did their predecessors in the earlier stages of church growth and development.[10] For a young professional to be made a Mormon bishop thus can be not only a heady experience but also the beginning of a long and gratifying avocational church career accompanied by considerable family pride (and the possibility of an eventual "second career" in full-time church leadership at the highest echelons).

Summary

Although the United States has constitutionally maintained a relatively open "religious market," American society has historically sought to assimilate new religious movements or else to repress and destroy those which remained too deviant to assimilate. New religions that have survived beyond a generation or two have thus typically lost much of their distinctiveness in the process of assimilation. The Mormon religion presents an anomaly to this pattern. Since about midcentury, a partial reversal of the assimilation process can be seen in a deliberate church policy of retrenchment. This policy is expressed in different degrees and in different ways in different locales. Yet the overall purpose seems to be the recovery of Mormon institutional distinctiveness, which had partially eroded during the first half of the century, and the renewal of a clear Mormon identity at the individual level. Contemporary theory in the sociology of religion would interpret these developments as enhancing the vitality and the future prospects of the Mormon religion by seeking for the optimum level of tension with American society.

Notes

1. The Hotel Utah, long owned by the church, was recently renovated and converted to offices, a visitors' center, and other church uses and renamed the Joseph Smith Memorial Building. The ornate lobby, however, remains.

2. On this point, see Doctrine and Covenants 29:31–35, McMurrin (1969:1–8), and O'Dea (1957:chap. 6).

3. For further elaboration and empirical demonstration of this point, see Mauss (1971). Of course, some social movements result in revolutions that totally displace existing regimes, but reference here is to the more common and less radical outcomes of social movements.

4. There is recent evidence that Roman Catholicism in the United States is moving back toward the pre–Vatican II posture of a "counterculture," according to the periodical newsletter *Religion Watch* (Feb. 1993), published by Richard P. Cimino in North Bellmore, New York. In this issue of the newsletter, Catholic publications of both a liberal bent (*National Catholic Reporter*) and a conservative bent (*Crisis*) are quoted about a growing perception among Catholics of a need to resist assimilation, rebuild a sense of Catholic community, and recover a disappearing Catholic identity vis-à-vis secular American society. For a somewhat different but generally compatible alternative interpretation of the Catholic predicament, see Kowalewski, 1993.

5. A profitable correspondence between Bushman and me on this matter is found in my personal files: his letter to me of Sept. 10, 1989 (in response to an earlier query from me); my response and proposed elaboration on his ideas in a letter of Sept. 18, 1989; and his response again to me of Sept. 24, 1989. While the three-part scheme discussed in this chapter has been borrowed from Bushman, he is not responsible for the sociological implications I have drawn from the three kinds of conditions.

6. A common "war story" from that era was the regular need each Sunday morning for early arrival at the rented Moose Lodge, or similar facility, so that the beer bottles and cigarette butts from the previous night's partying could be cleaned up before church services.

7. The U.S. West Coast would perhaps best exemplify this stage of development, especially after World War II, but so might the Washington, D.C., area (see full-page spread on D.C. Mormons in the *Washington Post*, May 16, 1992).

8. Note that a temple for Mormons is not an ordinary house of worship but a regional center for administering the most advanced and esoteric Mormon rites. Construction of a temple signifies a relatively large and durable Mormon presence in the immediate region.

9. Much about the above description of typical differences from one of these three stages to another, including the changing nature or quality of the Mormon experience, is nicely exemplified in a recent collection of personal remembrances about an LDS mission community in Maryland that finally became a full-fledged ward of the church in 1981 (with Richard Bushman, interestingly enough, as the new bishop); see Taber (1992, 1993).

10. This generalization might seem odd to anyone who knows how hard most Mormon bishops and other leaders work, no matter where their congregations. The point here is not that bishops today necessarily devote less time to their callings. It is simply that they have considerably less responsibility and autonomy than did their predecessors in earlier generations, especially in the more settled and entrenched areas of the church. Many functions once in the purview of local bishops have been increasingly centralized into the hands of regional and general echelons of the church bureaucracy, many of whom are paid, professional civil servants and thus not even ecclesiastical officers, as such. Fund-raising, the maintenance of church buildings, and various social and psychological services are among those responsibilities no longer done on a local basis. Record keeping is centralized, and all local bishops are given computers and standardized software from church headquarters for receiving and transmitting the necessary data. Even many of the strictly pastoral functions traditionally expected of bishops have been turned over to local "quorum leaders," who are now supposed to be the chief watchmen over the flock. Of course, in any situation, some bishops will work harder and assert more initiative than will others, but in general the scope of their responsibilities is much more constrained than in earlier generations. Also, since modern Mormon bishops tend to be recruited from the ranks of corporate business, their postures toward their congregations are often more managerial and distant than pastoral.

PART 2

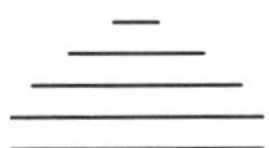

The Mormons as an Assimilated American Subculture

CHAPTER TWO

Mormons as a Case Study in Assimilation

While the theoretical pattern of oscillation between the two predicaments could probably be applied with some success to the entire history of the Mormon movement, it seems especially useful for understanding the transformations of the twentieth century.[1] As this century began, Mormons faced the predicament of disrepute to an extreme degree. The relative isolation of Utah during the entire second half of the nineteenth century had made possible the unrestrained development of the angel motif: The Mormons, under their own prophetic inspiration and leadership, had self-consciously cultivated institutions, both religious and secular, that were uniquely their own. Divinely inspired or not, the Mormon religion and way of life projected a national image of an un-American, even anti-American, insurgent counterculture (Arrington, 1968; Bitton and Bunker, 1978, 1983; Cannon, 1974; Davis, 1960).

The Predicament of Disrepute and the Quest for Respectability

The mood of the country was pretty well summed up by the 1879 Supreme Court ruling in *Reynolds*, which finally outlawed polygamy: The First Amendment, it said, guaranteed freedom of religious belief, but not necessarily freedom for any sort of practice or behavior (Firmage and Mangrum, 1988). A society can tolerate only so much "peculiarity" and no more, even in the name of religion. By the 1890s, the increasing repression from American society produced the desired result. As a condition for obtaining Utah statehood, and for enjoying peace and national toleration more generally, the Mormons were required to give up polygamy, theocracy, collectivist economic experiments, and any other flagrantly un-American institutions, and thus to abandon the path of charismatic peculiarity, except at the relatively abstract level of theology. Symbolically enough, the seal of the new state of Utah carried the logo of the beehive, not the angel (Lyman, 1986).

From the turn of the twentieth century on, this reversal was reflected in deliberate church policy, which was conspicuously assimilationist in most respects, at least for the first half of the century. Yet there was much to live down, and for decades the Mormons still struggled with the predicament of disrepute. How were they to achieve respectability in the face of almost universal national contempt? That question was answered by an astonishing success story (Alexander, 1986b; Shipps, 1985). With the consistent encouragement of church leaders, Mormons became models of patriotic, law-abiding citizenship, sometimes seeming to "out-American" all other Americans. Their participation in the full spectrum of national social, political, economic, and cultural life has been thorough and sincere, not only at the grass-roots level but also in the persons of many prominent leaders in national institutions.

Few American subcultures have realized the American Dream as fully or rapidly as have the Mormons. By midcentury, Mormons had risen in socioeconomic status from the very bottom among American religious denominations to the middle-class ranks, and, since then, to virtual parity with such high-status denominations as the Episcopalian and Presbyterian (Roof and McKinney, 1987:110). The point, though, is not that twentieth-century Mormons have necessarily been more preoccupied than their forebears with material things but only that they have become more successful in material terms, relative to the rest of the nation, and thus have begun to acquire a greater stake in the surrounding socioeconomic system than ever before.

The church itself, as a corporate entity, set the example starting early in the century. It has become awesomely involved since then in the American capitalist marketplace and in the rough-and-tumble of American politics (Gottlieb and Wiley, 1984; Mauss and Bradford, 1988; Robertson et al., 1991). Church publications have regularly featured as models for emulation a variety of accomplished Mormon figures who have achieved notoriety in government, business, athletics, music, arts, entertainment, and other fields, especially if they are inclined to credit their Mormon roots for part of their success. Such cases are sometimes summarized also in the biennial *Church Almanac* (see Deseret News, 1984:15–16, 306–13).

Church leaders at the general, regional, and local levels came increasingly during the century to be drawn from the ranks of prestigious professions, such as business, law, and education, especially if they had been successful in worldly terms. For example, a tabulation from the 1985 *Church Almanac* reveals that about a third of the general authorities at that point had come from the world of business administration and another third from law; the next largest category was educational administration (as opposed to the scholarly segment of academia), and the remainder came from medicine, dentistry, engineering, and miscellaneous other fields (Deseret News, 1984:18–37).

The system of governance evolving in the church began to be based far less upon the individual prophetic initiative of a Joseph Smith or a Brigham Young and far more upon the collective, collegial, and bureaucratic model usually associated with large corporations. While much of this bureaucratic development has been an inevitable concomitant of sheer growth, of course, the effect of it still has been to produce another kind of convergence with the corporate world. This has been even more true since the advent of the "correlation movement" aimed at greater organizational centralization and standardization in the church (Gottlieb and Wiley, 1984; Johnson, 1979; Tarjan, 1990; Woodworth, 1987). The church public relations enterprise has grown enormously in size, scope, and importance. The approval of the world has been courted not only through a growing corps of clean-cut young missionaries but also with the Mormon Tabernacle Choir, mass-market magazine ads, films, and television ads and specials (D'Arc, 1989; Editors of *Dialogue*, 1977; Fletcher, 1982; Lythgoe, 1968; R. A. Nelson, 1977; Stathis, 1981).

All of these involvements with the world have carried the constant risk of compromise with the teachings of the angel. Most forms of such compromise creep in so gradually that they are scarcely noticed. It eventually became obvious, however, that if the church were to own hotels and other businesses, then it would have to keep many of them open on Sundays, contrary to its own sabbatarian teachings. In some of those businesses, it would have to serve beverages that church members are enjoined not to drink. If the church is to own radio and television stations with major network affiliations, then they will sometimes have to carry ads for products that the Saints have been taught not to use or to carry both music and "adult" programs that church leaders have urged the Saints to avoid.

The point of all this, one hastens to add, is not that all involvements with the world of the beehive are subversive, for the Saints have always been counseled to embrace the good wherever they find it. Much that is in the world is fully harmonious with traditional Mormon values. Nor, for that matter, are all worldly borrowings materialistic in nature; they might even come from the other religions of the world, as, for example, have many LDS hymns, or from such wholesome secular sources as the Boy Scouts of America. The point is only that the Saints have not always been clear about where those culture traits have been acquired that are now such a conspicuous part of the Mormon way of life. Did they come from the angel or from the beehive, from within the Mormon heritage or from outside? And if from the beehive, then from what sorts of blossoms did the bees take their nectar? In whatever ways we might answer those questions, it does appear that the Mormon movement, even by midcentury, had coped well with the predicament of disrepute and has since then gone considerably farther toward achieving American respectability.

Signs of Assimilation within the Corporate Church

While assimilation is sometimes accomplished in part by increasing tolerance and other changes within the host society, it usually requires much more change on the part of the deviant movement itself. Some of that change takes the form of renunciation of especially controversial claims or characteristics. Though we scarcely need documentation for the extent of the Mormon renunciation of polygamy, of theocracy, or of economic communitarianism, recent scholarship has shed a great deal of light not only upon the forms of such renunciation but also upon the ideological and organizational evolution that has accompanied them (Alexander, 1986b; Gottlieb and Wiley, 1984; Lyman, 1986; Shepherd and Shepherd, 1984; Shipps, 1985).

The historical record of the general assimilationist thrust within the institutional church is far too extensive to encompass within this one chapter, but I can at least cite convincing samples from the scholarly literature of the many forms and dimensions of the process. Shepherd and Shepherd (1984), for example, have traced the assimilation process through the changing rhetoric in general conference sermons. They found, among other things, a steady decline after the late nineteenth century in such uniquely Mormon themes as Zion and kingdom building, eschatology, missionary work, the apostasy of other churches, the restoration, the corruption of outside governments, and the like. By contrast there was an increase during the same period in such assimilationist themes as the greatness of American institutions, patriotism, good citizenship, and fel-

TABLE 2.1. Changes in General Conference References to Separatist Mormon Themes

Themes	1830–59	1860–89	1890–1919	1920–49	1950–79
	Decreasing in Saliency after 1889				
Apostasy of Christianity	.030	.022	.019	.008	.007
Enemies of the Church	.060	.051	.035	.005	.002
Non-Mormons	.038	.068	.001	.000	.000
Church public image	.004	.008	.034	.005	.002
Plural marriage	.003	.079	.020	.007	.000
The last days	.036	.051	.025	.010	.011
Second Coming	.025	.020	.025	.006	.008
Millennium	.005	.005	.006	.000	.003
	Increasing in Saliency after 1889				
United States of America	.003	.004	.008	.012	.007
U.S. wars	.005	.004	.018	.015	.006

SOURCE: Compiled from Shepherd and Shepherd (1984), appendix C.

NOTE: Decimal figures here and in subsequent tables taken from the Shepherd and Shepherd data are *saliency scores* based on the proportions that the various themes constitute of all general conferences thematic references. Thus, the larger the scores the greater the relative saliency in the given time period. The figures might seem small in themselves but are quite meaningful in terms of the metric system on which they are based. See Shepherd and Shepherd (1984), appendix A, for an explanation of this system.

lowship with other faiths. The following excerpts from their work are illustrative (see table 2.1).

A similar trend toward accommodation and assimilation can be seen during the same historical period in Mormon hymnody (Hicks, 1989). Successive official hymnbooks during the first half of the twentieth century not only included increasing proportions of hymns "borrowed" from mainstream Protestantism but the words for even the classical LDS hymns were toned down to reduce the amount of peculiarly Mormon referents and militancy (e.g., in "Praise to the Man," about Joseph Smith, "long shall his blood . . . stain Illinois" became "long shall his blood . . . plead unto Heaven"). The increasing Mormon emphasis early in the century on the use of the Bible, particularly the King James Version, might be understood as part of the same process (Barlow, 1991).

Important doctrinal and ritual developments during the first half of the twentieth century were also consistent with this overall assimilationist trend in the corporate church. Alexander (1980, 1986b) has shown how the church doctrines on deity were codified early in the century to eliminate some of the chaos and some of the more outrageously "innovative" or heretical ideas that had characterized Mormon discourse on deity during the nineteenth century, such as the so-called "Adam-God" theory (Buerger, 1982). The official auspices and widespread dissemination of Talmage's *Jesus the Christ* can be understood as part of the same process of standardizing the LDS concepts of deity and Christology. While some uniquely Mormon ideas are obviously important in that book, its portrayal of the Christ was heavily influenced by prevailing Victorian theories in mainstream Protestant scholarship of the time (Thorp, 1988). The same trend during the same general period can be seen in the changes made in the temple endowment and undergarment, which rendered the Mormon temple experience somewhat less strange to the uninitiated (Alexander, 1986b:291–303; Buerger, 1983, 1987; Mauss, 1987).

The effort to bring the church into mainstream American life during the earlier part of this century was also reflected in the auxiliary organizations, beginning with the almost immediate adoption of the new national Boy Scout program in 1913 (Alexander, 1986b:144–45). Contemporary ideas and practices from the secular social welfare professions were introduced into the women's Relief Society, some of whose general officers during this period were known and appreciated in the church for their expertise and encouraged by church leaders to maintain contacts and collaboration with outside professionals (Alexander, 1986b:128–36; Derr et al., 1992; Hefner, 1982; Mangum and Blumell, 1993).

The Mutual Improvement Association (MIA) for the youth became almost an extension education program for the church by the mid-1930s, offering not only training in the arts, in drama, and in forensics but also lessons on the important social and ethical issues of the day, authored by noted church professionals and intellectuals (Alexander, 1986b:140–46; Kenney, 1978, 1987). Individual scholarly experts were often commissioned to write the lesson manuals for the Relief Society and the Sunday school, too (Alexander, 1986b:138–40; Christensen, 1987).[2] To all appearances, then, the social gospel movement abroad in the general Protestantism of the time was making its inroads in Utah, as well (Alexander, 1983, 1986b).

With the appointment of Franklin S. Harris as president of Brigham Young University, an effort was made to upgrade and enhance the respectability of that school as a legitimate institution of higher learning in the eyes of the nation (Christensen, 1987; Bergera and Priddis, 1985). A new religious education program of seminaries and institutes was inaugurated to help the youth of the church articulate and integrate their religious faith with the worldly learning which they were starting in large numbers to seek (Bennion, 1922). For a few years, prominent non-Mormon biblical scholars and theologians were brought to Utah during summers to instruct the faculties of the seminaries and institutes in the latest theological scholarship of the Protestant world (Lowry Nelson, 1985).

In a few cases, the church even sent away some of its own promising young scholars on stipends to seek advanced degrees in prominent centers of learning such as the University of Chicago in the expectation that they would return and bring to the church educational system some of the worldly professional credibility it was then lacking (Arrington, 1967; Sherlock, 1979; Swensen, 1972). To be sure, there was much ambivalence and some controversy among the presiding brethren about the wisdom of these and similar developments (Sherlock, 1979), but it seems clear enough that they were manifestations of the quest for respectability in the spirit of the beehive motif.

The religious education curriculum and textbooks reflected this commitment to a scholarly approach during those early years, even at the high school level. A good example would be the 1922 seminary textbook on the New Testament, *Outlines in Theology: New Testament Dispensation*, which was prepared by LDS seminary teachers themselves (under Superintendent—and later Apostle—Adam S. Bennion) during a 1921 summer school session at BYU. This textbook was based partly on the historical work of an English professor of ecclesiastical history at King's College, London. Its references included eight works identified for high school students as their "minimum library" and ten others as "recommended." These eighteen references included both LDS works (by, e.g., Talmage and McKay) and non-LDS works such as Dummelow's *Commentary*, Farrar's *Life of Christ* and *Life of St. Paul*, and Edersheim's *Life and Times of Jesus*.

The 1936 edition of Berrett's *The Restored Church* for high school students was comparably rich fare, embodying considerable non-LDS scholarship on American religious history and referring students both to non-LDS works and to rather weighty LDS works like B. H. Roberts's six-volume history of the church, Lucy Mack Smith's biography of her son Joseph the prophet, William Clayton's journal, and Tullidge's life of Brigham Young. Nor did this textbook in Mormon history for young minds shy away from controversial issues: It candidly acknowledged elements in the social environment of Joseph Smith's time and place that would have facilitated the spread of his ideas (including early American ideas about Native Americans); the unusual methods of "translation" used by Smith for the Book of Mormon and the errors in that translation; the understandable motivations of the non-Mormon enemies of the church in Illinois; the Mountain Meadows massacre; and many other controversial issues in Mormon history. Subsequent editions of the book attenuated this candor to some extent, but the book was used for several decades in the high school seminary system of the church.[3]

Signs of Assimilation at the Grass Roots

The first few decades of the twentieth century brought a time of great ferment for Mormons. The changes initiated by the leadership, which have been only superficially reviewed above, must have been mind-boggling for some of the Saints. In addition, the arrival of World War I presented an occasion for a more thorough reintegration of Utah with the rest of the nation in a common war effort. During and after that war, in particular, an outmigration of young people from Utah both contributed to the ongoing Mormon reintegration with America and led to the establishment of major Mormon outposts on the two American coasts. One social historian characterized this process as a hemorrhaging of Utah's "lifeblood" (Morgan, 1958:474; Meinig, 1965), but the emigrating young Mormons did well for themselves: Utah soon assumed (and maintained) top ranking among the states in the proportion of its men who achieved advanced academic degrees and professional eminence across the land (Thorndike, 1943; Hardy, 1974).

It would be fascinating to have had Gallup-type pollsters who could have surveyed Mormons at the beginning of this process and again later to determine the nature and extent of changes in Mormon grass-roots thinking about both religious and secular matters. In the absence of any such systematic data, we can still see signs that religion at the folk level was starting the kind of demystification process that we would expect of a people increasingly engaged with the world. One indicator was an apparent decline during the early decades of the century in the frequency with which traditional Mormon folktales circulated (such as Three Nephite stories) and concomitant modifications of those stories to fit more modern circumstances (William Wilson, 1988).[4]

Another indicator could perhaps be seen in the changing nature of certain ritual activities where grass-roots initiative (as opposed to ecclesiastical structure) could have freer rein. Knowlton (1991) is undoubtedly correct about the various functions of "testimony bearing" among the Mormons, including the ritual function. For generations, Mormons have been accustomed to the monthly "fast and testimony meeting," which people are expected to attend after a fast of at least two meals so that they might be more susceptible to the power of the Holy Spirit. Then, individually and in turn, as moved by such spiritual influences, they are encouraged to stand in the congregation and bear testimony.

The memories of many Mormons still living, together with diaries and proceedings from earlier days, all indicate that these testimony meetings often took on strongly charismatic overtones. It was common for individuals to testify about their own firsthand spiritual experiences and in other ways to validate each other's certainty about the "truth of the restored gospel" by bearing solemn witness to their own certainty, received through the promptings of the Holy Spirit. Only rarely would there be episodes of glossolalia, but testimonies about miraculous healings were common. Stories about the Three Nephites and about other miraculous encounters with spiritual beings were sometimes attested to.

Modern Mormon testimony meetings are certainly bland by comparison. Still monthly events, they nevertheless are carefully timed, since they occur as part of a series of three meetings, each allocated about one hour, so that the series can be finished in three hours. Long testimony meetings cannot be permitted, since they would encroach on the time required for the other meetings. Although the testimonies are presumably individual products, they nevertheless have acquired a strongly formulaic nature (Knowlton, 1991). For one thing, the prevailing theme of most modern testimonies has become one of gratitude rather than of personal witnessing itself.

To be sure, gratitude is an admirable sentiment to be expressed, but it is not at all the same as personally testifying to spiritual, ontological certainty about Mormonism or Mormon doctrines. Another common feature that once was uncommon is the involvement of small children in testimony bearing, often at the instigation of parents or of Sunday school teachers who, in effect, require all the children in a given class to participate, thereby marshaling peer pressure as well as other kinds of pressure. Some of these children are toddlers who can scarcely reach the pulpit or even have to be held by their parents while they speak. Following parental examples, these little ones tend to limit their "testimonies" to expressions of gratitude for Mommy and Daddy and the bishop. However valuable an experience it might be for little children to become accustomed to the pulpit early in life, the ritual in which they are engaging bears no relation to the proceedings of the early Mormon testimony meetings.

During one entire year (1974), I classified and tabulated the major themes of the testimonies expressed each month in an eastern Washington ward of some 500 members. Of 178 such testimonies, including children's, 167 were preoccupied with expressions of gratitude, primarily gratitude for the family or for family members. To be sure, some of the gratitude expressed was for the gospel or the church (38 cases), or for other church members and workers (33 cases), but the theme almost exclusively in these cases was still gratitude, not personal testimony to spiritual truth. In a few cases, the dominant theme was, indeed, a testimony, and in 66 cases a passing or perfunctory spiritual testimony was included in a delivery dominated by gratitude. In a third of the cases, no testimony at all was expressed, even implicitly or in passing. The average length of the testimonies was five minutes, with a testimony of ten minutes or more being very rare. For many children, of course, their testimonies lasted only seconds.

Since this little "survey" took place in the seventies and in only one ward, it is not really comparable, of course, with any earlier compilations known. It also comes from the seventies, rather than the thirties, so it would have to be understood as representing a much longer period of devolution in the Mormon testimony-bearing ritual than we would have seen with thirties data. Yet the direction of the devolution can be assumed from the end point represented by the 1974 findings, a trend that has continued during the past two decades. Although representing only the one Mormon ward, the same general pattern would almost certainly be confirmed by any informed observer of Mormon religious life, at least in the American West.

The general outlines of the assimilation process traced in this chapter have long been understood from the extensive work of many historians, including those who have been cited here. Somewhat less well recognized, perhaps, is the supportive evidence from sociology and anthropology I have introduced into this historical overview, such as the work of Shepherd and Shepherd on changing general conference themes, William Wilson on changing folklore twists, and Knowlton and myself on testimony bearing. There is yet another important observation inspired by the sociological theory of Stark and colleagues introduced in the previous chapter: As new religions are assimilated and thereby lose some of their tension with the surrounding culture, they tend to generate schisms or sects made up of disciples seeking to recover some of the lost tension. As might be expected, then, Mormonism generated a few sects focused on either polygamy or communitarian living (or both) even in the first half of the twentieth century (Baer, 1988; Hardy, 1992; Van Wagoner, 1986); but since 1960, probably the high point in assimilation, Mormonism has generated more sects than it did during the entire century prior to that year (tabulated from Shields, 1982). Utah, furthermore, has achieved the second highest rate of new sect formation in the nation (Stark and Bainbridge, 1985:145), an interesting "hidden cost" of the assimilation process.

Notes

1. As a sketch of how the same general pattern might apply to the nineteenth century, one could think of the New York, Kirtland, and Missouri years as especially innovative ones symbolized mainly by the angel. This period (1827–39) saw major political and economic experiments and increasing militancy in Mormon behavior (not just in rhetoric). The repressive response of the civil establishment, especially in Missouri, was quite understandable (though in retrospect the severity of that response certainly seems excessive). By comparison, Nauvoo represented a more successful accommodation in line with the beehive motif until the secret of polygamy became public. Up until 1844, at least, Mormons participated extensively in the normal political and economic life of Illinois and of the nation but had to make a number of worldly compromises. Thereafter, the combination of martyred prophets, a succession of crises in the leadership, a forcible expulsion from Illinois, and a grueling trek across the wilderness produced a collective trauma expressed in Utah's studied rejection of American society from the mid-1840s until the mid-1890s. The angel motif was thus again brought to the fore, as new and deviant arrangements in the name of religion flourished in the political, economic, and family realms. Again, the repressive response from American society was inevitable. The historian R. Laurence Moore (1986:31–32) has observed that this mutual rejection and hostility served certain political, psychological, and other interests of both the Latter-day Saints and the scandalized nation. Mormons, he says, frequently advanced their claims "in the most obnoxious way possible," while both sides seemed to go to some lengths "to stress not what Mormons had in common with other Americans, which was a great deal, but what they did not have in common." It was, of course, the reversal of this emphasis after the 1890s that brought back the beehive motif and the assimilation process.

2. Often these authors were top church leaders who could combine the authority of office with the authority of scholarship in the manuals they produced. See, for example, the 1927 MIA manual by Apostle John A. Widtsoe, "How Science Contributes to Religion," cited in Paul (1992:chap. 7).

3. I discovered these books among the possessions of my aunt Ruby Stauffer of Salt Lake City, who was kind enough to call them to my attention. She had used the New Testament book herself as a seminary student in high school.

4. The "Three Nephites" refers to one of the best-known folk legends in Mormon culture, based upon a passage in the Book of Mormon (3 Nephi 28:7) in which three of Christ's disciples in ancient America were promised that they would not "taste death" until his Second Coming but would linger to minister in various special ways to the inhabitants of the earth. Mormon tradition is replete with stories of such special ministrations and miraculous interventions of one or more of these Three Nephites, who suddenly appear to resolve serious crises and then suddenly disappear. See, for example, Fife (1940), Fife and Fife (1981), and William Wilson (1988).

CHAPTER THREE

Mormon Religious Beliefs at Midcentury

Surveys as Data Sources

The brief review of Mormon assimilation in the previous chapter dealt with the corporate or institutional level, where the evidence is fairly easy to trace in the historical record. It is not so easy to trace changes across time in the minds of people. Sometimes we can follow changes in individuals from diaries, journals, and letters kept during their lifetimes; but how do we learn about general or average changes in populations, or at least in cross sections of populations?

In recent decades, social scientists have developed a survey technology, based upon interviews, questionnaires, or both, with representative samples (or "cross sections") of entire populations. This technology has gradually become rather highly refined by well-known professional organizations like Gallup and the National Opinion Research Corporation (NORC), as well as by many university-affiliated research centers and institutes. Just what constitutes a truly "representative" (or otherwise appropriate) sample is always an important issue in any survey. Professionals who forecast the outcomes of important elections have often demonstrated an uncanny precision in their predictions with national samples of only about 1,500 respondents, when such samples are carefully drawn with certain key population traits and locales in mind.

Careful surveys can tell us much about what a given population is thinking and feeling on certain questions at a given point in time. If we want to know how the thinking of that population changes across time, we can either survey the same sample at different points in time in a "longitudinal" study or we can periodically survey the same population with different samples in a series of cross-sectional "taps," or studies. The longitudinal approach is probably the more accurate, but it is also very complicated and expensive, so it is not often undertaken. More common, even for Gallup or NORC, is the periodic cross-sectional survey with different (but presumably highly comparable) samples of the same general population.

Any kind of sampling can be quite complicated and expensive. To be truly "representative" in accordance with statistical theory, a sample must be drawn strictly "randomly," which does not mean the same as "haphazardly." A random sample is a given fraction of the population drawn on a systematic basis. As an illustration, if one wanted a random 10% sample of all the people in a given telephone book, one would simply choose every tenth name. (Such would not, incidentally, give one a random sample of all the people but only of those with telephones and listed telephone numbers.) Sometimes it is necessary first to divide a population into segments, or strata (say, by race), and then draw the samples separately for each segment (otherwise there might be an insufficient number of black respondents, as an example). Besides such stratified random samples, there are many other variations on the issues of randomness and representativeness that need not concern us here.

Because it is often impossible, as a practical matter, to get full access to a given population for truly random sampling, many surveys are conducted with samples that are less precise or systematic. Some such samples might be defensible as reasonable approximations to representativeness, especially if they are quite large and contain at least some degree of randomness. Others might be strictly "opportunity" samples, meaning just whatever is available. However a sample is put together, if it is not truly random or systematic, the researcher carries some burden of argument in defending the sample as at least "typical" or "not unrepresentative in any known ways" or "purposive" (drawn for a specific purpose not necessarily requiring randomness). Samples drawn in these ways might still be very useful, even if the survey results must be cautiously interpreted.

Early Surveys on Mormons

Corporate or institutional changes are fairly easy to trace, but changes at the individual level across a population are much harder to gauge. Survey data from the 1960s, the apex of their assimilation, will give us at least a close approximation to the grass-roots thinking of Mormons. By this time, all of the major institutional and doctrinal accommodations of the Mormon church to mainstream America had been achieved, except, of course, for the race issue that was then only starting to become a Mormon public relations problem (Bush and Mauss, 1984: chap. 1).

The church during the fifties and sixties was led by President David O. McKay, a prophet with an image and reputation for outreach, humanitarianism, patriotism, relatively liberal thinking, and a conciliatory approach to all kinds of conflict. (In these respects, he was the Mormon counterpart of his Roman Catholic contemporary, Pope John XXIII.) Partly through his efforts, furthermore, the Mormon church had been enjoying a level of favorable coverage in the mass media that was historically unprecedented (Lythgoe, 1968). Yet how much did Mormons resemble their American neighbors in their actual thinking about religious and social issues?

To get some meaningful answers to this question, we can turn to data collected from three surveys of Mormons in Utah and in California between 1964 and 1969:[1] (1) a 1964 survey of Mormons in three wards covering an entire suburban area of several hundred square miles lying about thirty miles northeast of Oakland, California (N = 249); (2) a 1967–68 survey based on a systematic random sample of Salt Lake City Mormons (N = 958); (3) and a 1968–69 survey of Mormons living in two wards comprising the entire eastern half of the city of San Francisco (east of Golden Gate Park—the most diverse and transient part of the city—N = 296).[2]

The two California samples quite clearly fall into the "settlement" pattern discussed in chapter 1, but they, in turn, represent two different modes of settlement. The 1964 East Bay suburban sample would be the more "normal" of the two, since it was comprised mainly of families more or less typical in age, in occupational distributions, and in other demographic traits. Spatially or ecologically, this sample was distributed across an area that included both newly settled suburbs and small towns on the suburban fringe. The latter had just begun to become bedroom communities for nearby Oakland and San Francisco but were still largely inhabited by more traditional small-town folk.

By contrast, the later San Francisco sample had a disproportionately large component of young, single, transient types living in downtown apartments and working in secretarial and other clerical jobs. Taken together, the East Bay and the San Francisco samples would offer a fairly typical mix of the Northern California Mormons of the sixties, so for some purposes they are combined in the tables that follow.

These cross-sectional surveys will not, of course, permit longitudinal comparisons—no longitudinal samples exist on Mormons starting in that time period and virtually none do for any later periods. These surveys from the sixties, however, provide important and enduring benchmark data that can be used as a basis for comparison in any later surveys of Mormons conducted in urban Utah or in the California Bay Area. Also, fortunately, directly comparable data are available that were collected from representative samples of Protestant and Catholic church members in the California Bay area during the same period. These data come from the extensive survey of Charles Y. Glock and Rodney Stark conducted through the Survey Research Center of the University of California during 1963 and 1964.[3]

What the Surveys Say about Mormon Religious Assimilation

While *assimilation* may be given a variety of sociological definitions, some of them rather technical, it is being used here in the simple dictionary sense: the process by which one people (in this case, Mormons) come to be similar to another (in this case, other religiously affiliated Americans). The survey data do not really permit us to study the process as such but only to assess the similarities or differences between the two peoples at a certain point in time. Implicit is the assumption that Mormons at an earlier time were less similar (assimilated) than they had become by the sixties. We seem to have solid enough historical grounds for such an assumption, given the documentary and observational data surviving from earlier generations (e.g., Arrington, 1958; Arrington et al., 1992; Leone, 1979; Logue, 1988; Lowry Nelson, 1952; O'Dea, 1957; Vogt and Albert, 1966).[4] For example, table 3.1, based on a similar one from Stark and Glock (1968:28), shows the extent of Mormon similarity to others in levels of belief in God.

The ten denominational groups in the original Stark and Glock table arranged themselves in a continuum of increasing levels of orthodox belief, with the Congregationalists (Cong) as the least orthodox (on average), the Southern Baptists (SoBap) as the most orthodox, and the Presbyterians (Pres) in about the middle. As we can see, the level of unequivocal belief in God among the Mormons (LDS), at 84%, would rank a little beyond that of the moderate Presbyterians (75%), well beyond the Protestant average (Prot; 71%), and close to both the Missouri Synod Lutherans (MoL) and the Roman Catholics (Cath; 81% each), but not as high as that of the Southern Baptists (99%).

TABLE 3.1. Beliefs about God, 1960s (percentages)

Belief Options	LDS	Cong	Pres	MoL	SoBap	Prot[1]	Cath
I know God exists and I have no doubts about it.	84	41	75	81	99	71	81
While I have doubts, I feel that I do believe in God.	11	34	16	17	1	17	13
I find myself believing in God some of the time but not at other times.	1	4	1	0	0	2	1
I don't believe in a personal God, but I do believe in a higher power of some kind.	1	16	7	1	0	7	3
I don't know whether there is a God and I don't believe there is any way to find out.	1	2	1	1	0	1	1
I don't believe in God.	1	1	0	0	0	<.5	0
Other or no answer	1	2	<.5	0	0	1	1
N (100%)	249	151	495	116	79	2,326	545

SOURCES: Compiled from Stark and Glock (1968:28) with the addition of my 1964 sample.

1. In this and other tables involving Stark and Glock data, "Prot." (or alternatively "Ave.") refers to the average responses of *all ten* Protestant denominations in their sample, not just the average of the four denominations selected for this table.

In most of the Stark and Glock data on religious beliefs, the Presbyterian figures (as here) run close to the Protestant averages. By comparison, the Mormon figures for various religious beliefs tend to fall somewhere between the moderate middle of the continuum, represented by the Presbyterians or the Protestant average, and the conservative extreme, represented by the Missouri Synod Lutherans, the Southern Baptists, and certain fundamentalist sects. Accordingly, in these tables the Mormon samples are being compared only with denominations along the *moderate to conservative half* of the Stark-Glock continuum, though "Ave." refers to the average for *all* Protestants (see Stark and Glock, 1968:chap. 2 for the entire range of their continuum and the implications thereof). Table 3.2 offers a more elaborate comparison of the various Mormon samples with each other and with the selected Stark and Glock moderate-to-conservative denominations.[5]

On the basis of tables 3.1 and 3.2, we would seem justified in concluding that the levels of Mormon belief in God, despite a somewhat unique definition of God, are very similar to those of moderate Protestants. Those

TABLE 3.2. Belief in God, 1960s (percentages)

God's Existence	Mormons				Protestants				Catholics
	SLC	SF	EBay	CombCal	Pres	MoL	SoBap	Ave.	
No doubts	77	58	84	70	75	81	99	71	81
Some doubt	5	6	11	8	16	17	1	17	13
N (100%)	958	296	249	545	495	116	79	2,326	545

SOURCES: Compiled from Stark and Glock (1968) with the addition of my 1964, 1967–68, and 1968–69 samples.

NOTE: For the SLC and SF samples, the question about belief in God was worded somewhat differently to make it more specifically Mormon in content, and the responses were based upon a Likert scale ranging from "definitely true" to "definitely not true."

levels are somewhat lower than the corresponding figures for the more conservative Protestant groups and for the Catholics.[6]

Besides belief in God, there are many other religious beliefs, of course, that Mormons might or might not share with the more traditional denominations. Among these are beliefs about life after death, about Jesus, and about the devil. In addition, there are beliefs that distinguish Mormons from others, including the belief that Joseph Smith was a true prophet, who actually conversed with God and angels, and a derivative belief that contemporary Mormons are led by a prophet who is God's exclusive spokesman. This latter belief might reasonably be considered a Mormon counterpart to the traditional Catholic concept of papal infallibility.

In table 3.3, we can see a pattern resembling that in the two earlier tables: The Mormon levels of belief tended to lie between the moderate and conservative Protestant levels and close to the Protestant and Catholic averages. The Utah sample tended to show somewhat higher levels of belief than did the California samples in the visions of Joseph Smith ("JS") and in the exclusive prophetic role of the contemporary Mormon prophet. Yet even the Utah Mormons did not subscribe to the latter belief any more fully than the Catholics subscribed to papal infallibility (and the California Mormons not as much so). To the extent that reservations about the prophet's (or the pope's) exclusive role might indicate some openness toward ecumenicity, the Mormons (especially in California) showed as much or more such openness as the pre–Vatican II Catholics did.

Belief-by-belief comparisons, however, can be quite complicated and tedious. Also, even the most devout believers hold some of the prescribed beliefs more fully and definitely than they hold others. For example, it is apparent from table 3.3 that the beliefs in Joseph Smith's visions or in a literal devil are less fully accepted by Mormons than are the beliefs in God or Jesus; it is apparent also that the levels of belief among the San Franciso Mormons are generally lower than among the Mormons in the other samples. Sometimes an overall *index* can give a general or composite picture of how levels of acceptance of all such beliefs simultaneously average out.

For example, Stark and Glock (1968:chap. 3) concluded that four key traditional beliefs defined basic orthodoxy for Christians: belief in God, belief in the divinity of Jesus, belief in a literal devil, and belief in life after death. They gave each respondent in their survey one point for each of those four beliefs held definitely or unequivocally but zero for any degree of doubt or rejection. They thereby created an index of orthodoxy ranging from a score of 4 (full acceptance of all four beliefs) down to 0 (full acceptance of none).

For Mormons, belief in a God of flesh and bones, belief in the literal divinity of Jesus, belief in a literal devil, and belief in Joseph Smith's visions would seem to be four key indicators of orthodoxy. An index based on these four is not fully comparable to that created by Stark and Glock, not only because the component beliefs are somewhat different, but also because a somewhat different system (statistically weighted) was used to create the Mormon index (see the Appendix). However, it is comparable

TABLE 3.3. Definite Acceptance of Various Religious Beliefs, 1960s (percentages)

	Mormons				Protestants				
Beliefs	SLC	SF	EBay	CombCal	Pres	MoL	SoBap	Ave.	Catholics
Afterlife	82	67	83	74	64	84	97	65	75
Jesus divine	83	64	82	72	72	93	99	69	86
Devil exists	72	54	78	65	31	77	92	38	66
JS saw God	78	59	*	*	*	*	*	*	*
LDS pres. God's only Prophet	74	52	62	56	*	*	*	*	*
Pope infall.	*	*	*	*	*	*	*	*	74
N (100%)	958	296	249	545	495	116	79	2,326	545

SOURCES: Compiled from Stark and Glock (1968) with the addition of my 1964, 1967–68, and 1968–69 samples.

* = This question was not asked in the applicable questionnaire.

enough to give us at least a general idea of how orthodox the Mormons were about their religion in the sixties compared with how orthodox the Catholics and Protestants were about their religions.

About two-thirds of the Salt Lake City Mormons accepted with some certainty all four key tenets of their faith, thereby ranking at the very top of the orthodoxy index. By contrast, fewer than half of their San Francisco coreligionists did (not shown in tables). When averaged, the high orthodoxy figure for the two Mormon samples was 59%, which stood between those for the Presbyterian moderates (or the Protestant average) and the more conservative Protestant denominations on a similar index. The SLC and average Mormon percentages were actually closest to those for Catholics or Missouri Lutherans (Stark and Glock, 1968:60).

Of course orthodoxy is only one way of being "religious." Another dimension of religiousness, or "religiosity," is practice. Practice can take either a public form (such as attendance at church), called "ritual practice," or a more private form (such as personal prayer), called "devotional practice" (Stark and Glock, 1968:chaps. 4, 5). There are actually many ways to practice a religion, but perhaps we can get an adequate comparison of Mormons with others by looking first at the figures for church attendance (table 3.4) and then at the figures for three kinds of personal devotion: offering "grace" or "blessings" on meals, regular personal prayer, and regular scripture reading (table 3.5).

Mormon church attendance figures, whether in Utah or California, tended toward the Protestant average and were considerably lower than for the Catholics. San Francisco Mormons were especially low, bringing down the combined California average. In more private devotions, Mormons were considerably more likely to say grace or blessings at meals than even the more conservative Protestants and Catholics, but in private prayer and in scripture reading Mormons were about as regular as people in the other denominations. (Pre–Vatican II Catholics were not encouraged to read the scriptures at all, which probably explains the extraordinarily low Catholic figure for that kind of personal religiosity.)

Stark and Glock have identified at least two more dimensions of religiosity, religious experience and religious knowledge (1968:chaps. 6, 7). The first of these they measured (and indexed) by reference to items in their questionnaire about certain spiritual experiences their respondents claimed, such as a feeling of being in God's presence or of being saved in Christ or of being tempted by the devil, and the like. Religious knowledge was measured by whether or not respondents could give accurate

TABLE 3.4. Church Attendance, 1960s (percentages)

	Mormons				Protestants				
	SLC	SF	EBay	CombCal	Pres	MoL	SoBap	Ave.	Catholics
Weekly	37	19	34	26	29	43	59	36	70
Nearly weekly	21	14	23	18	29	30	25	27	10
Total	58	33	57	44	58	73	84	63	80
N (100%)	958	296	249	545	495	116	79	2,326	545

SOURCES: Compiled from Stark and Glock (1968) with the addition of my 1964, 1967–68, and 1968–69 samples.

NOTE: For Mormons, "church attendance" refers to "sacrament service." For Catholics and Protestants, it refers to "Sunday worship services."

answers to general Bible questions like which disciple denied Christ three times, whether the Book of Acts is an account of the ministry of Jesus, and so forth.

Many of these same questions (and others more directly tapping the Mormon tradition) were included also in the questionnaires for Mormons. To summarize the comparisons of Mormons with others: For spiritual experiences, Mormons claimed to have received "a sure testimony, through the Holy Ghost," of the truthfulness of the gospel at rates very similar to those at which the Stark and Glock Protestants claimed a "sense of being saved in Christ." From a third to a half of the various Mormon samples claimed to be sure of having had such a spiritual witness, as did like proportions of Protestants, on average. Only the most conservative Protestant denominations and sects claimed higher rates (90% or more), and the Catholics claimed a considerably lower rate (about a fourth). In other kinds of spiritual experiences with God, Mormon claims tended to run at or below the rates for the Catholics and the Protestant averages. In knowledge of the Bible, all Mormon samples showed lower rates of correct answers than did the Protestants and Catholics, on average, although the Utah Mormons were very close to these averages.

The differences in the Mormon responses by locale were largely as would have been expected from the differences between entrenched (Utah) Mormons and settlement (California) Mormons. For the most part, the Utah Mormons showed higher rates of religiosity on the various measures than did their California counterparts, especially as compared with the San Francisco Mormons. This is suggestive both of the greater incidence of converts in the California samples (less seasoned in Mormon

TABLE 3.5. Private Devotions, 1960s (percentages)

	Mormons				Protestants				
	SLC	SF	EBay	CombCal	Pres	MoL	SoBap	Ave.	Catholics
Grace/blessing at meals daily	68	38	64	49	26	21	20	23	22
Personal prayer weekly	76	64	56	61	77	82	92	75	83
Scripture reading weekly	28	25	19	23	23	21	63	24	6
N (100%)	958	296	249	545	495	116	79	2,326	545

SOURCES: Compiled from Stark and Glock (1968) with the addition of my 1964, 1967–68, and 1968–69 samples.

NOTE: Frequencies are at least as great as those indicated here. They should be read as daily or more and weekly or more.

ways) and of the greater tolerance in California for maverick Mormons of various kinds, at least in the sixties.

So how fully assimilated or Americanized were the Mormons of the sixties in their religious beliefs, practices, and other dimensions of religiousness? All things considered, the data presented in this chapter indicate rather a high degree of similarity between Mormons, Protestants, and Catholics, at least on average. Naturally there are a few specifically Mormon truth claims, such as belief in Joseph Smith's visions, the Book of Mormon, and modern, living prophets. Incredible (or galling) as these peculiarities might be to non-Mormons, they would rarely come up in interactions between Mormons and others. For one thing, though Mormons have always claimed a miraculous origin for their religion and for their Book of Mormon, they have also claimed that the book is simply another testament of Jesus Christ. Furthermore, in the actual teachings of the Book of Mormon, there is nothing that non-Mormon theologians would not recognize as part of the mainstream Christian tradition.

Of course, Mormons have always been known for their successful proselytizing efforts, but these have been primarily the efforts of the full-time (and rotating) young missionary corps, not of the grass-roots members. Despite the urging of President McKay that every member be a missionary, grass-roots Mormons in the sixties were no more likely than most of their non-Mormon neighbors to try to convert others. In a question about that in the Glock and Stark 1963 survey, 9% of the Catholics and Protestants (on average) claimed that they "often" tried to convert someone to their own faith.

The corresponding figure for Mormons was almost identical: Only 10% of either Utah or California Mormons claimed they often tried to convert others (another 40%, approximately, of Mormons, Catholics, and Protestants claimed to make conversion efforts "once in awhile"). It is probably fair to observe also that by the sixties, most Americans had become quite atheological in their approach to religion in general (except, perhaps, for the most fundamentalist Protestants), caring but little about the theological peculiarities of Mormons or any other denominations; and grass-roots Mormons, for their part, were also generally in a mood of "live and let live."

To claim that by the sixties the Mormons were pretty well assimilated, however, is to speak primarily for the Mormon side of the relationship; that is to say, the Mormons could not claim many distinctive religious beliefs, practices, or experiences that mattered to others. This does not mean, however, that the Mormons were fully accepted by others. Despite a remarkable improvement in the Mormon public image by this time, and a general ignorance or indifference about Mormon religious beliefs and practices, there remained (and still remains) a certain residue of the nineteenth-century aura of disreputability, with occasional remarks, whether snide or in jest, about polygamy, theocracy, or other perceived Mormon traits. By the sixties, furthermore, outsiders were just beginning to discover that Mormons had an obsolete racial policy.

Probably for reasons that were mainly historical, however, 50% of the Protestants and Catholics in the Glock and Stark survey said that they would feel at least somewhat uncomfortable in attending a Mormon church service (1964:32). This proportion was almost as great as the 56% who felt the same way about attending Jewish services and was significantly exceeded only by the 68% who felt that way about visiting the services of the Jehovah's Witnesses (the corresponding figure was only 39% for the Baptists). This reticence about association with Mormons apparently continues down to the present (Brinkerhoff and Mackie, 1986; Brinkerhoff, Jacob, and Mackie, 1987b; Brinkerhoff et al., 1991). One is reminded here of an observation by Rodney Stark (1984:27) that even academics make comments in public about Mormons that they would not dare make in polite company about Jews.

Summary

Yet this chapter has been concerned not with how popular Mormons were at midcentury but with how similar they were to others in basic religious beliefs and practices. A high degree of similarity is apparent from the comparisons of the California and Utah samples with the Protestant and Catholic ones surveyed at about the same time. Comparisons of the Mormon samples with each other, however, revealed a tendency for the Utah Mormons to be somewhat more orthodox in beliefs and practices than their California counterparts, although the differences tended to be greater between Utah and San Francisco than between Utah and the suburban East Bay. Some gaps between Utah and California Mormons would be expected from two theoretical considerations: the differences in Mormon experience and outlook as between the "entrenched" and "settlement" locales, respectively, and the more general tendency for church members of all denominations to be somewhat less "religious" along the West Coast than in other parts of the country (Stark and Bainbridge, 1985:chap. 4).

Notes

1. Here it might be appropriate to mention that these were the first large-scale, systematic surveys ever conducted on Mormon populations. They were carried out with the cooperation (but not the surveillance) of the Presiding Bishop's Office of the LDS Church and of the local bishops whose wards were included in the sample. For more information on these surveys, see the Appendix. A few earlier surveys had been conducted (e.g., Cline and Richards, 1965; Wilford Smith, 1959; and Vernon, 1955, 1956), but these were primitive and pioneering efforts flawed by relatively small, unsystematic opportunity samples, and perhaps even contaminated by church influence.

2. The questionnaires for these three surveys went to every household in all of the sample wards, addressed alternately to the husband and to the wife, in the case of married couples, or otherwise to the single individual of record. The response rate reached 60%, after repeated follow-up, and the remaining 40% differed from the respondents mainly in a greater likelihood of being male, working-class, and inactive in the church. The data can be considered reasonably representative of the adult Mormons residing in the locales specified. See the Appendix for more details.

3. The data from the Glock and Stark survey have appeared in various places, but mainly in two important books (Glock and Stark, 1966; Stark and Glock, 1968). Most of their data have remained unpublished. However, the general, or "marginal," distributions for the various questionnaire items can be found in an unpublished codebook from the project (Glock and Stark, 1964), a copy of which was generously furnished me by these two authors. The comparisons in this chapter are drawn from one or the other of their two published books, where appropriate, but otherwise from the marginals in the unpublished codebook. I am deeply grateful for the cooperation of these two scholars, not only for sharing their work in these respects, but also for their guidance years ago in the Mormon surveys that I conducted, which in general followed their methodology and design.

4. For the purposes of this book, it might be less important whether Mormons actually became more like others or simply came to recognize themselves as more like others, since the main concern in this book is with Mormon reactions to the recognition. Still, we must at least demonstrate that there was some similarity (assimilation) there to be recognized.

5. In this case, however, table 3.2 is abbreviated, showing only the more "believing" responses, rather than the full range illustrated in the previous table. This will be the pattern, incidentally, in most of the tables yet to be presented—i.e., only the one or two most definite or revealing responses will be compared so as to keep the tables simple; the labels too will be much abbreviated. For some purposes, the two California Mormon samples will also be combined ("CombCal") to provide average figures somewhat more "balanced" as between the transient and diverse San Franciscans and the more settled and stable East Bay suburbanites.

6. The believing figures for the SLC and SF samples (77% and 58%) are somewhat smaller than the one for the East Bay sample (84%), shown in tables 3.1 and 3.2, probably because they represent responses to a somewhat more restrictive definition of God as having a "body of flesh and bone." They still represent, however, the most orthodox *Mormon* response. In assessing the Catholic figures, it is important to remember also that the data in these and other tables from that period would not yet reflect the impact of Vatican Council II and all that has derived from that council during the past twenty-five years. Incidentally, in this and in subsequent tables, the identical *N*s of 545 for Catholics and for California Mormons (combined) are, of course, entirely coincidental.

CHAPTER FOUR

Mormon Social and Political Beliefs at Midcentury

Social Status

In assessing the extent of assimilation, it is not enough to know only whether Mormons' religious beliefs and practices made them stand out among their neighbors (which apparently was seldom the case). Other characteristics can also make a people seem different from their neighbors or, in the extremity, even unassimilable. Chief among these are ethnic differences of the kind still associated with Jews and once associated with Roman Catholics when they were disproportionately immigrants from southern and eastern Europe. Although Mormons might once have become a separate ethnic group in America, they never actually did. Mormon converts who were not American in the nineteenth century came almost entirely from the easily assimilable English, Scandinavian, and German stock.

Always related to ethnicity, however, or at least to historical factors such as recency of immigration, have been social status differences among religious denominations. At least until fifty years ago, some denominations, such as the Anglican or Episcopal, were made up disproportionately of people with advanced education and professional or white-collar occupations, which helped to add an aura of national respectability to their denominations. Other denominations earlier in our history, such as the Roman Catholic, Mormon, and Pentecostal, had constituencies with very modest education levels and largely blue-collar or working-class occupations, which seemed to verify the public image of these denominations as appealing to the simple-minded, the untutored, or the un-American. Such was even more the case for those religious groups who, like the Mormons,

TABLE 4.1. Educational Attainment, 1960s (percentages)

Educational Level Completed	Mormons SLC	Mormons SF	Mormons EBay	Non-Mormons[1]
Postgraduate	16	18	10	14
College degree	12	13	6	16
Some college	27	35	28	31
High school grad.	28	21	34	22
< H.S. Grad.	15	11	22	15
N (100%)	958	296	249	2,871

SOURCES: Compiled from Glock and Stark (1964) with the addition of my 1964, 1967–68, and 1968–69 samples.

1. In this and other tables involving distributions from the Glock and Stark codebook (1964), "Non-Mormons" refers to their entire sample, with Catholic and all Protestant denominations averaged together.

Mennonites, Hutterites, and some Bible-belt sects, were concentrated in remote or rural areas, and thus often regarded as "country bumpkins."

If such characterizations might have fitted the Mormons earlier in the twentieth century, the gap in social status between Mormons and others was pretty well closed by about midcentury, especially after the returning Mormon war veterans had gotten the full educational benefits due them under the GI Bill. By the sixties Mormons closely resembled other Americans, on the average, in educational attainment, in occupational distribution, and in the sizes of the communities in which they had been reared.

On the whole, as we can see from table 4.1, Mormons were about as well educated as Protestants and Catholics (Non-Mormons), though East Bay Mormons (EBay) tended to have a little less education. Similarly, though again with relatively minor variations, the Mormon samples are quite similar to each other and to the Protestant/Catholic average. The Mormons were only slightly less likely to be in the higher-status professional and technical occupations (see table 4.2). The San Francisco Mormons (SF) were considerably more likely than any of the other samples to be in clerical roles, probably reflecting the disproportion among them of clerical workers living in inner-city apartments. The mixture of suburban and small-town inhabitants probably explains the greater number of blue-collar workers in the East Bay Mormon sample. All in all, though, we see a high degree of similarity between Mormons and others in the ways in which they were assimilated into the work force. In community size of origin, it appears that the Mormons (except the San Francisco sample) were considerably more likely than the others to have been reared on farms or

TABLE 4.2. Occupations and Professions, 1960s (percentages)

	Mormons			Non-
Occupational Category	SLC	SF	EBay	Mormons
Clerical and related	7	27	7	9
Craftsman, foreman	15	8	31	18
Laborers	4	3	6	3
Operative and related	3	3	7	4
Private household worker	1	1	1	<1
Professional and technical	27	28	24	33
Proprietor, manager	18	15	8	13
Sales worker	10	4	5	10
Service worker	4	5	5	3
Agriculture and misc.	<1	0	2	<1
N (100%)	958	296	249	2,871

SOURCES: Compiled from Glock and Stark (1964) with the addition of my 1964, 1967–68, and 1968–69 samples.

TABLE 4.3. Community of Origin, 1960s (percentages)

Size and Nature of Community in Which	Mormons			
Respondent Was Reared	SLC	SF	EBay	Non-Mormons
Farm	21	12	28	16
< 2,500 pop., not suburb	19	17	24	14
< 15,000 pop.	12	16	16	16
<50,000	5	9	11	10
<100,000	7	6	6	6
<250,000	24	16	8	8
<750,000	4	14	4	13
1 million or more	2	4	2	6
Suburbs	3	4	10	7
N (100%)	958	296	249	2,871

SOURCES: Compiled from Glock and Stark (1964) with the addition of my 1964, 1967–68, and 1968–69 samples.

in small towns or in cities of 250,000 or more (see table 4.3). Again, however, these differences are not great. Already during this period, Mormons were about as urbanized in their upbringings as were other Americans on the average.

Civic and Political Attitudes

The relation between the assimilation of a religious denomination and the political party preferences of its membership is complicated by historical factors, among other things. Rarely if ever have the basic teachings of any religion in the United States implied a preference for one political party over another. The rank and file of a given denomination, furthermore, do not necessarily share the political preferences of the clergy or leadership. American Jews and Catholics have tended to prefer the Democratic party in the United States for reasons related mainly to their earlier urban immigrant experiences, though with increasing assimilation Catholics have become somewhat more likely to vote Republican. Episcopalians and other mainline Protestants have tended to prefer the Republican party (though their clergy does not necessarily do so), primarily out of class interest rather than from any particular religious motivation.

Mormons usually remained aloof from commitments to any national parties throughout the nineteenth century. In Utah, they formed their own People's party to protect their interests against the growing power and encroachment of non-Mormons moving in, who, for their part, formed the rival Liberal party. One of the conditions, however, under which Utah was finally granted statehood at the turn of the twentieth century was that its people adopt the two-party system common to the rest of the country, which was expected to cut across the acrimonious religious boundaries of Utah (Lyman, 1986). As the twentieth century progressed, Mormons in Utah and elsewhere tended to favor the Democratic party more often than the Republican, though the top church leadership was apparently somewhat more Republican in inclination (Alexander, 1986b; Shipps, 1967).

With the arrival of the New Deal era, however, Mormons began to see the Democratic party increasingly as representing big government and big labor, rather than the common people per se, and so began to move toward the Republicans. This was especially true of the church leadership. All in all, though, by the sixties Mormons (especially those outside Utah) tended to be about equally divided between Democrats and Republicans and tended to follow the majority of the nation in presidential elections. Even those in the Bay Area followed this trend despite the well-earned reputation of that area for political liberalism. By the criterion of a balanced distribution between the two major parties, therefore, Mormons by the sixties were certainly more fully assimilated politically than were Catholics or Jews (see table 4.4).

Political party preference is not a bad measure of general political orientation, but it tells us little about how people of either party might respond to specific social and political issues. The Mormon surveys, like the one of Glock and Stark, posed to the respondents certain questions

Table 4.4. Self-described Political Party Identifications, 1960s (percentages)

	Mormons			
Party	SLC	SF	EBay	Non-Mormons
Democrat				
Liberal	6	15	9	10
Moderate	16	20	36	25
Democrat Total	22	35	45	35
Republican				
Conservative	19	15	15	12
Moderate	35	30	20	41
Republican Total	54	45	35	53
Independent	18	16	12	8
N (100%)	958	296	249	2,871

Sources: Compiled from Glock and Stark (1964) with the addition of my 1964, 1967–68, and 1968–69 samples.

about their attitudes toward some nationally prominent issues, including support for the United Nations, support for Medicare, concern about the power and control of large companies, and opposition to prayer in the public schools, all of which would have been indicative of a politically liberal orientation during this period. A more conservative orientation, however, would have been indicated by opposition to admitting communist China to the UN, a concern about communism as an internal threat, and a concern about the power of labor unions.

One thing that is apparent from table 4.5 is the great diversity among the Mormon samples on these various issues. Were we to examine the non-Mormon data by denomination or region, no doubt we would also see much diversity. This diversity indicates that the religion itself really offers no prescriptions on specific political issues, so that other influences probably determine such responses. As we compare the various Mormon samples with the non-Mormon ones, we find Mormons about as liberal as the non-Mormons on foreign policy issues. Indeed, perhaps surprisingly, the Utah sample was the least likely to oppose admission of China to the UN.

In domestic policy issues, Mormons tended to be somewhat more conservative than non-Mormons on some issues but more liberal on other issues. The East Bay Mormons, furthermore, were often very similar to the non-Mormons. Considering both the diversity among the Mormon samples and the comparisons with the non-Mormons, it is difficult to make a case from these data that Mormons were either unusually liberal or unusually conservative on the major issues of the sixties.

A potential exception to that conclusion must, however, be considered, and that is the political posture of the Mormons on race and civil rights. As has been thoroughly explained elsewhere (Bush and Mauss, 1984), the Mormon church maintained until 1978 a racial restriction on access to its lay priesthood: Those church members having any black African ancestry (a minuscule proportion of all church members, in any case) could not be ordained. This anomaly in a church with an otherwise strongly egalitarian tradition was scarcely noticed by other Americans until the crest of the civil rights movement in the early sixties. For a decade thereafter, Mormons at both the corporate and the individual level were regularly criticized by liberal and civil rights exponents and were very much on the defensive. Virtually all other major denominations had dropped their own

TABLE 4.5. Attitudes on Prominent Political Issues of the 1960s (percentages)

	Mormons			Non-
Percentage agreeing	SLC	SF	EBay	Mormons
Domestic Issues				
Communism is as big a threat inside as out.	85	79	85	63
Unions do more harm than good.	73	59	26	39
Big companies control too much business.	58	71	44	40
Government ought to have medical care for the aged.	54	73	55	51
Better not to have prayer in public schools.	31	46	22	29
Churches should stick to religion and not be concerned with social or political issues.	37	40	26	22
Foreign Policy Issues				
U.S. should give strong support to the UN.	78	83	79	85
Red China should not be admitted to the UN.	28	45	54	52
N (100%)	958	296	249	2,871

SOURCES: Compiled from Glock and Stark (1964), with the addition of my 1964, 1967–68, and 1968–69 samples.

NOTE: For the Mormon samples, the figures represent combined responses of "agree strongly" and "agree somewhat" on a 5-point Likert scale. For the non-Mormons, the figures are for those choosing "agree" on a 3-point scale (agree/uncertain/disagree).

TABLE 4.6. Attitudes toward Blacks, 1960s (percentages)

	Mormons			Protestants				
Attitude	SLC	SF	EBay	Pres	MoL	SoBap	Ave.	Catholics
It's a shame that Negroes are so immoral.	27	22	31	28	36	33	26	28
It's too bad, but in general Negroes have inferior intelligence compared to whites.	43	36	37	31	38	38	30	29
Most Negro neighborhoods are run down because Negroes simply don't take care of property.	64	59	50	52	66	58	50	53
Suppose you owned your own home and several Negro families moved into your block. Would you be apt to move elsewhere if you could get a fair price for your home? (Yes, would move.)	48	34	44	43	48	43	42	40
It would probably be better all around if Negroes went to separate schools.	30	22	27	20	29	46	22	18
It would probably be better for Negroes and whites to attend separate churches.	12	12	28	28	34	67	29	15
N (100%)	958	296	249	495	116	79	2,326	545

SOURCES: Taken from Glock and Stark (1966:168) with the addition of my 1964, 1967–68, and 1968–69 samples.

NOTE: The percentages refer to respondents answering "definitely agree" or "agree somewhat."

equally racist practices at the first sound of the civil rights trumpet, and the seeming obstinacy of the Mormons in this respect was hard for the nation to understand (Stathis and Lythgoe, 1977).

Two overlapping but separable issues were involved here for the Mormons: whether Mormons were more racist or less supportive of civil rights for blacks than were other Americans in the secular or civil realm, and whether Mormons were entitled to restrict access to their own priesthood on any grounds (including race and gender) as a private matter within their own church. During much of the civil rights era, Mormon leaders, as well as most of the rank and file, vehemently answered "No" to the first question and "Yes" to the second.

Neither response was terribly convincing to most political commentators and image makers in the country, so Mormons increasingly came to be suspected of harboring racism in their hearts as well as in their churches and thereby of lending at least passive resistance to the goals of the civil rights movement. Under these circumstances, we are entitled to wonder what surveys of this period would show about Mormon racial attitudes in comparison to those of non-Mormons. The Mormons were asked exactly the same questions to tap their attitudes toward "Negroes" (as African Americans were usually called at the time) as Glock and Stark asked Protestants and Catholics (1966:chap. 10).

The comparisons in table 4.6 again show considerable diversity even among the three Mormon samples, with the San Francisco Mormons (who presumably had more frequent contact with black neighbors or co-workers) the least likely of the three to hold negative attitudes. When we compare the three Mormon figures in each case to the Protestant and Catholic averages , the Mormons generally seem to hold negative attitudes with somewhat greater frequency. Yet Mormons do not seem more negative in general when they are compared with the moderate Presbyterians or with the more conservative Lutheran or Baptist denominations. The differences between Mormons and others actually disappeared, furthermore, when controls were imposed on the data for education and other secular influences (Mauss, 1966, 1970).[1]

Thus, whatever their peculiar internal ecclesiastical policies were in the sixties, Mormons could not be considered outside the national consensus in their external civic attitudes toward African Americans. Incidentally, Mormon rates of anti-Semitism during this same period were considerably lower than those of Catholics and of most Protestant denominations (for more detailed analyses of Mormon racial attitudes and their roots, see Bringhurst, 1981; Bush and Mauss, 1984; Mauss, 1966, 1968, 1970).

Aside from racial attitudes specifically, how accepting were Mormons of the American tradition of civil liberties more generally? By the 1960s, had Mormons grown so strong and smug in their traditional claims to exclusive truth that they would restrict the expression of religious "error"? Was their nineteenth century heritage of theocracy still with them? Apparently not. Mormons had become well enough assimilated politically (or perhaps had suffered enough persecution of their own) that they were strong exponents of civil liberties even for atheists, those presumably farthest beyond the American religious pale.

The data in table 4.7 illustrate that Mormon responses varied widely, with sometimes one sample and then another more conservative, depend-

TABLE 4.7. Attitudes toward Civil Liberties for Atheists, 1960s (percentages)

	Mormons			Protestants				
	SLC	SF	EBay	Pres	MoL	SoBap	Ave.	Catholics
A book he wrote should be removed from the library.	8	6	10	10	13	27	12	14
He should not be allowed to preach his beliefs to others.	13	15	24	23	32	32	24	28
He should not be allowed to teach in a public high school.	30	18	32	40	39	57	39	36
He should not be allowed to teach in a private university.	20	13	24	30	31	46	29	31
He should not be allowed to hold public office.	13	10	23	29	40	41	28	23
N (100%)	958	296	249	495	116	79	2,326	545

SOURCES: Taken from Glock and Stark (1966:88) with the addition of my 1964, 1967–68, and 1968–69 samples.

NOTE: The percentages refer to respondents answering "agree" in a dichotomous choice (agree/disagree).

ing upon the kind of restriction imposed. On virtually all of the proposed restrictions, however, the Mormon samples were among the least restrictive. Indeed, they agreed with the restrictions less often than did either the Protestants (Ave.) or the Catholics and a lot less often than those of the more conservative Lutheran and Baptist denominations. By the sixties, then, Mormons were thus already well assimilated into the American civil liberties tradition, if, indeed, they had not been earlier.

Life-style Differences

If the Mormons of the sixties presented a picture of such general assimilation in both religious and socio-political respects, where might we look for evidence of any residual Mormon peculiarity after all of that twentieth-century assimilation? Mormons self-consciously continued to remain distinctive in certain life-style behaviors: abstinence from alcohol, tobacco, coffee, tea, and, by implication, other addictive or mood-altering substances; sexual abstinence outside of marriage; and a strong familial orientation expressed in high rates of marriage, a preference for religious endogamy, and a relatively high birth rate.

We can compare attitudes toward alcohol of Mormons with those of Protestants and Catholics, although they were not asked exactly the same questions. Of the East Bay Mormons, 51% believed that abstention from alcohol and tobacco was "absolutely necessary" for salvation, which is scarcely different from the 48% of the Utah Mormons believing that drinking liquor would be "very serious" in God's eyes. For San Francisco Mormons, however, the "very serious" figure was only 30%. Both Protestants and Catholics were asked if drinking liquor would "definitely prevent salvation." Only the Southern Baptists reached even two digits (15%) in the percent believing that alcohol use is such a serious matter, with the other Protestants and Catholics bringing up the rear at only 1% or 2%.

Even drinking coffee or tea was a serious matter for many Mormons. Almost as many East Bay Mormons believed that the coffee habit was dangerous to their salvation as felt that way about the use of liquor (45% versus 51%). Salt Lake and San Francisco Mormons were less concerned about coffee. Only 22% of Salt Lake Mormons and 15% of San Francisco Mormons viewed drinking coffee as a "very serious" weakness in God's eyes.

Unfortunately Glock and Stark did not collect any data about sexual practices in their surveys, but Harold Christensen, a real pioneer in the study of the relation between religion and sexual behavior, published several articles based on data from surveys of college students (e.g. Christensen, 1960, 1973, 1976; Christensen and Carpenter, 1962). His samples from the Intermountain West and other regions of the United States allowed him to make a number of comparisons between Mormons and others, and we can use his data to infer behavioral patterns among Mormons as a whole.

Of Christensen's Mormon university students in Utah, on average only about 18% approved of premarital sex (22% of men and 16% of women). This corresponds well with the adult Mormons in my Salt Lake City survey since 74% of them considered premarital sex a "very serious" failing in God's eyes, which would leave only 26% of them somewhat less concerned. (Only 53% of the San Francisco Mormons agreed that premarital sex was "very serious.") Similarly, on average only 2% of Mormon college students (3% of men and 1% of women) felt extramarital sex was acceptable while 90% of Salt Lake City Mormons, and 79% of even the San Francisco Mormons, considered this behavior unacceptable. Non-Mormon college students, however, widely diverged from this pattern. They were much more likely to approve of premarital sex (55% of the men and 38% of the women) and somewhat more likely to approve of extramarital sex (2% of the women versus 10% of the men).

What all of this suggests is that if we had comparable non-Mormon data on adults we would see similar patterns for these questions. In other words, in the sixties, all Mormons (whether adults or students) were far more likely than non-Mormons to disapprove, and far less likely to approve, of sexual relations outside of marriage. For premarital sex, non-Mormons, whether men or women, were more than twice as likely as Mormons to approve. Even for extramarital sex, the non-Mormon men were more than three times as likely to approve as the Mormon men (see also the other Christensen studies cited above and Wilford Smith, 1976).

The third and final category of expected life-style differences between Mormons and others is in family matters. Mormons profess a special proclivity for marriage, especially within their own religious fold (endogamy), and a special desire for children (pronatalism). To a limited extent, we can make some comparisons relevant to these issues between the Mormon samples and the non-Mormons surveyed by Glock and Stark.

From table 4.8 we can see that during the sixties the Utah and East Bay Mormons were no more likely to be married than were the Protestants and Catholics. The San Francisco Mormons, on the other hand, were disproportionately single, which simply emphasizes once again the somewhat skewed nature of the San Francisco sample as disproportionately young, urban, career transients.

The amount of comparative data available on attitudes toward religious intermarriage is fragmentary because of differences among the various questionnaires in the ways that the questions were asked. However, we can see that the East Bay Mormons, at least, were about as likely as Protestants and Catholics, on average, to disapprove of mixed marriages, but the Mormons were apparently more likely to disapprove for theological reasons (23% versus 1%). The Utah Mormons were also more likely than their San Francisco counterparts to worry about the eternal consequences of intermarriage with non-Mormons. The greater proclivity of the Utah Mormons for actually marrying within their church is quite understandable given the greater opportunity, in a state that was (and is) 70% Mormon, for finding a Mormon spouse. All in all, these data do suggest that marrying within one's own religion has been a fairly serious issue to the Mormons, perhaps more serious than for Protestants or even for Catholics.

The Catholics of this period, however, were still the most likely of all to regard artificial birth control as offensive to God. Although this specific information is not presented in the table, 23% of them thought it would definitely prevent salvation. Very few Protestants (1–5%), even among the Southern Baptists, worried about this question. The Utah Mormons, with

TABLE 4.8. Attitudes on Family Norms, 1960s (percentages)

Attitude	Mormons			Non-Mormons
	SLC	SF	EBay	
Married	79	40	85	80
Never married	4	34	6	8
Disapproves of mixed marriages	*	*	49	45
Salvation would "definitely" be prevented by marrying a non-Mormon.	*	*	23	*
Salvation would "definitely" be prevented by marrying a non-Christian.	*	*	*	1
Marrying a non-Mormon would be a "very serious" failure in God's eyes.	35	21	*	*
Those who married within the church	90	42	59	*
Had four or more children	36	13	34	14
N (100%)	958	296	249	2,871

SOURCES: Compiled from Glock and Stark (1964) with the addition of my 1964, 1967–68, and 1968–69 samples.
* = This question was not asked in the applicable questionnaire.

16% agreeing that birth control is a "very serious failing" to God, were a little closer to the Catholics than were the California Mormons, whose levels of concern about birth control reached only about half the level expressed by the California Catholics (12%). The number of Mormons in the table with more than four children, therefore, must not be attributable to a rejection of contraception; for despite the disinclination of more than 80% of the Mormons to worry much about God's view of contraception, the Mormons in Utah and in the East Bay were more than twice as likely as the Protestants and Catholics, on average, to have four or more children.

Even the relatively young and transient Mormons in the San Francisco sample achieved at least parity with the Protestant and Catholic average in the likelihood of having large families. (It is probable, of course, that if we could have separated the Catholics out of this average their figure would have been larger.) All things considered, we can easily glean from table 4.8 the usual image of the Mormons as an especially endogamous people who choose to have relatively large families.

From the data throughout this chapter, we can see also how the San Francisco Mormons tend to reflect the greater "maverick" posture more often found among the Saints living in the settlement stage of development than in the entrenched stage characteristic of the Utah Mormons (a tendency probably exaggerated by the relative youth and mobility of this sample). The San Francisco Mormons were generally the most tolerant toward atheists of all the Mormon samples, the least disapproving of the use of alcohol or coffee or of sex outside of marriage, the most likely never to have married, and the least likely to have had large families or to have disapproved of either birth control or of marriage outside of the church. Overall this group showed an even greater level of assimilation than did the other Mormons surveyed.

Summary

This chapter and the previous one have presented a picture of the Mormons of the 1960s generally as a highly assimilated group of Americans. In educational attainment, occupational status, and community size of origin, it would be difficult to distinguish most Mormons from others. In civic and political attitudes, too, Mormons were already well within the American mainstream. With some variations in party preferences among the Mormon samples, they were all generally quite close to their non-Mormon neighbors. In the specific domestic and foreign policy issues of the time, there was much diversity among Mormons, as among others, suggesting that civic and political attitudes were not much informed by religious beliefs or commitments. The main tendency of Mormon views was neither very liberal nor very conservative but quite centrist and moderate.

Only when we encountered the realm of "life-style," as it is sometimes called, did we see evidence of lagging assimilation. Mormons at midcentury, even in relatively liberal San Francisco, still derived from their religious heritage a strong aversion to alcohol and other mood-altering substances, and to sexual relations outside of marriage, as compared with other Americans of the time. At the same time, Mormons were more inclined than others to marry within their own religion and to prefer relatively large families, despite a general willingness to use contraceptives in planning their families. As important as such differences were, however, they did not give Mormons the distinctiveness of such truly unassimilated groups as the Amish or the Hutterites, or even of the Jehovah's Witnesses in the civic and political realm.

Note

1. Interestingly enough, these same general results were replicated in a survey of southern Mormons conducted during the seventies. Although the survey uncovered higher general rates of antiblack prejudice among Mormons in the South than among those in either Utah or California, which was a function of locale, the part played by religious beliefs per se in prejudice was about the same as for the western Mormon samples; see Ainsworth (1982).

CHAPTER FIVE

Midcentury Mormon Peculiarity and Its Prospects

From the beginning Mormons have been fond of referring to themselves as a "peculiar people," a phrase consciously borrowed from the Apostle Peter's characterization of the early Christians (1 Pet. 2:9). Throughout much of their history, the Mormons would probably have been regarded as peculiar by most of their neighbors, too, though the term no longer retains as benign a connotation as it had in the English of the King James Bible. American society, however, has generated a great many peculiar peoples in its history. Indeed, the modern historian R. Laurence Moore (1986) maintains that "outsider" status has been almost a cherished possession for new religions in America, validating simultaneously (and ironically) both their unique claims to heavenly sanction and their quintessential Americanness. In that sense, assimilation has been as much a problem for many other peculiar peoples as it has been for the Mormons.

That the Mormons were highly assimilated by the middle of the twentieth century is borne out by the data I have already presented in addition to numerous other studies by scholars who have convincingly examined this process in different ways and at different levels: at the economic level by Davies (1963) and by Leone (1979); at the political level by Larson (1971) and by Lyman (1986); at the cultural and institutional levels by Alexander (1986b); at the theological and mythological levels by Shipps (1985); and at the rhetorical level by Shepherd and Shepherd (1984), to mention only a few of these studies. The Americanization thesis has become the conventional wisdom.

Despite all of this evidence, Mormons continue to think of themselves as a peculiar people (DePillis, 1991). This might be reason enough to reconsider the conventional wisdom. In an attempt at such a reappraisal a few years ago, Grant Underwood (1986) offered evidence that the Mormons were neither so far outside the nineteenth-century American mainstream nor so highly assimilated into the contemporary culture as to justify an uncritical acceptance of the Americanization thesis. Though Underwood's caveats have generally gone unheeded, they certainly fit into Mormon-centered thinking about their peculiarity, which is, in fact, an article of faith that remains crucial to the Mormon identity, both at the public relations level and at the psychological or grass-roots level: If the Mormon church was unique and special when God established it, then it still is. If God does not change, neither does his church, at least not in any essential ways, and surely not in its basic doctrines. One sometimes hears in Mormon sermons or lessons the reassuring testimony that the church has "always been the same" since it was founded by Christ through the Prophet Joseph Smith (and even then, of course, it was presented to the world as a faithful replication of the primitive Christian church). Such a proposition is credible, of course, only among those lacking institutional memory (as all Mormon converts do by definition) or among those untutored in any but mythological Mormon history (as are nearly all Mormons at the grass roots).

The scholarly counterpart of the Mormons' continuing belief in their own peculiarity has been the discovery of Mormon "ethnicity." It was Thomas F. O'Dea at midcentury (1954, 1957; Vogt and O'Dea, 1955) who first characterized nineteenth-century Mormons as an emergent ethnic group or "incipient nationality." Although he was writing in the fifties, after most such Mormon separatist tendencies had long since been overwhelmed by assimilation, O'Dea tended to emphasize the historical culture traits of the Mormons that had set them apart from other Americans in the nineteenth century, with but little acknowledgment of how far those traits had already eroded by midcentury. Only toward the end of his 1957 book did he discuss the "sources of strain and conflict" accompanying the Mormon assimilation process. Similarly, the Rimrock studies of Vogt and others (e.g., Vogt and Albert, 1966), like O'Dea's own products of the Harvard "comparative cultures" project, portrayed a cultural heritage that was actually already in decline except perhaps in isolated rural locations such as Rimrock.

This tendency to exaggerate contemporary Mormon differences by dwelling on the cultural heritage of the past has served the public relations interests of the church, too; for continuity in the face of even drastic change is one of the essential myths of institutional Mormonism. The massive and successful church public relations campaigns that we have seen in more recent years had not yet gotten started in O'Dea's time, but during the forties two important occurrences did yield a great deal of favorable exposure for the Mormons. One of these was the 1940 film *Brigham Young*, with leading Hollywood actors of the time, which gave a very sympathetic portrayal of the Mormon exodus to Utah with scarcely a hint of polygamy (D'Arc, 1989). Another was the 1947 celebration of the centennial of the arrival of the Mormon pioneers in Utah, which made the cover of *Time* magazine in July.

These events were both very historical and retrospective in nature, of course, largely overshadowing the assimilation that had occurred during the intervening years, including the generally acknowledged contribution of the patriotic Mormons to two world wars. Even the religious tracts distributed by Mormon missionaries well into the fifties had been written decades earlier and emphasized traditional, rather than emergent, Mormon values and biblical interpretations.[1] With the arrival of the sixties, the internal Mormon struggle to retain a peculiar identity, and the external proclivity of scholars to see Mormons as "ethnic," both received intellectual support from other national developments.

From "Peculiar" to "Ethnic"

One of the by-products of the American civil rights movement of recent decades has been the fostering of pride in one's own ethnic heritage, whatever that might be. This pride was first asserted by black Americans in the sixties perhaps most conspicuously and significantly in movements for black nationalism or black separatism, religiously in the formation of the Black Muslims, and academically in the establishment of black studies departments, programs, and curricula on many college campuses (Breitman, 1965; Howard, 1970; Kurokawa, 1970; Petersen, 1980; Van den Berghe, 1981: chap. 1). Slogans such as "Black is beautiful" gained some currency, and Alex Haley's prodigious research on his family origins produced the best-seller *Roots* demonstrating that even the descendants of black slaves could recover their genealogical heritage to a large extent.[2]

Other American ethnic groups soon followed the black example with comparable or analogous expressions (Howard, 1970; Kurokawa, 1970; Levine and Lurie, 1970; Petersen, 1980; Servin, 1970; Steiner, 1968) and began to promote their own forms of ethnic pride and power (Glazer and Moynihan, 1970; Lokos, 1971; Novak, 1972; Petersen, 1980). One outcome of this collection of movements was a growing disenchantment with the classical American metaphor of the "melting pot" (Abrahamson, 1973; Gordon, 1964) and a newly fashionable emphasis on ethnic identity—indeed, in some quarters almost a desperation to establish such an identity. The Canadian counterpart could be seen in the rise of "cultural pluralism," both as slogan and as explicit government policy, in response to incipient separatist movements in Quebec and elsewhere (Bibby, 1990).

It was in this context that the Mormon church and culture entered a new scholarly and literary age of its own, called "Camelot" by Davis Bitton (1983). While Bitton applied this term mainly to the decade that began with Leonard Arrington's call as church historian in 1972, the flowering of the new Mormon scholarly literature more generally began actually a decade or so earlier, perhaps with the founding of *BYU Studies* but certainly by the time of the emergence of *Dialogue* in the midsixties. The prodigious output since then of historical and other studies of Mormon life and culture, virtually all of it by Mormon authors, can be understood in part as an expression of a renewed appreciation (if not, indeed, pride) for the unique cultural and religious heritage and identity of the Mormon people, however erstwhile all of that uniqueness might have become.[3]

Thus, by the sixties, even the Mormons, despite their highly assimilated northwest European genetic homogeneity and their thorough-going commitment to Americanism, could join in the increasingly fashionable celebration of unique ethnic identity. Such an identity was eventually even legitimated by the inclusion of the Mormons (May 1980) in the *Harvard Encyclopedia of American Ethnic Groups* along with Hutterites, Copts, and Muslims.[4] It seems ironic that an assertion of special Mormon identity—even ethnicity—should have begun just at a time when the Mormons were the least ethnic that they had ever been.[5]

The appropriateness of the terms *ethnic* or *ethnicity* in reference to the Mormons depends largely on whether one applies a "hard" or a "soft" definition of such terms. A hard definition is one that depends partly on a common genetic stock and kinship, along with such common cultural traits as language and religion (Keyes, 1976:202–13; Van den Berghe, 1981:35). A soft definition requires no genetic dimension but only "common cultural characteristics," language being especially important (Winick, 1969:193). In his introductory essay for the *Harvard Encyclopedia* Abrahamson (1980) comes close to saying that a distinctive religion is a sufficient basis for assigning ethnicity. A more recent glossary of anthropology requires little more than the "self-conscious awareness" of a people about key common traits in order for them to be considered an ethnic group (Pearson, 1985: 77). The professional literature of the social sciences, then, is by no means unanimous on the meaning of the term (Petersen, 1980:234–42; Thernstrom, 1980:v–ix).

As I have suggested elsewhere (1990) I suspect the self-interested *uses* made of such terms (by Mormons or others) are of greater interest than the controversies over the definition. Yet the danger remains that a term like *ethnic group* can lose all meaning if it is applied too promiscuously. If Mormons of all sizes, shapes, colors, cultures, and geographic origins can comprise an ethnic group, then who, one wonders, cannot? If the term has any meaning for Mormons, it is probably best understood not as categorical but as "emergent," that is, as waxing and waning under certain social-structural conditions like mutual institutional dependence, occupational and other kinds of homogeneity, residential concentration, and the like (Yancey, Ericksen, and Juliani, 1976).

The Mormon/Jewish Parallels

One of the more successful and meaningful applications of the term *ethnic group* is probably to the Jews, and one suspects that many who are inclined to use the same term for the Mormons will have the Jewish example at least in the backs of their minds (Goldscheider and Zuckerman, 1986:chaps. 1, 10, 11). It is an attractive comparison, for there are certain compelling parallels between the Jews and the Mormons. Both claim literal, Israelite origin. Both claim a special status in the divine historical scheme. Both cherish a history of having endured and prevailed over persecution. Each identifies to some extent with a certain homeland. Both possess a worldwide sense of community based on common teachings, rituals, myths, and definitions of reality. Both continue to be viewed with a certain suspicion or hostility, sometimes organized (as with the anti-Semitic and anti-Mormon movements that still occur in North America), sometimes only subtle or muted (Mackey et al., 1985).[6]

On the other hand, we must not be so facile about drawing parallels that we overlook the considerable differences between Mormons and Jews. The Mormon claim to an ultimate common ethnic origin of an Israelitish or any other kind is an article of faith among believers, having no scientific, historical, or other external validation (Epperson, 1992). It might be that a certain identifiable genetic structure can be found among the Mormons in

Utah, a synthesis of the waves of nineteenth-century migrations from the countries of northwestern Europe (Jorde, 1982). Indeed, one journalist of dubious talent has caricatured a pervasive blond, hulking, Viking "look" found in Utah (Bart, 1981:255, 260, 302ff). That is a far cry, however, from the ancient common Semitic origins claimed by the world's Jews.

Even Mormon persecution, as cruel as it was in the nineteenth century, was of relatively short duration, more akin to that suffered by the various other heretical Christian movements of history, and far short of the Jewish experience in either duration, severity, or recency. It is true that the Mormon "homeland" has its parallels to that of the Jews in its arid climate, its two lakes (one salty) joined by a river, and its settlement after an exhausting trek under a modern Moses. Yet it is a homeland that is becoming less Mormon all the time, even as Israel has been growing more Jewish. After another hundred years, the Mormon homeland might well be seen in retrospect as paralleling more the erstwhile "Puritan homeland" of New England than that of modern Israel.

Another important difference between Mormons and Jews is in their sources of growth: For the Jews, growth comes almost totally from natural increase, enhancing the likelihood of a fairly homogeneous ethnic subculture from one generation to the next. In contrast, the Mormons are an aggressively proselytizing body, with converts accounting for a large proportion of each year's increase. These converts, furthermore, are coming increasingly from so-called Third World cultures that are quite exotic to that of the North American homeland.

Without meaning, then, to minimize the differences that also exist among Jews in various parts of the world, we would still expect the Mormon culture across time to be far more influenced than the Jewish one by recruitment from the outside. Indeed, Mormons already lack the kind of common historic language and literature that the Jews have in their Hebrew and Yiddish. The unifying ritual, doctrinal, and epistemological heritage of the Mormons certainly remains important, as it does for any distinct religious community, but in that respect Mormons parallel the Jews no more than they do, say, the Catholics, whom we would not ordinarily consider a single ethnic group.

What is it, then, that ultimately has identified Mormons with other Mormons, beyond a shared religion, however distinctive that religion might be? To Martin Marty (1987), Mormons are best understood as "a people" rather than as a church or a religion, and it is a common "story" that makes a people, he says. Surely it begins to become ludicrous if we go far beyond the common religious tradition (story) and attempt to define Mormons from all the cultures and colors of the world as somehow constituting a new and separate ethnic category. Why not just call it a new world religion, as Jan Shipps (1985) or Rodney Stark (1984) would have it? Indeed, there is something incongruous and antithetical about thinking of the Mormons as a world church and as a separate ethnic group at the same time.[7]

Prospects for Peculiarity from the Midcentury Perspective

While scholars such as Thomas O'Dea and Dean May have made the case for a separate Mormon "peoplehood" or "ethnicity" about as convincingly as it can be made, it remains essentially a historical case. True as it might have been that nineteenth-century Mormons were an emergent ethnic group, with a subculture increasingly divergent from the American mainstream, such trends were obviously reversed during the twentieth-century assimilation of Mormons in North America. To be sure, there have recently been some strenuous and partially successful efforts by Mormons, at both the official and the folk levels, to resist this assimilation and the growing convergence with American culture more generally. Nevertheless, the assimilation proceeded apace during at least the first half of this century.

If we were to go back a generation and stand at the apex of Mormon assimilation in the sixties, what prospects might we have seen for the perpetuation of Mormon peculiarity, ethnicity, or any other kind of distinctiveness in future generations? Both the conventional sect-to-church model in social science and the historical experience of virtually all other religions would have led us to expect the continuing assimilation of Mormons. Similarly, Mormon history together with the evidence of the sixties surveys would have led us to see the process of assimilation as occurring right on schedule. Surely we would have predicted that American Mormons, at least, would become even less distinctive, less ethnic, by the end of the century than they had been in the sixties.

Our expectations about this process of assimilation would have been based on a number of factors. By the sixties the distributions of Mormons in the various categories of education, occupation, and community size of origin closely approximated those of the non-Mormons, although historically they had come disproportionately from lower-status occupations and rural upbringings (O'Dea, 1957). A traditional emphasis on education among Mormons had meanwhile produced a relatively high educational level in Utah; and there was some evidence that Mormon war veterans had taken advantage of the educational opportunities under the GI Bill at a rate somewhat higher than that of their non-Mormon contemporaries. All of this suggests a trend that would have made American Mormons even more thoroughly urban, educated, and high in occupational status by the end of the century than they had been in the sixties, perhaps even outstripping their non-Mormon neighbors in those respects.

The relatively high birth rates that our surveys reported would also have suggested an increasingly youthful Mormon population compared with the rest of the American population. What would we get with this combination of youth, education, and a preference for urban living—particularly during a period when the entire nation, especially in the cities, would be undergoing a wholesale liberation movement? Our urban San Francisco sample offered us the closest approximation to what we might have expected from the most youthful, urban, and potentially liberated Mormons of that time. It would be fascinating to see how those youthful urbanites have turned out by now. Even then, however, they demonstrated considerably lower levels than the other two Mormon samples of conformity to traditional Mormon religious teachings and life-style prescriptions. Would that comparison suggest a further narrowing of the differences between Mormons and others by the end of the century?

Some of the survey data enable us to predict how these factors might affect religious belief. For example, if, in the sixties, Mormons could have been expected to continue improving their average educational attainment, should that have led us to predict also a concomitant loss of Mormon commitment to their religion in favor of greater assimilation? In table 5.1 we can see how the percentages of Mormons high in orthodoxy varied with increasing levels of education.

Some of these samples might be too small for reliable results, but the general picture is the same whether we are looking at the San Francisco sample, the Salt Lake City sample, or the two of them combined: There is no appreciable variation in orthodoxy across the educational categories, certainly not enough to make the results statistically significant. In other words, educational level has no impact upon religious belief for Mormons (a finding, incidentally, replicated in more recent years—see Albrecht and

TABLE 5.1. Mormons High in Orthodoxy by Education Level, 1960s (percentages)

	Salt Lake City		San Francisco		Combined	
Educational Level	%	*N*	%	*N*	%	*N*
< Grade school	74	47	40	10	68	57
< High school	60	268	49	61	58	329
Tr./technical	65	100	42	26	60	126
Some college	69	260	41	102	61	326
B.A./B.S.	65	112	35	37	58	149
Some graduate work	68	73	53	36	63	109
M.A./M.S.	55	44	25	16	47	60
Doctoral degree	61	33	0	3	56	36

SOURCE: My 1967–68 and 1968–69 samples.

NOTE: Some of the items in the orthodoxy index were not the same for the 1964 East Bay sample as for the Salt Lake City and the San Francisco samples, so it is omitted from this and subsequent tables.

Heaton, 1984). We would thus not have been on firm ground in the sixties to have predicted any loss of Mormon commitment or peculiarity on the basis of greater education.

Yet we must not overlook one other important feature of table 5.1: Whatever the educational attainment, the levels of orthodoxy are consistently lower, usually by a third or more, for the San Francisco sample than for the Utah one. This suggests that the surrounding non-Mormon environment, especially in a highly urban area (or selective migration to such an environment), might have more to do with religious commitment than education does. On that basis, we might have been justified in the sixties if we had predicted greater assimilation for Mormons living in cities outside Utah than for those living within Utah. Here it might be useful to recall once again the distinction made between the entrenchment and the settlement phases of Mormon community life. It is not difficult to understand how the Mormon-entrenched environment of Salt Lake City would undermine distinctive Mormon beliefs far less than would the environment of San Francisco, where Mormons were well settled and numerous but still a small minority.

The amount of education, however, is only one aspect of the influence of education upon religious commitment. The *kind* of education is also very important, and no study has ever evaluated that issue, at least not among Mormons. In table 5.2, for those Mormons who had at least some exposure to higher education, we can see how the levels of orthodoxy differed according to their major fields of study in the sixties.

Once again, the number of respondents for several of these categories is too small to produce reliable percentages. However, the general picture is again quite clear. The consistent difference between the Utah and the San Francisco samples appears here just as it did in table 5.1. More important this time, however, are the differences by college major: Those Mormons who majored in the social sciences, the arts, and philosophy had the lowest levels of religious belief, whether we look at the two samples separately or at the combined percentages. The differences among the other majors in this table are not so noteworthy and probably not statistically significant. Why would the rates of religious orthodoxy be lower for Mormons in the social sciences, arts, and philosophy than for those in the other disciplines? The answer is probably that the other disciplines do not confront and challenge traditional religious beliefs, nor do they encourage a view of relativity about religion, as much as the social sciences, arts, and philosophy do.

Of course, from these data we can't tell whether training in the social sciences, for example, caused an erosion of orthodoxy or a strongly orthodox worldview led to an avoidance of college disciplines that would threaten traditional beliefs. Maybe both causal directions were at work. In any case, it is clear that we cannot draw facile conclusions about the lack of educational impact on religious belief without considering the kind of

TABLE 5.2. Mormons High in Orthodoxy by College Major, 1960s (percentages)

	Salt Lake City		San Francisco		Combined	
Major	%	*N*	%	*N*	%	*N*
Education	75	97	45	20	71	117
Liberal arts	71	38	38	16	61	54
Business	62	109	33	49	53	158
Mathematics	67	18	50	2	65	20
Physical sciences	62	39	40	10	57	49
Life sciences	73	63	69	16	72	79
Social sciences[1]	54	70	32	28	48	98
Arts	61	33	34	29	48	62
Philosophy and religion	33	3	100	1	50	4

SOURCE: My 1967–68 and 1968–69 samples.

1. Social science here includes history.

education in question. It seems clear, too, that on the basis of table 5.2 we would have been inclined in the 1960s to predict some erosion in the ethnic peculiarity at least of those educated Mormons identified with the three most relativistic college majors.[8]

Tables 5.1 and 5.2 provide only two examples of the kinds of analysis that could be done, step by step, to assess the prospects of future Mormon religious commitment and peculiarity in the face of many different secular influences. Besides educational attainment and college major, there are such potentially secularizing influences as occupational type or prestige, participation in professional and other nonreligious organizations, association with close friends who are not Mormon, and so on.

I created an index of cosmopolitanism to provide a general and composite measure of the extent to which the Mormons in the surveys of the sixties were exposed to a variety of "worldly" influences (see the Appendix for a complete description of the indexing process). This index combines measures of (1) educational attainment; (2) educational major; (3) occupational prestige; and (4) membership and weekly hours of participation in (a) professional/academic societies, (b) political clubs or interest groups, and (c) literary, art, or study clubs (see table 5.3).

The most striking feature of table 5.3 is the asymmetry between the two samples: There were no Salt Lake City Mormons in the three highest levels of the index and there were no San Francisco Mormons in the three lowest levels. The explanation for this asymmetry is found in the facts that the San Franciso Mormons were somewhat more likely than their Salt Lake City counterparts to be at least college graduates; considerably more likely to have majored in the social sciences, arts, or philosophy; and far more likely to have been actively involved in a variety of secular clubs, organizations, and societies. We would expect these outside involvements to be more important, of course, for those living in the settlement phase of Mormon community life, as the San Francisco Mormons did during the sixties, than for the Utah Mormons in the entrenched phase, where church activities and associations could more fully monopolize their lives.

But what difference does all this make? Is Mormon religious commitment affected by the combination of influences represented in the index of cosmopolitanism? The correlation of this index with the index of orthodoxy was −.063 for the Utah Mormons and −.238 for the San Francisco Mormons. The two indexes were thus inversely related, so that those high in cosmopolitanism were likely to be low in orthodoxy, and vice versa.

Notice, however, that the correlation for the San Francisco Mormons

TABLE 5.3. Distributions of Mormons on Index of Cosmopolitanism, 1960s

	Low 1	2	3	4	5	6	High 7	Totals
Salt Lake City								
%	27	27	22	24	0	0	0	100
N	259	258	214	227	0	0	0	958
San Francisco								
%	0	0	0	26	25	25	24	100
N	0	0	0	77	73	75	71	296
Combined								
%	21	21	17	24	6	6	6	100
N	259	258	214	304	73	75	71	1,254

SOURCE: My 1967–68 and 1968–69 samples.

was *four* times that for the Utah Mormons (.063 versus .238). Such a drastic difference suggests that the Mormon religion so permeated even the daily secular lives of the Utah Mormons that the kinds of influences measured by the index of cosmopolitanism had almost no impact on their religious beliefs (again, something that we might expect in the "entrenched" setting, especially when it is in Utah). The much more appreciable correlation for the San Francisco Mormons suggests that, as we might expect in the less entrenched "settlement" phase of Mormon community life, outside influences really did have the power to undermine traditional Mormon beliefs (or, alternatively, Mormons who had already experienced some erosion of belief were more likely to seek outside associations and influences).

In any case, had we been standing back in the sixties and making predictions about the survival of Mormon peculiarity, we would probably have expected that increasing assimilation would bring increasing erosion in the residual distinctiveness of the Mormon way of life. Of course, we could not expect the church to stand idly by and watch the erosion take place. One of the programs that the church already had in place by this time to help the members maintain their Mormon ways was "family home evening." To the extent that the parents themselves were active in the church, we might have expected them to give meticulous attention to home religious instruction through home evening activities or otherwise.[9]

Another weapon of the church in the struggle against the loss of religious commitment was religious education. By the sixties, the church had started providing in California and elsewhere the same daily program of

TABLE 5.4. Mormons High in Orthodoxy by Religious Training, 1960s.

	Salt Lake City Mormons			San Francisco Mormons		
	Parental Church Activity[1]					
	Father	Mother (or other)	Both	Father	Mother (or other)	Both
%	27	57	71	11	39	52
N	22	361	548	9	168	115
	Seminary Exposure					
	None	1–2 Yrs.	3+ Yrs.	None	1–2 Yrs.	3+ Yrs.
%	62	60	70	40	42	49
N	400	178	283	145	55	69
	Institute Exposure					
	None	1 Yr.	2+ Yrs.	None	1 Yr.	2+ Yrs.
%	57	72	79	28	33	69
N	726	95	137	210	34	52

SOURCE: My 1967–68 and 1968–69 samples.

1. "Father" means that the father was active in the church while the person was growing up, but the mother was not. "Mother" means just the opposite, but this column includes also various other combinations for which orthodoxy was distributed very similarly as for "Mother" (one or both parents active in a different church, or neither parent active in any church). "Both" means that both parents were active members of the church while the respondent was growing up.

formal religious instruction for the youth that it had already had in Utah for two generations. At the high school level, this program was (and is) called "seminary," which would meet daily, usually in the early mornings before school. At the college level, the program was (and is) called "institute" because Mormon students at the various colleges (even junior colleges) would be expected to include in their academic schedules certain college-level religion courses offered at nearby LDS institutes of religion.

Could the church's family and religious education programs of this time be counted on to preserve a distinctive Mormon culture in future generations? We can see from table 5.4 how likely high orthodoxy was to be found among those with varying levels of exposure to devout parents and to formal religious education.

Upbringing in a home where both parents had been active Mormons was clearly of crucial importance to the religious orthodoxy of the sixties Mormons, whether in Utah or in San Francisco, but it was more important in San Francisco, where the percentages increased nearly five times (11% to 52%) depending on the nature and degree of parental religious activity. Even in Utah there was almost a threefold increase (27% to 71%). We would, of course, have expected home influences to have been more crucial in San Francisco, where they were competing with so many other influences, than in Utah, where much in the home is reinforced from the general cultural environment.

By comparison, exposure to the obligatory high school seminary program was much less important, having, indeed, minimal impact in either Utah or San Francisco (a finding replicated, but only in part, in a more recent survey—see Cornwall, 1987a). The college-level religious institute training was certainly accompanied by increased levels of orthodoxy, but in this case we can't be sure whether the institute training increased belief or the believers were more likely to choose institute as part of their college training.

Summary

This chapter and the previous ones have invited the reader, in effect, to step back into the sixties, review the extensive assimilation that had occurred by then in the Mormon subculture, and consider the prospects for continuing assimilation. The relatively few life-style distinctions that had survived were hardly stigmatizing and probably not a sufficient basis for defining the Mormons as a separate "ethnic group." Such "ethnicity" as had been discovered by O'Dea and others depended primarily on historic Mormon peculiarities that had mostly been lost or seriously eroded by midcentury, a process that has continued in many respects as Mormons have become even more cosmopolitan. Yet the rhetoric of ethnicity and related concepts still has its uses in serving the needs of Mormon church leaders, intellectuals, and even grass-roots members in their efforts to assert a special Mormon identity despite the manifest assimilation. Furthermore, there was evidence already in the sixties that the church had both the means and the intention of resisting this assimilation through special programs of family renewal and religious education.

Notes

1. In this connection, the Mormon missionaries of the forties, fifties, and even sixties, will recall the ubiquitous Penrose and Widtsoe series of missionary tracts.

2. Numerous biographies of Malcolm X (by Haley himself, among others), along with the 1992 Spike Lee movie on Malcolm's life, testify to the continuing appeal of black separatism for many African Americans.

3. This proliferation of scholarly literature is apparent from a bibliography by Mauss and Franks, 1984. More recent bibliographies, e.g., Mauss and Reynolds, n.d., and Allen, Walker, and Whittaker, n.d., will provide even fuller demonstrations of this proliferation. It must be emphasized here that by "scholarly literature" I am referring primarily to social science literature, including, to be sure, most of the so-called "new Mormon history." I do not mean, however, to slight the much earlier literary work of Mormonism's "lost generation," as it is sometimes called, or any of the (relatively few) serious historical studies like Brodie's or Arrington's that came well before the sixties.

Incidentally, an interesting parallel can perhaps be seen here to scholarly developments in the Jewish community, nearly all of the literature on which is written of, by, and for Jews. One informed scholar of this work (Heilman, 1982) has suggested that this represents in part an effort to legitimize Jewish studies in the minds of Jews and others. A comparable motivation might reasonably be attributed to many of the Mormon scholars.

4. Perhaps the recent publication by the Macmillan Company of the *Encyclopedia of Mormonism* (Ludlow, 1992) could also be seen as adding somewhat to the legitimation of an ethnic conception of the Mormons.

5. On the other hand, one of the themes of the subsequent chapters is that people are likely to make a renewed effort to reassert their identity precisely at those times when that identity seems the most ambiguous. Whether or not that identity has to take on "ethnic" dimensions, of course, is a different issue.

6. Indeed, I have been so struck with the parallel stereotypes applied to Mormons and Jews that I have come to think of the Mormons as the "Jews of the Rockies."

7. Jan Shipps (1994) has also revealed a tendency to continue thinking of even contemporary Mormons in ethnic terms. Drawing on the conceptualizations of Werner Stollars, Shipps employs the term *saintmaking* to refer to the process by which Mormon converts come to internalize Mormon ethnicity. Most social scientists, I think, would find it difficult to see what the neologism *saintmaking* adds to what we have for many years been calling "socialization" (or "resocialization"), or how that process somehow makes Mormons more ethnic than would the same process among, say, Roman Catholics.

8. A study of changes across time in the religious beliefs of Mormon scholars and scientists in various fields (Wooton, 1992) demonstrates clearly that those in the social sciences were far less likely to maintain their orthodox Mormon beliefs than those in the physical or biological sciences.

9. A separate study of the data from these same Mormon surveys indicated that family home evening experience in childhood was quite strongly predictive of religious commitment in adult life (see Gordon Mauss, "Religious and Secular Correlates of the LDS Family Home Evening Program," master's thesis, Brigham Young University, 1969).

PART 3

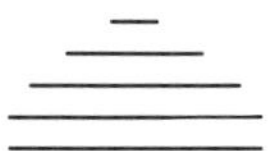

Coping with Assimilation and Respectability

CHAPTER SIX

The Official Response to Assimilation

The rest of the chapters in this book will develop the thesis that by the 1960s the Mormon movement had become so successful in living down the nineteenth century, and in dealing with the predicament of disrepute, that it had entered a new stage in its history, a stage in which the movement faced a new predicament of respectability (with the dominant symbol of the Beehive), rather than the old one of disrepute.

Faced with cultural assimilation, Mormons have felt the need since the sixties to reach ever more deeply into their bag of cultural peculiarities to find either symbolic or actual traits that will help them mark their subcultural boundaries and thus their very identity as a special people. Even the traditional Mormon theological teachings, considered heresies by other Christians, don't help much in a society that (in general) has grown indifferent to theology, a society that cares far less about how God is defined and revealed than about how personal fulfillment can be achieved. In such a predicament, how does a people so accustomed to thinking of itself as peculiar deny its domestication and successfully reassert its unique identity? The collective and individual efforts in this regard, contrived as well as authentic, constitute an interesting study in the adaptation of a successful religious movement to the predicament of respectability.

Certain caveats seem appropriate at this point concerning the historical theory being applied to the Mormon case. It is important that the reader not take the theory too literally. It is intended only as an "ideal type," a general framework that fits empirical reality only approximately. To discuss different "stages" in Mormon history is not to imply that history can be arbitrarily divided into discrete and independent segments in the way that sports events are divided into quarters, downs, or innings. Stages of history are a lot like stages of individual human growth and development, in which one stage imperceptibly gives way to another.

For example, when we speak of the "adolescent" stage of human development, we have a general idea of about when it starts and when it ends and what the chief features are. Yet we know that it can begin or end much later in some people than in others. We know also that many of the traits we associate with adolescence have their origins, genetic or psychological, much earlier in life. So it is with stages of history: We can arbitrarily impose demarcations that might prove more or less useful for certain kinds of analysis, but we know that such boundaries can never be more than approximate; that many forces set in motion during earlier stages can spill over into later stages; and that many features of a given stage are but the full flowering of seeds planted in earlier stages. Thus we can speak of forces or characteristics that are emergent in a given stage of history, as well as those that are dominant.

It is important to recognize too that no matter how valid any given conception of "stages" might be for a real and concrete case, the conceptualization of the stages is done only retrospectively by historians or other scholars. The actors in history typically do not have any sense of stages as history is unfolding. Theories about historical developments (in stages or otherwise) are based upon the naturalistic assumption that social processes do not require teleological intention or understanding by individuals in order for the processes to take place, any more than biological or physical processes do. In other words, no claim is intended that anyone has planned for one stage to end and another to begin. With these caveats in mind, let us proceed to assess the thesis that beginning in or around the 1960s, Mormons began to become increasingly aware of their new predicament of respectability,

This awareness is apparent on at least three levels: First is the official level, where we can identify renewed efforts by the presiding authorities to reassert the charismatic and prophetic element (represented by the angel) through new church initiatives, as well as through reemphasis, renewal, or retrenchment in existing programs and principles. Second is the folk level, which refers to the efforts of individuals and groups of Mormons in wards and stakes at the grass roots to identify and promote certain values and norms of behavior as uniquely Mormon, or especially Mormon, in reaction against the pressures of assimilation.

Third is the intellectual level, at which we can see a concentrated effort on the parts of Mormon academics and intellectuals to seek out, illuminate, and celebrate their unique historical and cultural identity. Such enterprises as the Mormon History Association, *Dialogue*, *Sunstone* (both symposia and magazine), *Exponent II*, and the "Camelot" days in the Church Historical Department can all be understood as part of this third level of effort (Bitton, 1983; Ludlow, 1992:1388–89). This chapter will be devoted only to discussing the efforts made at the official level to recover eroding peculiarity.

Seeds Planted in Earlier Decades

It is not likely that a Mormon president or other general authority ever arose among his colleagues to announce that the church was entering a new stage of history, with its "predicament of respectability." It is thus very difficult to say with any precision just when the assimilationist stage began to wind down and the current resistance to assimilation started in earnest. Assimilationist and retrenchment elements have always existed side by side, both at the various levels of church leadership and at the grass roots. Some openness to assimilation is obviously still present in the church, which continues to strive for at least a modicum of respectability, both within the nation and among the denominations of Christianity.[1]

Yet it seems clear in retrospect that at some point during the past three or four decades at least some segment of the church leadership began to become more concerned with the costs of assimilation than with the benefits; more concerned with the consequences of a muted Mormon identity, an ambiguous peculiarity, than with maintaining or enhancing a position of comfortable respectability. That segment of church leadership, furthermore, seems increasingly to have gained ascendancy during the most recent generation of Mormons.[2]

The seeds of change toward a renewed emphasis on Mormon distinctiveness might have been planted as early as the midthirties. A fertile environment for such seeds would have been provided by the Great Depression, which brought a sense of crisis in the Mormon community and perhaps a renewed sense of dependence on basic principles and on the church as a source of security. The newly organized church welfare program of that time, with its renewed stress on the value of Mormon communitarianism (however attenuated), might be understood as one expression of such a sense among the Saints (Arrington, 1964; Hinton, 1985).

The contemporaneous changes in American political culture, exemplified by the repeal of Prohibition and by the New Deal, were also threatening in certain ways, at least to many of the church leaders. President Heber J. Grant (and perhaps other church leaders as well) regarded the emergent political values as so subversive to the moral fiber of the nation that he switched his personal allegiance to the Republican party during this period. As liberalism in American politics came to be accompanied by liberalism in certain moral outlooks, especially during the sixties, the alarm of church leaders and members grew accordingly.

If indeed the decade of the thirties provided a fertile environment for the seeds of change, then many of them were sown by the determined hand of J. Reuben Clark. This is not to subscribe to a "great man" theory of history or to any comparably simplistic explanation for historical developments. Yet, a reading of the biography of Clark during his church years (Quinn, 1983) readily convinces one that his appointment to the First Presidency of the church in 1933 had a more profound impact on the future of the Mormon church and culture than did that of any First Presidency appointment in the twentieth century.

Much of the significance of President Clark's appointment lies in the fortuitous demise at about the same time of some of the great minds of the church who had been proponents of quite a different leadership orientation from his—e.g., B. H. Roberts, James Talmage, and Anthony Ivins. Equally significant and coincidental was the fact that for nearly two decades the presidents of the church to whom Clark was First Counselor were not in vigorous health (both President Grant and President George Albert Smith). These coincidental conditions in the top church leadership, in effect, left the vigorous, conservative, and eloquent President Clark as the most influential spokesman for the Presiding Brethren, both within and without the church, with but few, if any, of his colleagues possessing comparable personal or ecclesiastical power.

To some extent, Clark's colleague in the First Presidency, David O. McKay, provided a degree of balance, but President McKay disliked confrontations of any kind and tended to avoid engaging Clark directly. That Clark's arrival among the general authorities signaled the emergence of a distinct camp among the leaders is evident from the tendency among them, even in the thirties, to speak of each other as "Clark men" or "McKay men" (Quinn, 1983). In the early forties, with President Grant largely incapacitated, four crucial appointments were made to the Quorum of the Twelve, Harold B. Lee, Spencer W. Kimball, Ezra Taft Benson, and Mark E. Petersen, at least three of whom were recognizably Clark men.

Elder Lee, of course, despite the brevity of his later occupancy of the role of church president, was to have a powerful impact upon church organization first as the "father" of the Welfare Program (in the thirties), and later of the correlation movement, long before he became president (Goates, 1985; Gottlieb and Wiley, 1984; Shipps, 1994; Wiley, 1984–85). Elder Petersen, during much of his tenure among the Twelve, had the special assignment of keeping an eye on schismatics and other apostates and trying to protect the church from their influence.[3] Elders Lee, Petersen, and Benson have all been known in recent church history for their conservatism (theological and political), their preference for centralized and standardized leadership and control, their stress upon obedience, especially to the living prophet, and their suspicion of scholars and intellectuals (Poll, 1985; Quinn, 1992a, 1992b, 1993).

While we cannot be sure of the extent of President Clark's direct involvement in the calls of these three conservative brethren to the Twelve in the early forties (absent our access to the records of the relevant deliberations), we are justified in assuming that his influence must have been great, given that he was at this time (1941–44) de facto president of the church (President Grant was to die in early 1945 after a lengthy incapacitation). It is apparent also that the three above-mentioned conservative apostles shared President Clark's preferences for a church leadership style that was more formal, bureaucratic, and centralized than had been the case earlier (Quinn, 1983).

The Emergence of a New Leadership Orientation

The point here is not that Elders Lee, Petersen, and Benson conspired with President Clark to launch the church in a radically different direction of some kind. After all, the topmost leadership from this period on included such other important leaders as David O. McKay, Stephen L. Richards, John A. Widtsoe, and Matthew Cowley, clearly not Clark men. The point is only that as these Clark-sponsored brethren gained seniority and power (along with such like-minded and outspoken colleagues as Bruce R. McConkie, appointed to the First Council of Seventy also in the forties), they would have been disposed to support the renewal and retrenchment ethos that became increasingly apparent in the church leadership during more recent decades. Their support might or might not have been decisive, but it must have been important.

Particularly influential was Harold B. Lee. His correlation movement, which began in the church around 1960 (Allen and Leonard, 1992: chap. 20; Gottlieb and Wiley, 1984; Poll, 1985; Wiley, 1984–85), has functioned as the organizational expression of the renewal and retrenchment ethos just mentioned. As Richard Poll explains from personal knowledge and experience, Elder Lee, the "quintessential Iron Rod," was the prime mover of correlation, a program "originally intended to eliminate duplicate and inefficient programs," but which by the seventies had produced "a standardized and sanitized instructional curriculum [in which the] intellectual threat was being contained by eliminating intellectual inquiry from Church education" (1985: 17).[4]

In such a role, Elder Lee was not only "the right man in the right place at the right time," says Poll, to promote the new retrenchment thrust, but Lee "will surely be remembered as one of the ten most influential General Authorities in the history of the Church" (1985: 17). That should also qualify him as the single most important of all the Clark men brought into the leadership during the postwar era. Lee was remembered by Ernest L. Wilkinson, president of BYU 1951–71, as a determined man, seemingly arrogant at times, who was often able to intimidate his colleagues in the church hierarchy during (sometimes stormy) meetings of the BYU Board of Trustees; and Wilkinson himself, it should be noted, was no shrinking violet.[5]

Already in the early fifties, Elder Lee, along with colleagues J. F. Smith, Bruce R. McConkie, and others, were asserting themselves in such retrenchment efforts as trying to close down the "swearing elders" seminars at the University of Utah (Blakely, 1985; Poll, 1985); removing or transferring such "liberals" as George Boyd and Heber Snell from the Utah LDS institutes (Sherlock, 1979); and promoting the adoption of Elder Smith's anti-evolutionist *Man: His Origin and Destiny* as a textbook for the institutes of religion.

Whether or not through the influence of President Clark and the Clark men who followed him, the appointments to the Quorum of the Twelve Apostles since Clark's time have not included many men with scientific, scholarly training or experience. The contrast with the first half of the twentieth century is striking: Apostles appointed during that period included a generous proportion of men with demonstrated scholarly credentials and accomplishments in the world's terms – men such as David O.

McKay, James E. Talmage, Richard R. Lyman, John A. Widtsoe, and Joseph F. Merrill—who together constituted a third of all the apostles appointed in the twentieth century up to President Clark's time. These were men of undoubted religious commitment and church loyalty who nevertheless were comfortable with worldly learning and confident that Mormonism could not only hold its own in intellectual competition but perhaps even find some of its vindication therein.

Among the thirty or so apostles appointed since President Clark's arrival, those with backgrounds in business or law have been favored to the near exclusion of any with training in scholarly pursuits. Dallin Oaks, and perhaps one or two other recent appointments, would constitute exceptions to this generalization. Yet even those few with some academic backgrounds tend (with perhaps the exception of Oaks) to have earned their distinctions more in academic administration than in scholarship per se (Deseret News, 1990:15–18, 46–52).

This same tendency also permeates the next leadership echelons down: Tabulations compiled randomly from the weekly *Church News* during ten weeks in the spring of 1991 revealed that of seven general authority appointments, three came from careers in either business or law and the other four were already employees of the church's professional civil service bureaucracy. Of fifteen regional representatives, six came from business, two from engineering, two from agriculture, two from medicine, one was a NASA scientist, and the other two had already been in the professional church bureaucracy.

Of twenty-six mission presidents appointed, twelve came from business, three each from law and medicine, two from engineering, five from the church bureaucracy (usually the Church Education System), and one was an educational administrator. Of fourteen stake presidents appointed, seven came from business, three from the medical professions, three from law or law enforcement, and one that could not be classified.

Of fifteen new appointments to the Second Quorum of Seventy a year later (*Church News*, June 6, 1992, 3–5), six were already salaried employees of the church's professional bureaucracy, seven came directly from the business world, and almost all had degrees either in business fields or in educational administration. Of ten new stake presidencies reported in the *Church News* later in the same summer (Sept. 12, 1992, 13), including six in Latin America, almost all were recruited from managerial positions in business or government or from the church civil service bureaucracy. In the six Latin American cases, the resort to employees of the church bureaucracy (especially the Church Education System) was especially apparent (a common tendency outside the United States). Tabulations from nearly any cohort of new regional and general church appointments would yield similar results.

At this juncture, the reader might well wonder about the significance attached here to these changes across time in the career backgrounds of the church leaders (especially of the Twelve). Let the point be clear: It is not that scholars make better church leaders; indeed, anyone who has spent a career in academia would be more likely to argue that it is a rare academic scholar who is good at any kind of administration. Neither is the point that scholarly types have been deliberately and systematically excluded from church leadership. It is far more likely that their exclusion is a more or less natural and unintended consequence of the growing need for general authorities with the backgrounds and competence to manage the church's burgeoning commercial and industrial resources (cf. Robertson et al., 1991). Nor is all of this to be understood as special pleading on behalf of the academic profession, as though we feel slighted by our exclusion from the highest ranks of church leadership.

The point, rather, is much more sociological: Different kinds of education, training, and careers create different cognitive orientations or mindsets. People who are trained and work in practical fields, such as business, engineering, medicine, and public administration, are likely to approach problems (even church problems) in a pragmatic way. This does not imply any lack of values in even the most pragmatic decisions, but the decisions are likely to reflect primarily cost-benefit analyses.

Such analyses are not usually hospitable to abstractions or to considerations of relativity. They tend to be based upon discrete and categorical realities: what's real and what isn't, what works and what doesn't. Those with advanced education and experience in the more scientific (as opposed to applied) disciplines, on the other hand, are more comfortable with abstractions and ambiguities, more likely to recognize the differential realities that derive from different theories, and thus more likely to appreciate the importance of various kinds of relativity in human affairs. Such a difference in outlook is no doubt part of what lies behind the relationship, reported in chapter 5, between religious orthodoxy and college major.

The near-total disappearance of leaders with the more scientific or scholarly orientation from the topmost ranks of the church leadership thus implies that with the passage of time there would be a corresponding diminution within that leadership of their collective capacity to accommodate diversity, relativity, or ambiguity in church policies or programs, to say nothing of doctrines. Such a leadership would naturally be increasingly hospitable also to proposals for greater correlation, centralization, and other forms of retrenchment in the face of growing ambiguity about what assimilated Mormonism really "stands for" in the modern world. There is no need to postulate intent or calculation in any of this, to say nothing of conspiracy. It is a simple matter of a leadership with a certain collective outlook coming together with a certain new predicament in Mormon history. It can be taken for granted that the overwhelming majority of church leaders at all echelons and at any given time are conscientiously trying to do what they see as serving the best interests of the church and its membership.

The Five Major Thrusts of Retrenchment

In any case, it is against the background of such historical developments in the church during the forties, fifties, and sixties that we can see certain new initiatives by the leadership in more recent years to reassert the distinguishing features of the Mormon heritage, almost as if to declare, "Assimilation has gone far enough. Let's start remembering the things that have made us a peculiar people." Five of these initiatives, in particular, seem especially apparent and worthy of review here: renewed assertion of the claim of continuous revelation through modern prophets; renewed emphasis on temples, temple work, and genealogical research; expansion and standardization of the missionary enterprise; family renewal and retrenchment; and expansion of formal religious education in the service of parochial indoctrination.

Reassertion of the Principle of Continuous Revelation through Modern Prophets

Though one of the classical principles of Mormonism, the ideal of continuous revelation through modern prophets has received renewed emphasis in recent years. One form of this new emphasis is the increased frequency with which one hears the plea "Follow the Brethren." Once again, the Shepherd and Shepherd study (1984) of changing themes at general conferences proves instructive here.

Six themes they studied in five periods from 1830 to 1979 exhibit a similar pattern of changing prominence at these conferences. In the fourth

TABLE 6.1. Changing Saliency of Themes Related to "Follow the Brethren" at Mormon General Conferences

Themes	1830–59	1860–89	1890–1919	1920–49	1950–79
Absolute truth	.002	.003	.002	.001	.005
Obedience to authority	.019	.017	.008	.001	.005
Disobedience/rebellion	.015	.018	.013	.005	.029
Prophets	.041	.052	.056	.042	.050
Revelation (esp. modern)	.049	.056	.035	.013	.026
Priesthood	.077	.042	.068	.024	.044

SOURCE: Compiled from Shepherd and Shepherd (1984), appendix C.

period, between 1920 and 1949, when the assimilationist motif among the Mormons was approaching its apex, or even between 1890 and 1919 when assimilation was just beginning, these traditional Mormon ideals dropped in significance and then rose again during the fifth period between 1950 and 1979, when retrenchment was setting in. Some of the increases in saliency from the fourth to the fifth period are quite dramatic: a fivefold increase (.001 to .005) for absolute truth and obedience, a sixfold increase for the dangers of disobedience, and a doubling for the themes of revelation and priesthood authority. It seems clear enough that after a few decades of reduced emphasis on the importance of obedience to the living Mormon prophets, the general authorities of the church began once again at midcentury to call the Saints back to that traditional ideal (table 6.1).

During those same decades of assimilation and reduced emphasis on the uniquely Mormon prophetic claims (1920–49), the church also moved increasingly toward its own de facto canonization of the King James Version of the Bible, which had earlier been regarded as the common Bible for Mormons, but not necessarily their official Bible (Barlow, 1991). In the most recent decades, however, the church has integrated its own printing of the King James Version into a complex of other scriptures, footnotes, and reference works in such a way as, in effect, to Mormonize the Protestant Bible retroactively as part of the new reassertion of Mormon prophetic claims.

Another manifestation of the reassertion of Mormonism's prophetic tradition has been the addition of three new revelatory sections and a new Official Declaration to the latest edition of the Doctrine and Covenants (after a hiatus of nearly a century), as though to remind the world that Mormon prophets can still get revelations. The renewed emphasis upon the Book of Mormon in recent years can also be seen in this light. On the one hand, the assimilationist motif of the church can be seen in the new subtitle of the Book of Mormon as "Another Testament of Jesus Christ" (thus stressing the common Christian heritage with the rest of America); yet, on the other hand, that book is given more emphasis than ever as the most concrete evidence available of the prophetic claims of Joseph Smith. The increased attention to the Book of Mormon has been especially noteworthy during the administration of President Ezra Taft Benson.

Clearly related to this new emphasis, especially under the influence of Spencer W. Kimball (though somewhat attenuated lately), has been the increased focus on Native Americans as descendants of the Lamanites of the Book of Mormon, and, indeed, the expansion of the "Lamanite" designation officially in recent years to cover all Polynesians as well.[6] The establishment a decade or so ago of the Foundation for Ancient Research and Mormon Studies at BYU might be seen as a scholarly, or even a semi-official, expression of the same renewed emphasis on the Book of Mormon. All of these developments, in one way or another, seem to testify that the prophetic claims of Mormonism are being renewed in an effort to recover some of the traditional grounds of Mormon distinctiveness.

This effort has extended also to a reassertion of Mormon particularism after a period of doctrinal convergence with Protestant Christianity. The Shepherd and Shepherd research (1984) on sermons at general conferences illustrates this renewed focus on uniquely Mormon claims and scriptural interpretations. The Book of Mormon itself actually remained quite a stable topic across time, but the renewed emphasis on the Lamanites increased sharply from virtually zero at the turn of the century. The saliency score during the most recent period was fourteen times what it had been in the immediately previous period. Other special Mormon doctrines also showed noteworthy increases in emphasis after 1950 (table 6.2).

Mormon particularism (the antithesis of ecumenism or assimilation), seen especially in the notion of the Mormon church as the one true church or as the kingdom of God, actually more than doubled during the retrenchment period. Even Christ and his divinity, always important in Mormon doctrine, got renewed emphasis in the modern period, probably contra the erosion of the divinity theme perceived in liberal Protestantism during the present century. Satan and the literal resurrection, two other themes fallen into disuse in certain Protestant circles, also received Mormon reemphasis recently. It is as though the Mormon leadership of the past three decades has been making sure the members know that this church, at least, still promotes "that old-time religion," no matter how unfashionable it might have become elsewhere.

Even some of the unpopular positions of the Mormon leadership in

TABLE 6.2. Changing Saliency Scores of Special Mormon Doctrinal Themes in General Conference Sermons

Themes	1830–59	1860–89	1890–1919	1920–49	1950–79
Book of Mormon	.010	.010	.011	.015	.014
Lamanites	.003	.004	.000	.001	.014
One true church	.003	.003	.008	.003	.006
Mormon church as Kingdom of God	.114	.151	.029	.004	.010
Satan	.019	.027	.013	.014	.023
Jesus Christ	.036	.022	.050	.042	.104
Resurrection	.011	.003	.007	.002	.006

SOURCE: Compiled from Shepherd and Shepherd (1984), appendix C.

national politics in recent years can be understood as efforts to maintain the integrity of the prophetic office (Mauss and Bradford, 1988). For example, the official response to criticisms of the church's pre-1978 racial policy took the form mainly of reasserting the divine legitimacy of the prophets' leadership, and that issue, from early on, displaced the racial issue itself in the minds of the church leaders and probably in the minds of most members, as well (Mauss, 1981). Similarly, the more contemporary resistance at the official level to the Equal Rights Amendment, and to many other claims of the feminist movement, is not necessarily so much an expression of sheer patriarchal obstinacy as it is yet another assertion of the integrity and charisma of the prophetic office in the face of pressures for political expediency.

Renewed Emphasis on Genealogy and Temple Work

Few characteristics are as uniquely and authentically Mormon as genealogy and temple work. Both have received an enormously increased official church emphasis in the past two decades especially. Genealogical research, hopelessly slow and tedious as long as it was left mainly in the hands of a reluctant laity, has been increasingly computerized and turned over to a cadre of professional experts and to specially trained volunteers at widely dispersed local genealogical libraries. The "name extraction" program greatly facilitates the process of generating and approving names of the deceased for temple work, which can now be done on an individual basis, irrespective of demonstrated family ties either to the researcher or to other individuals of record.

At the same time, however, the Saints at large are kept involved in the genealogy program, at least in principle, through the continued call for each individual to maintain a four-generation group sheet and through the expansion of the meaning of "genealogy" to include the compiling of family history more generally. (Indeed, the genealogy program and library of the church were renamed "Family History" during the eighties.) One important effect of all this for purposes of the present discussion is to foster the continued sense of connection to a unique identity and heritage among the members, including even the converts to some extent.

Inseparably connected with the genealogical commitments of the church is, of course, the temple work. Since 1950, there has been a tremendous increase in the emphasis given to temples and temple work in general conference sermons, as Shepherd and Shepherd (1984) have demonstrated. The changing emphasis on genealogical research itself does not conform to our usual theoretical expectation of decline followed by eventual renewal; from 1890 on, this topic has remained quite stable. For the topics of temples and temple work, however, we see again the predicted pattern. As the Mormon assimilation process began, these related topics declined but then, in the modern period, increased sevenfold and elevenfold, respectively (Shepherd and Shepherd, 1984:255).

The rhetoric has been matched by temple-building activity: Until 1950, there had never been more than eight temples in operation throughout the world. Five more were built in the next fifteen years. The *1991–1992 Church Almanac* (Deseret News, 1990) lists some fifty in operation and still others under construction. This sharp increase in the number of temples has been accompanied by a streamlining of the temple endowment ceremony, both substantively and technologically, and by a drastic modernization of the temple undergarment (Buerger, 1987).

While such changes have in part been concessions to modernity, they have also made temple work more accessible geographically, logistically, and even psychologically to a vastly larger proportion of the church membership than ever before. There might be some question about how much increase proportionately has occurred in actual temple participation (Buerger, 1987), but the very presence of temples in the new locations around the world, and the potential for increased participation in the unique and esoteric temple rites, enhance the sense of distinct identity among Mormons who are living near the growing numbers of temples and wearing the undergarment (modernized or not) as a symbol of resistance to assimilation by the world (Mauss, 1987).

The Missionary Program

While Mormons have always been a proselytizing people, the slogan "Every Member a Missionary" symbolizes the renewed emphasis on missionary work since World War II and especially during the past three decades. Earlier in the century, mission calls to young men were by no means routine, and a relatively small proportion of them received calls. A mission call was such a special event, indeed, that the "missionary farewell" services were rather long and elaborate, complete with printed programs, imported speakers and musicians, and other forms of celebration. If held during a regular worship service (sacrament meeting), a missionary farewell program would totally preempt the normal worship proceedings and greatly prolong the meeting. Often, though, the farewell would be held on a totally separate occasion, and invitations would be sent far and wide.

Somewhat ironically, the modern scaling down and routinizing of the farewell service, and the elimination of the attractively printed programs and other fanfare, symbolize well the attempt of the church in recent years to routinize and universalize the expectation of a mission call, at least for the young men, and increasingly for the young women, as well. Though only about a third of the eligible young men actually serve missions these days, and a much smaller proportion of the young women do, that is a tremendous increase over the proportions that were called earlier in the century. With almost fifty thousand maintained in the field these days, there are as many Mormon missionaries serving in the world now as are sent by all of the American Protestant denominations combined (see Ludlow, 1992:910–20).

The standardization, centralized control, and routinization of Mormon missionary work since midcentury all combine to make the mission experience a vastly different one for today's young missionaries from that which their parents would remember. Until about 1960, mission presidents were called for indefinite time periods (sometimes lasting many years), and they were given enormous autonomy by the general authorities over both the missionaries and the church members in their jurisdictions. Very few instructions were given to the mission presidents, except to draw close to the Lord and lead by the Spirit. Since some presidents were much more spiritual, competent, or conscientious than others, there was always much variation in rules and procedures from one mission to another and from one president to his successor in the same mission.

These differences, in turn, were reflected both in the fluctuating conversion rates of the various missions and in the nature of the mission experience for the individual missionary. There was no special training for missionaries beyond a few days of orientation in Salt Lake City. They were expected to pick up the requisite languages after they arrived in their foreign missions, and a remarkably large number of them succeeded in doing so. During orientation, they were given a cram course in key Bible references, usually out of context in a "proof-texting" approach, a few words of advice about getting along with partners, and some inspirational messages from especially charismatic church leaders. They were given tracts and scriptures, but no teaching plans or other aids. They were expected to "teach by the Spirit," which meant that they had to devise their own approaches and arguments and create their own teaching opportunities (usually through door-to-door contacts). Of course, much lore in such matters was passed along from the senior to the junior partners, but the variation from one missionary to another was enormous in proselytizing style, content, energy, and effectiveness.

Starting in the sixties, the church began to increase both its commitment to missionary work and its control over the missions and missionaries. Mission presidents began to be called to specified terms of office (usually three years), frequently from the ranks of retirees or full-time church employees, whose careers would suffer only minimal disruption from such a call. Mission presidents are now given standardized training and leadership manuals, which they are expected to follow with great care. They are also given much closer supervision than before by general authorities, and their jurisdiction over church members in their missions has been much reduced by carving regular stakes and wards out of formerly mission territories, even in some fairly remote Third World locations.

The autonomy of the missionaries themselves has also been greatly reduced, starting with their training at the appropriate missionary training center (MTC). As of 1990, there were fourteen of these training centers throughout the world, the largest and most extensive being the one in Provo, Utah, adjacent to the BYU campus. Before "graduating" to their missions from these centers, the new missionaries are expected essentially to memorize a series of "canned" lessons, in a foreign language if necessary. Those headed for foreign missions are given a condensed two-month course in the appropriate language. The MTC experience includes many of the well-known attributes of a military boot camp, though in actual content the military elements are, of course, replaced by intensive training in a foreign language and in the use of the proselytizing materials. The extraordinary stress felt by most missionaries in training derives from the regimentation and peer pressure that permeate that experience, as well as from the necessity of learning the proselytizing program, usually in a foreign language (Miller, 1985). From all accounts, relatively few new missionaries flunk out of the MTC, and most leave with a greatly enhanced zeal and esprit (Bergera, 1988; Ludlow, 1992:913–14).

Once they have arrived in their respective missions, missionaries are assigned to specific proselytizing areas, which they are not supposed to leave without the mission president's permission. Through regular written reports, phone calls, and visits, the mission president maintains rather close surveillance over all the missionaries in his jurisdiction. The increased control exerted over both the missionaries and the mission presidents has made mission life much more standardized and routine than it was before midcentury. In many ways, the retrenchment, control, and standardization emergent throughout the church in recent decades reaches its logical extreme in the experience of its young missionaries (which might be just as well, given that most of them are boys barely beyond adolescence!).

The intensification of the church commitment to missionary work in recent decades can be seen also in the frequent experimentation with new standardized proselytizing plans, in the ongoing sociological research on the conversion process and determinants of missionary success (Cornwall and Cunningham, 1989), in the increased efforts to recruit missionaries from among women and retired couples, and even in the constant remodeling of the missionary program to increase the involvement and cooperation of local church members in partnership with the missionaries sent to areas already containing appreciable numbers of Mormons.

The phenomenal growth of the Mormon church, especially since 1960, has been the result of this increased proselytizing commitment and control. Mormon membership has doubled twice since then. Furthermore, the proportion of growth attributable to converts (as opposed to baptized children from member families) has shifted to the point where new converts between 1986 and 1990 accounted for more than three-fourths of all baptisms (*Ensign*, Aug. 1991, 78).

Mormons have always been proselytizers, but the increased missionizing campaign of the past generation, in addition to all else that it might mean, contributes much to the more general retrenchment response. It makes Mormons visible, it makes heavy demands on the missionaries and their families (as per the theories of Festinger, Kanter, and Iannaccone), and it thereby enhances the distinctive Mormon identity on both sides of the subcultural boundary.

Family Renewal and Retrenchment

Like the other features of church efforts to reassert a peculiar Mormon identity, the focus on family is not in itself a new Mormon idea. The sanctity and solidarity of family life have always been recognized, by Mormons and by others, as the foundation of both church and nation (Heaton, 1987a). Yet a new emphasis on strengthening the family is clearly visible in the recent history of the church, beginning at least with the introduction of the family home evening program in 1964. Shepherd and Shepherd (1984) studied these family topics as well in their assessment of general conference sermons, and the results follow the familiar pattern (table 6.3).

During the three most heavily assimilationist decades (1920–49) the family, marriage, parenthood, motherhood, patriarchal order, women, youth, and sexual sin took a pronounced drop in discussion levels and then made an equally pronounced recovery during the most recent retrenchment decades. Minor variations in this pattern occur: Church leaders apparently felt for a long time that they could take patriarchy and motherhood for granted, but the sudden upturn in emphasis on those themes between 1950 and 1979 indicates that the leaders had begun to find these issues somewhat problematic. In any case, the Mormon family, and family-related behavior, are now an essential focus of the ongoing retrenchment motif in contemporary Mormon life.

Epitomized in the well-known McKay dictum that "no success in life can compensate for failure in the home," the new family emphasis can be seen also in a variety of official initiatives: church-published family home evening manuals placed in every home; the official expectation of a special family relations course in Sunday school each year; the regular family features in the monthly *Ensign* magazine ("Family Handbook" and "Family Home Evening") along with special articles on practical problems of modern family life, such as divorce, infidelity, and single parenting; and the general prochild ethos of church life that expresses itself (among other ways) in a tolerance for a level of infant noise in worship services that would be appalling in most other denominations.

Periodically church leaders at various levels give sermons urging Mormon families and couples to stay with the old traditions confining women

TABLE 6.3. Changing Saliency of Family-Related Themes in General Conference Sermons

Themes	1830–59	1860–89	1890–1919	1920–49	1950–79
Family	.010	.006	.018	.007	.028
Marriage	.004	.020	.015	.005	.042
Parenthood	.013	.048	.070	.020	.060
Motherhood	.000	.000	.000	.002	.010
Patriarchal order	.000	.001	.000	.000	.003
Women	.003	.014	.007	.004	.015
Youth	.000	.003	.026	.006	.027
Sexual sin	.002	.014	.012	.005	.023

SOURCE: Compiled from Shepherd and Shepherd (1984), appendix C.

mainly to domestic roles, despite the contemporary economic and political pressures to the contrary. The same philosophy is explicitly promoted in the lesson manuals for teenage boys (Inglesby, 1985) and girls (Gunnell and Hoffman, 1985). Nevertheless, "official" church policy on this matter, as opposed to the personal preferences of individual leaders, remains somewhat ambiguous. In 1987, President Ezra Taft Benson (1987a, 1987b) issued a pair of sermons in which he advocated the traditional roles with considerable sternness. Yet a year later his First Counselor, Elder Gordon B. Hinckley (1988), delivered instructions to regional leaders in which he commended Golda Meir and Margaret Thatcher as examples to the sisters and emphasized the potential for reconciling domestic and extradomestic roles for Mormon women.

As part of its retrenchment thrust in the family realm, the church has also attempted to influence sex education, and even sexual practices, within the family. In 1985, *A Parent's Guide* was published by the church and distributed to all wards. Though one would not be able to guess from the title, this is essentially a sex education manual for parents, the first such ever issued by the church. A content-analysis of this manual has shown it to contain considerable ambiguity in the valuation placed upon sexual intimacy, even between married partners, with negative valuations outnumbering positive ones by a considerable margin (Day, 1988).

In the same vein, the First Presidency (1982) issued a letter instructing all bishops and others in pastoral roles to warn the members (in personal interviews) against "unnatural, impure, or unholy" sexual practices, even in marriage, with oral sex mentioned as a specific example. Leaders were warned not to be too intrusive, to "scrupulously avoid indelicate inquiries which might be offensive to the sensibilities" of an interviewee, since, in the final analysis, such matters were to be left to the individual conscience. Nevertheless, the letter instructed, "If a person is engaged in a practice which troubles him enough to ask about it, he should discontinue it." Such ambivalent and intrusive guidance from church headquarters soon proved ill-advised and was revoked in a matter of months, much to the relief, no doubt, of all Mormon bishops. Nevertheless, the episode is indicative of the intensity of the retrenchment motif in family matters.

Religious Education

It is clear from the historical record that during the fifties and sixties, the Church Education System (CES) underwent two major changes: an enormous increase in size and a fundamental transformation in pedagogical philosophy. The commitment of the church to the growth of CES is indicated by the estimate of BYU president Ernest L. Wilkinson in 1959 that the proposed CES budget for 1960 amounted to 45% of the total budget for the entire church.[7]

The past thirty years have thus seen a greatly increased emphasis in the church upon religious education at both the high school and the college levels. Even junior colleges, at least in the West, are likely to have LDS institutes nearby. The nonreleased time or early morning seminaries have spread to nearly every corner of the United States and overseas as well. The seminary program, in particular, is extraordinarily expensive, both in the demands it places upon participants and in the money it costs the church (Lambert, 1985). Surprisingly, there has not yet been a systematic cost-benefit analysis of this program to see whether it achieves its putative goal of enhancing the religious commitment of its students. The data we saw in chapter 5 about the relation between adolescent seminary exposure and adult religious commitment would not make one optimistic about such an impact from seminary.

Yet that concern might be secondary, in a sense, to the important symbolic significance of seminary and institute as Mormon identity-maintenance institutions, or in other words, as a means of asserting one's Mormon identity to one's peers, both Mormon and non-Mormon. (The choice of BYU for one's college career probably has a similar function, quite apart from its educational one.) More recent research by Cornwall (1987a) has indicated that although the religious education programs of the church do not have a direct effect, through actual instruction, on later adult religious commitment, they do seem to have an indirect influence by channeling Mormon youngsters together in peer groups that provide social supports or "plausibility structures" that help to maintain the faith.

Whether or not the expanded religious education program of the church has had its intended effects, it has functioned increasingly during the past three decades both as an exemplar and as a vehicle for the expression of retrenchment. In this respect, the CES now represents quite a different philosophy from that on which it was originally based during the twenties, when the church was still very much in the assimilationist mode. Then the CES curriculum was much more inclined to make use of non-Mormon scriptural and theological scholarship and to stress the articulation or "reconciliation" of Mormon doctrine with the best in the "wisdom of the world" (Arrington, 1967). As mentioned earlier, promising young faculty members, with church financial support, studied at the University of Chicago and at other worldly centers of scholarship, while visiting Protestant theologians taught summer sessions in Provo for CES faculty (Lowry Nelson, 1985; Sherlock, 1979; Swensen, 1972).

J. Reuben Clark of the First Presidency opposed this trend as early as 1938 (Bergera and Priddis, 1985:60–62; J. Reuben Clark, 1938), but most of his colleagues in the leadership at that time retained the vision of CES as a vehicle for promoting the reconciliation of the Mormon spiritual and theological heritage with the wisdom of the world. Periodic incidents brought occasional confrontations between the two visions of the CES mission, the one of reconciliation and the other of indoctrination, with uneasy resolutions. The Heber C. Snell case is an illustration (Sherlock, 1979): Snell, a prominent CES scholar with outside training, published a modernist interpretation of the Old Testament in his 1949 *Ancient Israel.* Highly acclaimed by professional scholars, both Mormon and non-Mormon, and widely circulated among CES faculty, the book generated considerable controversy.

Snell's lectures had been stirring up controversy at least since 1937, and he finally attracted the wrath of Apostle Joseph Fielding Smith. Although the First Presidency remained publicly aloof, Apostle Mark E. Petersen supported Smith's position, while Apostles John A. Widtsoe, Joseph F. Merrill, and Elder Levi Edgar Young took the other side. With their protection, Snell retained his CES position until a face-saving but involuntary retirement in 1950 at the age of sixty-seven.

A few years later, in 1954, Apostle Harold B. Lee, with the support of Joseph Fielding Smith, personally took over the instruction of seminary and institute faculty in the annual CES summer school at BYU, using Smith's *Man: His Origin and Destiny* as a textbook. They required all the teachers in attendance to submit term papers on the book and urged that it be taught in the seminaries and institutes of religion (Bergera and Priddis, 1985:152–55; Poll, 1985). To the relief of many CES faculty, and with no little irony, it was President J. Reuben Clark himself who, a few days after this incident, came to BYU and countermanded such an intrusion of unofficial doctrine into the curriculum. In an oft-reproduced speech, Clark (1954) reminded his listeners that only the President of the Church may define official doctrine, and then only when he is speaking as a prophet. Nevertheless, certain church leaders almost immediately tried to transfer the institute faculty members who had openly opposed the Smith and Lee enterprise, including George Boyd and Lowell Bennion (both at the University of Utah Institute), to more remote locations.[8]

A struggle thus ensued within CES between the original philosophy of reconciliation with outside learning and the emergent philosophy of particularistic indoctrination. To some extent that struggle still goes on, but the latter philosophy has by now gained clear ascendancy through natural faculty turnover. Recent years have seen the selective recruitment increasingly of teaching personnel much more amenable to the indoctrination philosophy. Naturally the "old-timers" resisted this trend but found themselves fighting a rear-guard action as time went on.

One such CES pioneer, George S. Tanner, director for many years of the first LDS institute of religion (University of Idaho), recorded in his journal his impressions of the 1962 CES staff summer school, where three apostles came and made clear the new philosophical thrust. The remarks of Elder Mark E. Petersen seemed particularly memorable to Tanner, who summarized them in his journal rather like this: CES instructors are to teach the pure gospel and nothing else; they are to instill in their students faith and testimony, for nothing else matters; they should not try to "steady the ark" by intellectualizing; there is no academic freedom in CES, and faculty who don't like that should simply resign; the LDS neither need nor want the learning of the world, and those who once went off to Protestant divinity schools to seek such learning were ruined by the experience; the LDS understand the Bible better than any others because of guidance from direct revelation; if others believe differently, they are simply wrong; in CES, loyalty takes preference over learning.[9]

Another such CES pioneer, George T. Boyd, shared Tanner's perceptions about the 1962 CES summer school and felt concerned enough to write a letter about the situation to Elder Hugh B. Brown, then a member of the First Presidency of the church under President David O. McKay. In his letter (which was sympathetically acknowledged by Brown) Boyd described his perceptions of the content of the 1962 summer school as including not only the anti-intellectualism deplored by Tanner but also the injection of theology more reminiscent of Protestant fundamentalism and Calvinism than of the Mormonism with which he had been reared. He referred particularly to a negative view of humankind as "depraved," and he was distressed at the informal support given to all such ideas by some of the general authorities in attendance.[10]

Since that time, the pedagogical posture of the CES has become increasingly antiscientific and anti-intellectual, more inward-looking, more intent on stressing the uniqueness and exclusiveness of the Mormon version of the gospel as opposed to all other interpretations, whether religious or scientific. Lesson manuals occasionally take gratuitous swipes at scientists, intellectuals, and modernist ideas, which are blamed for jeopardizing the faith of the students. The 1981 CES institute course on the Book of Mormon (Religion 121–22) provides several examples: The anti-Christ Korihor (lesson 29) is personified as an academic intellectual ("Professor Cochran") trying to lead his students astray spiritually. The same manual quotes Ezra Taft Benson, Joseph Fielding Smith, and Bruce R. McConkie as criticizing humanism, evolutionism, and birth control (8, 114, 379), promoting a highly literal interpretation of the Fall of Adam (72–73), and perpetuating a racist characterization of the Lamanites (112). With the exception of the last reference, the Book of Mormon itself does not speak to any of those issues; thus, their injection into this lesson manual is entirely gratuitous.[11]

Even where the discussion of a scientific or social issue is quite relevant to the CES curriculum, the commentary in the student textbooks is likely to reflect a fundamentalist or antimodernist position. In an analysis of the 1980 CES two-volume textbook on the Old Testament, for example, Erich Paul (1992: chap. 8) has shown how the discussion of the age of the earth (1:28) borrows from the scriptural numerology so popular among Protestant fundamentalists, and in so doing follows the dubious but popularized notions of Velikovsky, deliberately ignoring the broader consensus of informed scientists who reject such calculations (1:28–29). Throughout CES publications, non-Mormon sources and resources are rarely used and highly suspect, and those cited are usually taken from Protestant fundamentalist scholarship. CES personnel are strongly discouraged from participating in privately sponsored conferences of Mormon scholars, such as the annual meetings of the Sunstone Symposium and the Mormon History Association.[12]

Although the CES has its administrative headquarters under the church commissioner of education in Salt Lake City, one could make the case that its intellectual headquarters is found in the department of Church History and Doctrine at Brigham Young University, which sets the tone for much that happens throughout the CES. A recent collection of essays by several members of that department provides a fair overview of the anti-intellectual retrenchment response dominant in the department and increasingly throughout CES as well (Millet, 1987; see also Bergera, 1991; Woolley, 1990). As both an expression and a vehicle of the dominant indoctrinationist thrust in religious education, CES must now be considered one of the most important exhibits in the case being made here for the retrenchment response at the official church level.

Summary

It seems clear from the material in this chapter that an emerging generation of church leaders, with somewhat different backgrounds from those of earlier generations, became increasingly uncomfortable with the assimilation of Mormons and determined to resist that assimilation through a deliberate policy of retrenchment. At least five major expressions of that retrenchment can be seen in the contemporary church: a reemphasis on continuing revelation and obedience to modern prophets; new advancements in genealogy and increased stress on temple work; an expansion and standardization of the missionary system; a family renewal and retrenchment program; and an expanded program of religious education with a new mandate for indoctrination rather than intellectual reconciliation. These general forms of retrenchment have had their impact as well on many specific institutional changes, two of which will be considered in the next chapter.

Notes

1. The continuing LDS interest in acceptance by the religious world more generally can be seen in certain deliberate ecumenical initiatives taken by the church in recent years. This ecumenism is by no means theological or ecclesiastical, of course, but it is genuine and effective in an operational sense. That is, the LDS Church is not only willing but anxious to cooperate with other religions in ven-

tures of mutual interest, including political and humanitarian ventures. For example, see issues of the *Church News* covering an LDS regional leader's visit to the Pope (May 22, 1993, 3), humanitarian work by Mormon missionaries in Thailand (May 22, 1993, 6), and LDS participation in interfaith councils in Virginia and in California (Feb. 6, 1993, 9). It is also common now for the legal staff of the LDS Church to file *amicus* briefs on behalf of other religions in various court cases (including those brought before the Supreme Court) wherever a First Amendment issue seems to be involved, even if the case does not involve specific LDS interests at all.

2. Certainly a new spirit of resistance to assimilation was apparent among the general authorities by the time they began serious and comprehensive implementation of the correlation program in the early sixties. It is clear from the contemporaneous statements of Apostle (later President) Harold B. Lee and some of his colleagues that correlation was seen as a divinely inspired antidote, both to the organizational looseness that had developed internally and to the rising tide of corruption in the outside world. Clearly some of the leaders had begun to worry by this time about the impact of secular influences on the Saints, whether or not these influences were associated with assimilation as such. See, for example, the account of the rise and development of the correlation movement: *A Review of Priesthood Correlation*, an unpublished course manual for Religion 231 at Brigham Young University (first edition), Provo, UT: BYU Publications, 1968; also Goates (1985) and Mouritsen (1972).

3. This role later took Elder Petersen on a number of forays against the fancied faithless, such as his well-known initiatives against a certain list of *Dialogue* scholars (including the present author) in the spring of 1983.

4. Correlation as an administrative concept had actually been attempted to some extent much earlier in the century (Alexander, 1986b), but it became a major movement starting only in the sixties and in many respects has continued its gradual implementation even up to the present time (Allen and Leonard, 1992:chaps. 20, 21; Ludlow, 1992:323–25).

5. This characterization of Elder Lee is based upon numerous references to him in Ernest L. Wilkinson's diary, which reposes in the Archives and Manuscripts Division of the Harold B. Lee Library at Brigham Young University. A copy of the comprehensive index for that diary, with summaries of the various diary entries, is in my files. See also Bergera and Priddis (1985).

6. The term "Lamanites" has always been understood by most Mormons as referring in a general way to all the aboriginal inhabitants of the Western Hemisphere, although many LDS scholars have taken a considerably more restrictive view of the peoples covered by the "Lamanite" designation. Joseph Smith certainly thought that the term applied to the Native Americans of the states and territories of the United States, at least, and probably to those living under Latin American governments as well (Walker, 1993). He dispatched a party of missionaries as early as October 1830 to try to convert the Lamanites inhabiting (or forcibly relocated to) the U.S. Great Plains in the belief that they were literal descendants of the Book of Mormon peoples. Though there is a hint in the Book of Mormon that a seagoing party under one Hagoth might have migrated to Poly-

nesia (in Kon-Tiki fashion), it was President Spencer W. Kimball who most explicitly and fully expanded the Lamanite term to cover all Polynesian peoples, as well as the aboriginal inhabitants of North and South America. During his presidency, missionary work and educational scholarships were both greatly expanded among Polynesians as well as among Native Americans of this hemisphere.

7. This estimate appears in Wilkinson's diary for October 21, 1959, when the CES was under his jurisdiction. It is not certain that the proposal for such a large CES budget prevailed at the end of the budgeting process, but at least the figure indicates the seriousness of the growing church commitment to CES.

8. This brief account of the incident is based upon personal interviews in 1985 with George Boyd, Lowell Bennion, and Eugene Campbell, all of whom were participants in the 1954 summer school (interview notes in my files). Other participants might remember some of the details differently, but the general outline of the incident sketched here is well known. Readers not acquainted with Smith's *Man: His Origin and Destiny* should be apprised that it includes a vituperative rejection of any doctrine that would accommodate a theory of biological evolution, whether Darwinian or any other kind.

9. The late George Tanner was kind enough to excerpt this entry from his journal in a letter to me of May 25, 1985, now in my personal files.

10. George T. Boyd was for many years director of the LDS institute at the University of Southern California after his transfer from the University of Utah in the wake of the 1954 BYU summer school controversy mentioned above. He graciously shared with me a copy of his letter to President Brown and of the latter's reply. Both are in my personal files.

11. This manual has recently been replaced by a much condensed version, which has apparently eliminated such gratuitous references.

12. According to my numerous conversations and interviews with close friends on CES faculties, such directives to CES personnel are rarely put in writing but are spread by oral instruction at regular staff meetings. The independently published Mormon scholarly journals like *Dialogue* and *Sunstone* cannot be purchased for seminaries or institutes with church funds, and such personal copies as instructors might have are not supposed to be readily visible in their offices.

CHAPTER SEVEN

The Retrenchment Motif: Two Case Studies

The previous chapter, with its sweep across five different institutional arenas, has provided a fairly convincing general picture of the retrenchment reaction of the Mormon leadership to half a century of assimilation with American society. One could envision also a series of specific case studies that would add great depth to the general overview. For example an in-depth historical and contemporary study of the Church Education System would almost certainly demonstrate in great detail the gradual (and probably deliberate) transition from a pedagogical philosophy of intellectual articulation and reconciliation to one of indoctrination, in line with the general thesis of this book.

Some specific case studies have already been done: A book on the history of Mormon music (Hicks, 1989) unintentionally demonstrates the retrenchment thesis (among other things) through an examination of the greatly increased reliance on Mormon (as opposed to Protestant) music and lyrics in Mormon hymnbooks from the 1950s to the 1980s. Such a development might reflect many factors, including, to be sure, a natural accumulation during that period of acceptable literature by Mormon composers. Yet the effect is still to make Mormon hymnbooks more Mormon and less Protestant in content from the assimilationist to the retrenchment period of recent Mormon history (see also Ludlow, 1992:667–69 on this point).[1]

Another case in point, to which we will devote considerable attention in this chapter, is the changing Mormon posture toward the King James Version (KJV) of the Bible, also the subject of a book-length study (Barlow, 1991).[2] This work demonstrates the importance of an in-depth investigation of these trends. On a superficial level, one could easily get the impression simply that Mormons were KJV believers in the nineteenth century, in the early twentieth century, and perhaps even more so today, so no significant change has occurred in this respect. Such would certainly be the inference taken from the 1992 statement of the First Presidency (*Ensign*, Aug. 1992, 80), with its strong endorsement of the KJV over all other versions of the Bible (even if they are "easier to read"). It is only in the detailed research of Barlow that one can see the shifting posture across time of the church and its key leaders toward the KJV.

The Changing Mormon Uses of the KJV

The earliest official Mormon statement on the Bible can be found in the eighth Article of Faith written in 1842, which declares that the Bible is "the word of God, as far as it is translated correctly," a qualification that was not placed upon acceptance of the newly revealed Book of Mormon. Although significant numbers of Mormon converts came from Lutheran countries, the overwhelming majority were English-speaking people from North America and the British Isles. It is not surprising, therefore, that the KJV was always the common Bible for Mormons, even though it was not the official one. Joseph Smith even conceded once that the Lutheran version might be more nearly correct ([1902] 1980, 6:363–64); and his own lifelong project to produce a new "translation" of the KJV testifies fairly well to the mixture of feelings he had about it. Smith's was not a translation (or even a retranslation) in the usual scholarly sense but consisted of extensive redactions, interpolations, rephrasings, and redefinitions, believed to have been accomplished by divine revelation. The "Joseph Smith Translation" (JST), as Mormons call it, was never published during Smith's lifetime (except in fragments), but his followers have always regarded it as more reliable and authoritative than the KJV upon which it is based.

From the beginning, some Mormons have held rather inerrantist and literalist interpretations of the Bible but others decidedly have not. Brigham Young once quipped (in 1871) that some of the writers in the Bible were "lying and some . . . telling the truth; if you can believe it all to be the word of God, you can go beyond me" (*Journal of Discourses* 14:208). He more than once dismissed much of the Genesis creation account as "baby stories" (*Journal of Discourses* 1:237).[3] Although the early Mormon missionaries certainly appealed to a common Biblical heritage in their tracts and sermons (Timothy Smith, 1980), they remained Bible believers on their own terms.

In general, during the nineteenth century, the Mormon Church, while espousing a basic general appreciation and belief in the Bible, limited its authority in several ways: (1) by promulgating an extra-Biblical canon (the Book of Mormon); (2) by placing primacy on living prophets (and their "retranslations") over received scriptures; (3) by representing scriptures as but one source of truth among others; (4) by stressing the corruptions in the received text of the Bible; and (5) by dismissing portions of it as uninspired (Barlow, 1991). All of this was, of course, considered a very "fast and loose" use of the Bible by the mainstream evangelical contemporaries of the early Mormons; but it was consistent with the Mormon high-tension, culture-rejecting stance more generally.

As the Mormons entered the twentieth century their new assimilationist outlook had its implications also for their posture toward the KJV, along with everything else. Among the influences directly shaping this posture, two were especially germane: the growing national controversy over higher criticism and the deliberate Mormon public relations effort to broaden the common ground with American Protestantism more generally (Barlow, 1991).

It was not until their rapprochement with the rest of America that Mormons began to take a studied interest in the higher criticism controversy. Much in the inherited Mormon view of the Bible would have been compatible with some of the insights from higher criticism. On the other hand, there has always been in Mormonism a parallel strain of conservative literal-mindedness and a tendency to rely on church authorities, rather than on academic experts, in hermeneutical questions (Cummings, 1982; Hutchinson, 1982). The resulting Mormon ambivalence toward higher criticism was thus not so different from that found in Protestant America more generally.

Mormons did not, however, experience the deep cleavage that developed in Protestantism between the conservative and liberal camps, for among Mormons there would have been but few liberals as that term was understood in contemporaneous Protestant circles. Fundamentals like the divinity of Jesus were simply not open to question for Mormons. Yet there were several high-ranking Mormon leaders with scientific training during this period, some even with doctorates from eastern universities, and they were inclined to see some potential in science to vindicate, rather than undermine, religious faith (Roberts, 1911, 1929). The church leadership thus permitted considerable debate early in the century over issues of higher criticism, not only behind closed doors, but in the popular church periodicals as well (Ramseyer, 1908; Roberts, 1905; Sjodahl, 1929; Joseph

Fielding Smith, 1911; Webb, 1916a, 1916b; see also Alexander, 1986b; Keller, 1982; and Sherlock, 1979, 1980).

Although the debate among Mormons over higher criticism was never formally resolved, it can be understood as part and parcel of the increasing participation by certain Mormon leaders and intellectuals in the theological mainstream of the nation at that time. Such participation had the side effect also of focusing Mormon attention as never before upon the Bible as part of the culture shared with the rest of America and upon the question of which Bible to prefer. The process of resolving that latter question in favor of the KJV is another telling study in Mormon assimilation.

Well into the twentieth century, church publications continued to deny that the KJV was the official Bible for Mormons, and the more scholarly church leaders continued to urge due consideration for the results of scientific and linguistic research (Barlow, 1991). With the passage of time, however, a kind of drift occurred toward an increasing preference for the KJV in church lesson manuals, reference works, and sermons. In part, this growing tilt toward the KJV can be understood as a safe and reasonable resort in the face of the unresolved controversies surrounding higher criticism early in the century and the resulting proliferation of new Bible translations.

Against this background was launched a personal crusade by President J. Reuben Clark to achieve de facto canonization of the KJV. Paradoxically, Clark combined an enormous erudition and eloquence with a fundamentalist and somewhat anti-intellectual posture (Quinn, 1983). Having long associated with the Protestant establishment during his diplomatic career, Clark had acquired a deep and growing preference for the KJV and had even compiled a personal file of sermons and documents in support of that preference.

When the Revised Standard Version of the Bible appeared in 1952 under the auspices of the National Council of Churches, Clark reacted with the same hostility that characterized conservative Protestantism more generally. His response was *Why the King James Version* (1956), the product of many months of scholarly energy and commitment. Since he read no ancient languages, Clark relied on secondary sources, primarily those of conservative Protestant scholars. Like them, he argued for the superior reliability and purity of the sources used by KJV scholars (Barlow, 1991).

Although Clark was explicit in disclaiming official church status for his book, and it was privately criticized (to no avail) by church president

David O. McKay, the book quickly acquired authoritative, quasi-official status at both the grass-roots and the leadership levels. Since then, no serious consideration has ever been given to the use of any other English version of the Bible in the Mormon church, and subsequent apologias for the KJV have depended primarily on Clark's book (Barlow, 1991). Any doubt that the KJV has been canonized de facto by the church was removed by a 1992 First Presidency declaration that even alludes to "latter-day revelation" (otherwise unspecified) in support of official LDS adoption of the KJV (*Ensign*, Aug. 1992, 80).[4]

The main difference in outlook on the Bible between nineteenth-century Mormons and their early twentieth-century descendants was not a difference so much in which Bible was most commonly used. The KJV was the common Bible all along. The main difference, rather, lay in the uses or functions which the KJV served in the two periods. During the nineteenth century, the KJV provided a vehicle (along with such institutions as polygamy) for asserting the distinctiveness of the Mormons, their special and unique place in the world: The KJV was there to be explored, to be compared with the new scriptures coming through the modern Mormon prophets, to be questioned, and to be revised, as necessary, no matter what the rest of the world might think.

By contrast, during the first half of the twentieth century, the KJV served as a vehicle for Mormon assimilation. It provided the common scriptural ground for Mormons with the rest of the country (or, at least, with the Protestant establishment, which largely controlled the Mormon public image). The KJV had thus become a sacred emblem of the shared American civil religion, to be cherished and preserved, not questioned and revised. Beginning at about midcentury, however, still another phase has become apparent in the evolving Mormon relationship with the KJV and another function for the use of it.

The general Mormon retrenchment of the past few decades has been accompanied by a complementary modification in the Mormon uses of the King James Version of the Bible. This process has expressed itself primarily in two developments: (1) a retroactive "Mormonizing" of the KJV, once it had received de facto canonization, and (2) the official imposition of conservative Protestant hermeneutics upon the Bible.

During the seventies, the church undertook to review and reconsider its entire scriptural canon for the first time since 1920. After several years of work by a joint committee of religious leaders and educators, the church published its own edition of the KJV in 1979, followed two years later by a completely reedited publication of the other scriptures in the total church canon (Ludlow, 1992:110–11). The main purpose of these projects was to integrate the entire set of scriptures more completely and to link them all through a common concordance and cross-referencing system. The educator who chaired the working committee acknowledged that it never seriously considered any version of the Bible but the KJV in this process (Matthews, 1982:388). There is a touch of irony here: Having spent most of its formative years in conflict with the Protestant establishment, the Mormon church had now canonized the Protestant Bible. Another irony, however, must be noted from the Protestant point of view: Having canonized the KJV, the Mormons have since then retroactively Mormonized it, displacing much of the traditional Protestant hermeneutical content with Mormon counterparts.

This new publication includes a collection of extensive excerpts from the nineteenth-century JST, the shorter excerpts appearing as marginal notes to the KJV text itself and the longer ones reserved to a special section at the end, to which the reader is referred by the marginal notes. This clearly represents a rehabilitation of the JST, which had been entirely abandoned by the Mormon church during its assimilationist phase in the early twentieth century. It represents also, of course, the official imposition on the KJV text of Joseph Smith's own emendations and redactions.

The committee also prepared an extensive topical guide, actually a kind of concordance, which integrates Bible references with corresponding references to the Book of Mormon and to the other special Mormon scriptures and which is also tied to the Bible with marginal notes in the actual KJV text. The effect of these marginal notes is to impose on the Bible text certain meanings and interpretations derived partly from the conservative Protestant scholarship favored by the working committee and still other meanings and interpretations derived from the extrabiblical Mormon scriptures usually considered heterodox by Protestants (Ludlow, 1992:110–13).

The new scriptural package includes a special Bible dictionary, also prepared from a conservative viewpoint, so that the people, places, things, and doctrines in the dictionary reflect either traditional Mormon interpretations or conservative Protestant ones (or both, where these are not in conflict). It is a telling fact that this new dictionary replaced one based upon the classic *Cambridge Companion to the Bible,* reflecting mainline Anglican scholarship, which had been bound with the earlier Mormon editions of the Bible (Ludlow, 1992:111–12).

The ultimate effect of this extensive work on the new Mormon edition of the KJV was thus both to Mormonize it retroactively and to impose hermeneutics that one informed scholar has called "fundamentalist" (Ashment, 1990). Such a label might seem an exaggeration, but Ashment's careful analysis leaves little doubt that modern Mormon biblical hermeneutics are at the very least much closer to Protestant fundamentalism than to the American Christian mainstream (see also Ludlow, 1992:112–13). Nor is such an observation merely an expression of a liberal scholarly bias: The late Apostle Bruce R. McConkie, who oversaw the working committee responsible for the new edition of the KJV, and for all the resources bound with it, commended the package to the CES faculty as part of a lecture during which he predicted the eventual destruction "of the whole theory of organic evolution" and reminded his listeners that the "key to an understanding of Holy Writ lies not in the wisdom of men, not in cloistered halls, not in academic degrees, (and) not in a knowledge of Greek and Hebrew" (McConkie, 1984).

The ascendancy of a fundamentalist strain in Mormon hermeneutics more generally, especially since midcentury, has been noted, of course, in many other contexts, as well (Barlow, 1991; Cummings, 1982; Keller, 1982; Sherlock, 1979, 1980; and White, 1987). Both in the new edition of the Bible itself, then, and in the official and unofficial commentary about it, we can see another expression of the recent Mormon retrenchment trend.

To this point the chapter has had an internal focus. We have been concerned with a case study of a specific development within the church that can serve as a kind of "marker" for the general retrenchment trend sketched earlier. Now we change to an external focus with a case study of the evolving political posture of the church toward the nation outside and how that posture has come increasingly to reflect the same retrenchment trend.

The Changing National Political Posture of the Mormon Church

The cultural tension the Mormon church felt with America expressed itself perhaps most of all in the political arena. In probably no other arena is the relationship of the nation with any of its subcultures as overt and explicit. The more deviant a subculture appears in the public eye, the more difficulty that subculture can expect to have in its political relationships. Political conflict in a given instance might occur over symbolic issues, rather than over those of real political substance, but it is likely that the substance is just below the symbolic surface. For example, the nineteenth-century Mormon struggles with the U.S. over polygamy and noncapitalist economic experimentation were at least partly symbolic of a deeper national concern over the separatist and theocratic tendencies of the Mormon church at that time (Ludlow, 1992:1098–1103; Lyman, 1986). The level of political tension thus was a direct and faithful reflection of the underlying cultural and sectarian religious tension between the Mormons and the nation.[5]

Yet, as an institution, the Mormon church has only rarely injected itself into national political issues since Utah achieved statehood in 1896 (Ludlow, 1992:1107–9). The Mormon church did receive considerable publicity during the 1980s for its public opposition to the federal Equal Rights Amendment and to the basing of a MX missile system in Utah, and it proved to be on the winning side in both of those issues. Mormons as individuals do participate, however. They are known for rather conservative political leanings and for political participation (especially voting) that probably exceeds the national average (Ludlow, 1992:1106–9). Mormons are also somewhat overrepresented in Congress (Duke and Johnson, 1992).[6]

The church's involvement in Utah (as opposed to national) politics is, of course, a different question. Officially and unofficially, the Mormon church has always been an important political player in Utah and, to a much lesser extent, in the neighboring states (Croft, 1985; Jonas, 1969). We would be naive to expect otherwise, and one could argue that the church itself would be remiss in its civic obligations if it did not attempt to influence civil, social, and cultural developments in its own heartland. The same could be fairly said of Catholic church involvement in much of New England or Southern Baptist involvement in the Bible Belt.

Therefore, it is not Utah politics that is of interest here, but U.S. politics. Just as we cannot tell much about a person's global or national political orientation from his or her participation in neighborhood political skirmishes, so we must look beyond Utah and the West to assess the significance of the Mormon political posture toward the nation. The changes in that posture follow the same pattern we have already seen: rapprochement politics earlier in the century followed by the retrenchment politics of more recent decades. This pattern is best understood as a product of the changing relationships between the church and the nation, since it cannot reasonably be attributed either to ideological factors or to other internal matters.

There is little in Mormon doctrine or ideology that would bear upon national political issues (Ludlow, 1992:1103–8). In common with most other religions, Mormon teachings have always favored peaceful as opposed to military resolutions of foreign policy issues. When war is fought at all, it must be defensive in purpose and keep bloodshed to a minimum. Pacifism is acceptable on religious grounds, but not required (Book of Mormon, Alma, chaps. 43–55; James R. Clark, 1975:89–91; Firmage, 1983; Quinn, 1983, 1984, 1985). In domestic matters, Mormon doctrine implies (but with considerable flexibility) support for property rights, individual rights, and the state (Janosik, 1951); it also favors policies that promote conservative family values and discourage gambling or the use of alcohol, tobacco, and other addictive substances.

On the basis of such preferences, church leaders will sometimes speak out on what they call "moral issues" as distinguished from "political issues," a distinction not valid to social scientists, of course. While Mormon history is somewhat ambivalent on the separation of church and state, official church scriptures and pronouncements sound Jeffersonian enough, although church leaders are likely to invoke Jefferson's "wall of separation" more often to keep government out of the church rather than vice versa (Cannon et al., 1962).[7]

Like doctrine, internal polity and governance play a somewhat ambiguous role in church political posture. On the one hand, church organization has the appearance of a very tight ship with a command structure that reaches all the way down to the family level (Johnson, 1979). Mobilization for political or other purposes can thus be quite thorough and rapid (Gottlieb and Wiley, 1984). Rifts in political values between leadership and laity, so common in other denominations, are not common in the Mormon setting, since the lay priesthood (even at the top) is recruited from the same general social strata as the membership.

On the other hand, there is no tradition in Mormonism of prophetic infallibility, even for the church president (Capener, 1984), and there have always been many questions about the legitimacy of church leaders' pronouncements on purely secular matters (these being quite rare, in any case). Mormons cannot reasonably be considered a disciplined and monolithic political bloc, even in Utah, to say nothing of the rest of the nation (Alexander, 1986b; Jonas, 1969; Ludlow, 1992:1103–8; Miles, 1978). The major political parties are well represented among both laity and leadership. Occasional embarrassments to the church from the political overzealousness of individual local or regional leaders has led to a general policy, reiterated from all pulpits with the approach of every election, that church meetings, facilities, publications, membership lists, or other resources are not to be used for any political purpose.[8]

Early in the twentieth century, political controversies among the general authorities were sometimes aired in public (Alexander, 1982). This tended to undermine the prophetic charisma of the leadership, so all apostles and other top leaders were asked to submit to a pact whereby they would avoid making their political preferences public and would refrain from seeking public office without the collective approval of their colleagues (Lyman, 1985). Since then, public political partisanship has rarely been seen among the general authorities, and when it has occurred it has usually been "neutralized" informally by the circumspect comments in public of a designated colleague in the leadership with opposing views (Quinn, 1993). On those rare occasions when a national issue seems to require an official church pronouncement, it will be issued by the First Presidency (a triumvirate), usually after the unanimous consent of the Twelve Apostles. This dependence upon collegial consensus obviously provides inherent restraints on official political involvement in the name of the church.

What, however, does "political involvement" really mean, and when is it "official"? Such terms can obviously mean different things operationally. As used here, *official* refers to a church expression or action promulgated by the First Presidency, by the Quorum of Twelve Apostles, or by the Public Affairs Department of the church. The latter would never take action not approved by one of the other two. This does not mean that church leaders, high or low, might not speak or act on their own preferences behind the scenes, but they are not acting for the church when they do so, and the savvy citizen or church member will realize that.

Political "involvement," as understood here, has two dimensions: political content (the precise issue being addressed) and tactical strenuousness (how much and what kinds of effort are exerted on behalf of the church position). Tactics can run the gamut, of course, from comments in church meetings or publications (and these can be for either limited or extensive audiences) to lobbying (in person, by mail, by telephone) to raising and contributing funds to organizing and supporting pressure groups. The more of these tactics that are used, and the more resources they involve, the more strenuous is the church's involvement. No matter how crucial the issue, or how "official" the church's initiative, the "involvement" cannot be considered very serious if it is limited to sermons or passing comments.

Mormons and National Politics in the Twentieth Century

The cultural tension with America, the "predicament of disrepute," with which the Mormons began the twentieth century, expressed itself perhaps most of all in the political arena. Accordingly, the sincere and thorough efforts of church leaders to reintegrate the Mormons into the political life of the nation dominated the first half of the century. Then, at about midcentury, as our "retrenchment hypothesis" would lead us to expect, the Mormon political posture toward the nation began to stiffen, and the church asserted itself more or less strenuously against certain national political trends. A detailed case study of this process will once again support the main theoretical argument of this book.

Once the church had finally settled on a policy of rapprochement with the United States and thereby obtained statehood for Utah, a succession of Mormon presidents led the church deliberately toward increasing assimilation and Americanization (Alexander, 1986b; Davies, 1968; Larson, 1971; Leone, 1979; Lyman, 1986). The first part of that period, up into the twenties, was a transitional period, as Alexander (1986b) and Shipps (1985) have both pointed out, with the church feeling its way around the shoals of actual and potential political embarrassment toward the calmer open waters of national respectability (Alexander, 1982). Accordingly, the church tried to keep its political posture during this period generally in harmony with dominant national trends, including those associated with the progressive movement.

The first national political issue to face Mormons at the beginning of their Americanization was the Spanish-American War of 1898. Here the long tradition of Mormon aloofness from the "unrighteous wars of gentile America" was pitted against a desire to prove to a skeptical country that the Mormons were, after all, loyal Americans. After a vigorous debate among the church leaders, and despite the serious misgivings of several, the leadership finally urged Mormons to enlist (Mauss and Bradford, 1988:55–56; Quinn, 1984). In the two world wars, the Mormon leadership again followed national public opinion, beginning with an aloof and isolationist stance but eventually joining the "patriotic" mainstream in support of the war effort.[9] In general, this patriotic posture in foreign policy has continued to the present: In the two anticommunist wars in Korea and Southeast Asia, as well as in the more recent Persian Gulf conflict, church spokesmen have been less reluctant in their support for U.S. policy, while still condoning conscientious objection for individual Mormons inclined to invoke it.[10]

It is more in domestic policy that we see the hypothesized pattern of convergence with national trends, followed by divergence. The early twentieth century saw the growing political assimilation and Americanization. A good, old-fashioned American political machine was established in Utah led by the church president, Joseph F. Smith, as de facto boss in close alliance with Republican senator Reed Smoot. This relationship with a major national party was understood by the Mormon leadership as an important vehicle of national acceptance and leverage, and deference to that relationship clearly influenced church political stands on Prohibition, on the League of Nations, and on other issues as well (Alexander, 1986b; Gottlieb and Wiley, 1984; Sillito, 1992).

Despite the long-standing church requirement for total abstinence from alcoholic beverages, but in accordance with Republican policy, President Smith opposed a national prohibition law or amendment until 1916. Only when support for a national amendment crystallized in the nation more generally did President Smith and his colleagues in the leadership throw their support behind the Eighteenth Amendment, although they had favored state and local laws all along (Alexander, 1986b).

The next president of the church, Heber J. Grant (1918–45) was uncomfortable with the role of political boss and anyway had political preferences more Democratic than Republican until the advent of the New Deal (Alexander, 1986b; Gottlieb and Wiley, 1984). As his presidency began, the church (along with the rest of the nation) was in the midst of a controversy over U.S. Senate ratification of the League of Nations treaty. President Grant personally favored the treaty. Yet he refrained from promulgating any official church policy on it, while denouncing the efforts of his Republican colleagues in the leadership to marshal scriptural support for their opposition to it. The October 1919 general conference devoted considerable discussion to the issue. When all was said and done, however, Mormons and their leaders remained, like the rest of the nation, divided on the issue (Allen, 1973; Clark, 1971:137–42; Mauss and Bradford, 1988:57).

On another major issue of the time, the Nineteenth Amendment and female suffrage, the Mormons again were clearly part of the national consensus. As a federal territory, Utah had voted in female suffrage as early as 1870, despite the church institutions of patriarchy and polygamy (Alexander, 1970; Van Wagenen, 1991). Critics of that time had accused the church of simply trying to double the size of the voting population controlled by the church, but such a motive would not explain the inclusion of female suffrage later in the new Utah constitution nor the Mormon support for a national suffrage amendment (Alexander, 1970, 1986b).

The thirties brought the Great Depression, the repeal of Prohibition, and the New Deal. The Mormon response to all of these was in line with the national consensus. Mormons at the grass roots voted consistently for Roosevelt and the New Deal throughout the thirties and forties, just as the rest of the nation did, and many of them found careers in federal government during this period. This was despite the hostility of President Grant and much of the Mormon hierarchy to the New Deal and to its exponents, such as Utah senator Elbert Thomas (Alexander, 1986b; Gottlieb and Wiley, 1984).

Yet their resistance to the New Deal was muted by a genuine commitment to national respectability and a desire to avoid raising again the specter of a Utah theocracy by strenuous and conspicuous interventions in the political process. Even the opposition of the church leaders to the repeal of Prohibition, while no doubt sincere, was rather perfunctory. It was limited to a First Presidency statement and other occasional public comments but nothing like the efforts made earlier in the century to control Utah's support for the Eighteenth Amendment. Presumably the leaders were counting on their ability to control the liquor laws of Utah, no matter what happened nationally. As the thirty-sixth state to vote for repeal, Utah and its Mormons ironically put the Twenty-first Amendment across the line (Alexander, 1986b; Clark, 1971:338–40; Croft, 1985; Gottlieb and Wiley, 1984; see also Allen and Leonard, 1992; Arrington and Bitton, 1979; and Shepherd and Shepherd, 1984:58, 186).

During the final decade of President Grant's administration, his counselor J. Reuben Clark was the main spokesman for the church hierarchy in political and other matters (Quinn, 1983; Williams, 1966). Clark's political interventions were frequent but were limited mostly to Utah politics (Lythgoe, 1982). Occasionally he would denounce socialism and communism as diabolical counterfeits for early Mormon communitarianism (Clark, 1975:16–18, 151). In doing so, he was, of course, well within the ideological mainstream of the nation. Less well remembered are Clark's eloquent denunciations of universal military training and American imperialism in 1945 and 1946, also well received at the time by a war-weary public. The onset of the cold war, however, soon made that issue rather moot.[11]

The fifties brought to power the Eisenhower administration in Washington, D.C. (1953) and the administration of church president David O. McKay in Salt Lake City (1951). Still very much in an assimilationist posture, the Mormon hierarchy was pleased to contribute one of its own number as the first Mormon ever named to a federal cabinet (Apostle Ezra Taft Benson as secretary of agriculture). During occasional visits to Utah, Benson sometimes took advantage of his combined church and government standing by making public statements that were both partisan and strongly right-wing in their nature (Quinn, 1993). President McKay, in response, would often prevail informally upon another member of the hierarchy with opposite political leanings (especially the eloquent Hugh B. Brown) to give a public address with contrasting political views, and the president often went to some pains to assure the world of the church's political neutrality (Croft, 1985; Mann, 1967; Williams, 1966).

In short, the history of Mormon political involvements in national politics up to about 1960 provides few, if any, exceptions to dominant national trends. Even where the church leaders were displeased, as with the coming of Prohibition repeal and the New Deal in the thirties, their reactions were certainly not strenuous. Members of both major parties were prominently represented in the hierarchy, and Mormon votes were about evenly divided between the two parties. All of this bespeaks an interest in normalizing relationships with the rest of the nation and accepting a high degree of assimilation.

Such a posture cannot be explained by reference to Mormon doctrines, values, or other internal imperatives, since these have been invoked on both sides of several political controversies, including both war and peace, both feminism and (more recently) antifeminism, and even for and against national prohibition of alcohol. The church posture during this period was, however, consistent with a policy of assimilation, of living down the disrepute of the nineteenth century (see also Mauss and Bradford, 1988: 58–59).

One of the earliest indications of a new political stance for the Mormon church was the overt political involvement of church leaders in a national controversy over the right to work in 1965 and 1966. Section 14b of the Taft-Hartley Act permits states to pass their own right-to-work laws and thus prevent closed-shop agreements. Pro-union forces in Congress tried to repeal 14b, an attempt that ultimately failed. However, the Mormon First Presidency, citing the traditional church belief in "free agency," intervened overtly in these congressional deliberations on the side of keeping 14b. Utah has never been hospitable to labor unions, and most Mormon leaders and members have tended to look on unions with some suspicion, so the feelings of the church on 14b were not surprising (Mangum, 1968; Wirthlin and Merrill, 1968).

What was surprising was the overt and strenuous nature of the intervention. The First Presidency not only issued a public statement on the matter but church leaders contacted personally each and every Mormon in the House or Senate and lobbied them all to vote against repeal of 14b. The effort backfired, since most of the congressional Mormons were Democrats and favorably disposed toward repeal, so they resented the intervention of their church leaders. Some of them reported the incident to the press, which made for a certain amount of public relations embarrassment. Church opponents charged that the Mormons were motivated simply by regional economic interests, hoping to induce corporations to locate in Utah by keeping wages relatively low (Davies, 1968; Frederickson and Stevens, 1968). Whatever the motives, such overt intervention in national politics represented a departure from the more insecure and docile assimilationist posture of the past.

More recently, in 1981, the church leaders (especially President Spencer W. Kimball) showed a willingness to bite the hand that fed them, politically speaking, when they turned against a very friendly Republican administration in Washington to oppose the basing of an MX missile system in southern Utah and Nevada. In doing so, the church leaders reverted to the antimilitarist posture seen in earlier times and leaders (especially J. Reuben Clark), condemning not merely the intrusion of megaweapons into their own homeland but the resort to weapons of any kind in the search for world peace (Blais, 1984; Firmage, 1983; Glass, 1993; Hildreth, 1982; Gottlieb and Wiley, 1984; and Quinn, 1983, 1985). As in the Taft-Hartley issue, the Mormon political intervention in the MX controversy was not crucial to the outcome, but it did, once again, reflect a new Mormon resistance to co-optation by the political establishment.

Three other issues during recent decades, however, have been far more important as indicators of the Mormon willingness to take on the nation politically. The first of these was the painful race relations issue of the sixties and seventies. The others (the ERA and abortion issues) can be seen in the still-ongoing Mormon opposition to some of the goals of the contemporary feminist movement, particularly ironic in comparison with the nineteenth- and early twentieth-century progressiveness on women's issues (Beecher, 1982; Beeton, 1978; Derr, Cannon, and Beecher, 1992).

The race issue is well known and has been discussed at great length in other places (e.g., Bush and Mauss, 1984; Mauss, 1981; McMurrin, 1979a). Although the church had long withheld its lay priesthood from members of black African ancestry (of whom there were very few), this priesthood policy did not really come to national attention until it was forced to the surface by the burgeoning civil rights movement (Lythgoe, 1968; Stathis and Lythgoe, 1977). Earlier in the century, national disapproval and public pressure might well have been enough to cause the assimilating church to drop its unpopular race policy; indeed, some effort was made to do just that by President McKay in 1954–56 (Mauss, 1981). However, by the sixties and seventies, the church and its members were far less interested in popularity, or even racial equality, than they were in maintaining the integrity of their own practices and traditions.

Such an explanation accords well, of course, with the general argument of this book. It accords also with the observations of Leone (1979) and Shepherd and Shepherd (1984) in seeing the reluctance of the church to change its race policy as primarily an assertion of its own right to be peculiar and to depend on its own revelations, rather than upon popular trends. Such, indeed, was explicit in the official statements issued by the First Presidency on this issue in 1963 and again in 1969 (Mauss, 1981; McMurrin, 1979a). Consistent with this explanation (but somewhat ironically), when the church finally dropped its traditional racial restrictions in 1978, there had been no significant outside pressure to do so for several years.

Women's issues, however, continue to complicate the church's political relationships and are likely to do so yet for some time. As in all its public controversies, the church can be expected to cite selectively certain traditional Mormon doctrines, values, or institutional concerns as the basis for its policies. Sincere as such explanations undoubtedly are, there is simply no compelling doctrinal basis in Mormonism for the church's public opposition either to a national Equal Rights Amendment or to a pro-choice abortion policy, except perhaps the general profamily and prochild traditions that have always been important in the Mormon cultural heritage.

The ERA controversy was especially acrimonious for Mormons, both within the church and in relations with the outside. Almost three-fourths of the states had ratified the ERA by the time the Mormon leadership finally began speaking out against it in the midseventies. Mormons in the legislatures of Utah, Nevada, and other states had, in fact, been supporting ratification until church leaders publicly opposed it. At that juncture, many Mormon legislators reversed their position, which, of course, made church opposition even more conspicuous and controversial. From then on, church representatives lobbied in key state legislatures against ratification, raised and disbursed money for anti-ERA campaigns in several states, and orchestrated the opposition to ERA and other feminist issues among Mormon delegates to the International Women's Year meetings from 1976 onward (Gottlieb and Wiley, 1984:chap. 1; Huefner, 1978; Sillitoe, 1990; White, 1983, 1989).

All of this went far beyond the routine public statements of church leaders that had characterized earlier church involvements in political issues and even beyond the kind of remonstrances with individual Mormon legislators in the 14b labor law controversy. Indeed, church involvement in the ERA controversy may well have exceeded legal boundaries for tax-exempt institutions, at least in some states (White, 1983). It certainly represents the most strenuous church political involvement of the twentieth century for Mormons.

It is truly difficult to understand both why the church opposed the ERA at all, especially so late in the ratification process, and why its opposition was so strenuous. The ERA was seen by some Mormons as undermining family values by encouraging women to work outside the home. Others criticized the unduly brief, vague, and sweeping language in which the ERA was written. Yet, in Canada and in the states that had ERAs of their own, neither of these concerns would have been justified by the empirical realities. Whatever the ultimate rationale consisted of, it still reflected clearly a Mormon political posture of retrenchment and distinctiveness.[12]

On the abortion issue, the church position is more difficult to locate with respect to the national consensus. Both the pro-choice and the pro-life camps claim majority support in the nation for their positions (at least among women). Yet both claim too much. First of all, there is no appreciable difference between men and women on this issue nationwide. Second, public opinion is not simply dichotomous on the issue. National surveys, like the annual General Social Surveys of the National Opinion Research Corporation, that pose the abortion question in terms of differing circumstances or scenarios all find that only from 10% to 15% of the population opts for either the pro-choice extreme (abortion without restraint during the first two trimesters) or the pro-life extreme (no abortions under any circumstances). The great majority of the U.S. population distributes itself between these extremes along a continuum representing different kinds and degrees of restriction (Davis and Smith, 1990).

On such a continuum, both the leaders and the members of the Mormon church would stand mostly on the conservative side of the middle, but just how far from the middle is harder to define. The entry on *abortion* in the new *Encyclopedia of Mormonism* (Ludlow, 1992) quotes official church policy as limiting acceptable abortions for church members to cases where the pregnancy resulted from rape or incest, where the fetus is extremely deformed, or where the health or survival of the mother is in serious jeopardy. Other abortions are considered by the church as strictly elective and as sins second only to murder.

Current Utah law tends to reflect the church policy. Federal policy, based as it is on *Roe vs. Wade*, is currently much more liberal than this, and the laws of other states are somewhat mixed (many are now in flux as federal policy has become more ambiguous in light of some of the latest Supreme Court applications of *Roe*). Until the more conservative turn of public opinion on abortion in very recent years, the Mormon policy was clearly outside the national policy expressed in *Roe*, and it might be so characterized even now (though less so). Furthermore, the church has used its political influence in various states and at the national level in support of conservative national abortion policy (Daynes and Tatlovich, 1986; Richardson, 1984; Richardson and Fox, 1972, 1975).[13]

Here again, the church policy has no clear theological basis, for there is no Mormon counterpart to the Catholic doctrine that life begins at conception. Indeed, while different church leaders have had different opinions on when life begins, the church has operationally, at least, held that the "spirit enters the body" only at parturition (Keller, 1985). For example, stillbirths are not counted on church records as ever having lived (Ludlow, 1992:1419). Furthermore, the fetuses the church does allow to be aborted cannot be distinguished theologically from those that must not be aborted (Bush, 1985; Sherlock, 1981).

The Mormon abortion outlook thus seems to derive from a more vague and general profamily and prochild tradition, with perhaps an element also of requiring personal responsibility and consequences for sexual indulgence. Such an ideological orientation has aptly been characterized as more Victorian than Mormon in its origins (Foster, 1979; Hansen, 1981). The point is not that this ideology is by definition inauthentic in Mormonism but only that it is not a necessary or inevitable derivative of Mormon doctrine, scripture, or other ecclesiastical imperatives. Although the theological bases for political opposition to abortion seem selective and ambiguous, as they do for resistance to the ERA, in both cases they follow the pattern of a changing posture from assimilation to retrenchment.

Summary

This chapter has demonstrated how case studies of specific institutional changes can illustrate and validate large-scale programmatic trends of the five kinds discussed in the previous chapter. The church's relationship to the KJV Bible changed not so much in the *extent* to which the Mormons used that Bible (which was always considerable), but rather in the ways that the KJV *functioned* to express the changing Mormon relationship with American society. Ultimately the retroactive Mormonization of the KJV, through its absorption into a hermeneutical framework dominated by the JST and other modern LDS scriptures, marked a partial return to the nineteenth-century Mormon subordination of the Bible to modern revelation. This process was but another way of reaffirming the primacy of latter-day prophets as over against the shared American biblical heritage.

The same motif of prophetic primacy can be seen in the stiffening political posture of the church toward the nation. Reflected especially in racial and feminist issues, the new willingness to stand athwart the national consensus, if necessary, has reasserted the integrity of the Mormon tradition of change through continuous revelation, rather than through expedient responses to political pressure. The church leadership has thereby shown a new confidence, too, that its extensive missionary and public relations efforts will suffice to maintain the growth and success of the church around the world, despite any national U.S. judgments that Mormon views are politically unfashionable.[14]

Notes

1. Other fairly recent examples also come to mind of scholarly works that were prepared entirely separately and independently from the present study but unintentionally offer strong corroboration for the assimilation-to-retrenchment thesis advocated in these pages. I would include, for example, Shepherd and Shepherd (1984), which has already been much cited; White (1987), cited in chapter 11 in connection with doctrinal developments; and Paul (1992) on changing attitudes among Mormons and their leaders on scientific issues. When so many studies, independently conceived and executed, converge in support of a given thesis, then an author like myself can claim persuasive corroboration going far beyond the (perhaps biased) treatment in one's own work.

2. Philip L. Barlow's *Mormons and the Bible: The Place of the Latter-day Saints in American Religion* (1991) was given the 1992 Francis and Emily Chipman Award for Excellence in a First Book at the annual meeting of the Mormon History Association. Parts of it were later included in a co-authored article (Mauss and Barlow,

1991) on which the discussion here is based. I am deeply grateful for the contribution of Dr. Barlow to our fruitful collaboration in the article and derivatively in this chapter. Obviously, this part of the chapter could not have been written without the work he had already done.

3. For other references to similar expressions by Brigham Young on the Bible, see the *Journal of Discourses* 2:6, 79, 88, 90; 3:335–36; 13:45, 264; 14:208; and 16: 71–77.

4. This is another of those perplexing examples of the difficulty which the Mormon leadership still has in applying the perspective of a "worldwide church" to specific cases. One wonders how this official insistence in the *Ensign* on the KJV is managed in countries where Mormon converts read the traditional Lutheran or Catholic Bibles.

5. Much of the material in this second part of the chapter appears in Mauss and Bradford, 1988. The indispensable contribution of Dr. M. Gerald Bradford, both to that article and to this chapter, is hereby gratefully acknowledged.

6. Mormon overrepresentation continued in the 103d Congress after the 1992 general election, not only on the strength of senators and representatives from the Far West, as one might expect, but even with representatives from Oklahoma and New Hampshire, plus a delegate from American Samoa. Several on the slate, furthermore, were Democrats. See the list in *Church News*, Jan. 9, 1993, 6. Yet the Mormon overrepresentation in Congress is not great in comparison with that of the Jews or the Episcopalians.

7. For recent and authoritative statements on how the LDS Church views its legitimate prerogatives with respect to moral and political issues, see Avant (1992:3, 11) and also the long statements by Apostles Oaks, Ballard, and Faust in the *Ensign*, Oct. 1992, 60–71.

8. For an official statement of this policy, see the 1989 issue of the *General Handbook of Instructions*, 11:2, 3, which is disseminated to all priesthood leaders.

9. Early in World War I, President Joseph F. Smith condemned the Germans and the English more or less equally, but when the United States entered the war in 1917, he urged support for the Allied side (Clark, 1971:50–52, 61–62). A similar pattern occurred in World War II, with the First Presidency first condemning this "unholy war" in 1939 and then, in 1942, regretfully supporting the U.S. war effort, while still renouncing war in general (Clark, 1975:116–19, 139–40, 157–63, 182–89, 216–19). Church leaders at first considered, but ultimately rejected, a policy of conscientious objection in World War II (Quinn, 1985).

10. Until his death in 1961, President J. Reuben Clark was something of an isolationist. He was a strong opponent of virtually all U.S. military involvements and of the standing, conscripted military establishment that made them possible (Quinn, 1985). The generation of church leaders recruited since World War II have reflected a much more hawkish and "patriotic" tendency toward U.S. military adventures. Also, the official church position during the Korea and Vietnam eras was complicated and compromised by the fragile and restrictive arrangements with the government over draft deferments for Mormon missionaries; see Allen and Leonard (1992:part 4), Arrington and Bitton (1979:251), Firmage (1983), and Walker (1982). As recently as the Persian Gulf War, Elder Thomas Monson of the

First Presidency spoke publicly in glowing, patriotic terms about the commitment of Mormon military personnel to the service of their country. While allowing for conscientious objection on the parts of individual Mormons, Monson emphasized the patriotism of the Mormon troops, noting that of the 35,000 Mormons currently in the military, 5,400 were serving in the Persian Gulf. See *Deseret News*, Mar. 10, 1991, 6B.

11. Clark's ideas were made official in a letter from the First Presidency dated Dec. 14, 1945, to Utah's entire congressional delegation (Clark, 1975:239–42). Another such letter to all church officials on June 28, 1946, urged them to write their respective congressional representatives in support of the First Presidency's antimilitarist policy. Legislation providing for a drafted standing army was, however, eventually passed (Quinn, 1983, 1985).

12. Some of the Mormon wariness about the sweeping implications of the ERA might well have derived from alarm over the efforts of federal agencies during the seventies to interpret existing civil rights statutes (which did not even have constitutional status) as disallowing Brigham Young University's administrative control over the living arrangements (and thus the sex lives) of its students. Some Mormons might have seen a national ERA also as the opening wedge in a campaign to gain access to the Mormon priesthood for women, but that issue was never raised by any of the official church commentary on the ERA. For more discussion and documentation on the ERA controversy and related issues, see Mauss and Bradford (1988:esp. 59–60) and also Arrington and Bitton (1979:234–40), Oliphant (1981), Richardson (1984), Shepherd and Shepherd (1984:38–39, 206–7), and Winder (1980).

13. For more on the abortion issue and Mormon political relationships, see Hill (1981), Mauss and Bradford (1988), Oliphant (1981), Richardson and Fox (1972, 1975), and Sherlock (1981).

14. Critics of this argument, as it is applied to church political initiatives, have pointed to a tendency in this analysis to underemphasize the importance not only of church doctrine but also of the personal and collective political and economic interests of the church leaders during times of political controversy. I do not mean to ignore such obviously important factors, but rather to consider them in the larger theoretical context of the struggle to maintain an optimum tension between assimilation and distinctiveness. Viewed from this more abstract perspective, the "wishes of the Brethren," while always important, are not necessarily determinant. They can be muted, modified, or augmented by such other considerations as the amount of internal resistance from dissenting colleagues in the leadership, or from the Mormon grass roots more generally, as well as by external pressures from the national political and economic establishment. Thus, it is the overall thrust of corporate ecclesiastical responses to the environment, across fairly long time periods, that must provide basis for the argument here.

CHAPTER EIGHT

The Grass-Roots Response to Official Retrenchment

The Mormon retrenchment motif, whether in its official or its folk manifestations, has not, of course, occurred in a cultural vacuum. The intraorganizational, ecclesiastical context has been nested in an evolving American culture to which it has had to respond. The retrenchment is thus best understood as a reaction both to internal and to external developments of the past few decades. The main internal conditions have been the well-known mushrooming of the Mormon membership (an eightfold increase since World War II) and the erosion of Mormon distinctiveness through assimilation.

The main external conditions have been the sweeping moral and cultural revolution of the sixties and seventies, sometimes called "the Age of Aquarius," and the subsequent resurgence of conservative religious denominations, sects, and styles, new and old, as if in reaction to this era. Different scholars and researchers have undertaken to explain in different ways this rather unexpected new awakening in American religion, but all agree that somehow conservative religion has increased its powers of recruitment and retention, probably at the expense of the more liberal mainline religions, whose memberships have declined in recent decades (Hoge and Roozen, 1979; Kelley, 1972; Perrin, 1989; Perrin and Mauss, 1991; Roof and McKinney, 1987; and others). Considering such drastic internal and external changes, it ought not to be too difficult to understand the various manifestations of Mormon retrenchment as efforts to retain (even regain) control of an overloaded ship in turbulent waters.

The moral and cultural upheavals of the Age of Aquarius are too well known to require detailed consideration here. Many of these developments would be regarded in hindsight by most Americans (and most Mormons) as desirable: various liberation movements that have strongly mitigated the traditional racial, ethnic, and gender inequality and bigotry in our society; an expansion of religious toleration to include everything from Roman Catholicism to New Age spiritualism; and a greatly increased access to higher education even for people with very modest means. On the other hand, Mormons and their leaders (along with many others) have watched with increasing alarm the spread throughout society of such "liberating" innovations as the normalization of nonmarital sexual behavior; the concomitant rise in abortion, illegitimacy, divorce, and child neglect or abuse; the regular resort by many youth to dangerous recreational drugs; and the rise both in serious crime and in dependency.

If Mormon retrenchment is in part a reaction to these changes, so too is the Protestant retrenchment that is reflected in the growth of conservative and fundamentalist denominations (old and new) at the expense of the more liberal Protestant mainstream. Such differential church growth might be attributable also, in part, to a process sometimes called the "southernization" of American religion, because (1) religious fundamentalism has been historically associated with the South, or Bible Belt; (2) denominations with southern origins (most conspicuously the Southern Baptist and Assemblies of God) have been the chief exemplars of the disproportionate growth; and (3) southerners in recent decades have been migrating to the west and the north, bringing their denominations and their religious conservatism with them.

The migration patterns have actually gone both ways, so that people moving to the South from elsewhere have been recruited to southern religions even as migrating southerners have been partially Americanized. Even so, the net result has been a greater southernization of American religion than obtained before 1960 (Egerton, 1974; Shibley, 1991; Stump, 1984). Even the Mormons have been included somewhat in this southernization process, as more southerners than ever before have become Mormons. As an interesting side effect, the Mormons and the more conservative or fundamentalist denominations, which have always competed for a similar segment of the religious market, have in recent years been encountering each other more extensively (and somewhat more acrimoniously), as southerners have moved west into Mormon country and Mormons (with their large missionary corps) have become more visible in the South.

The "Grass Roots" versus the "Official" in the Mormon Setting

The Mormon polity is somewhat unusual in the Christian tradition because there is not a clear distinction between clergy and laity and thus no clear distinction between officials of the church and its grass-roots followers. The Mormons have a male lay priesthood but no professional clergy. The ecclesiastical polity is hierarchical and episcopal in nature, but only the general authorities at the very top (including the First Presidency, the Twelve Apostles, and the Seventy), totaling barely one hundred, are full-time, salaried church leaders. Priesthood officers at all lower echelons, down to and including the local pastors (called "bishops" by the Mormons), have other occupations and render their church service gratis as an avocation.

Working under the general authorities, however, and reporting to them, is a large, professional, and salaried "civil service" bureaucracy. This bureaucracy has a "staff" relationship to the church hierarchy, rather than a "line" relationship, so it is theoretically bypassed in the top-down extension of priesthood authority. However, key members of that bureaucracy will sometimes claim to be speaking for the general authorities (often called "the Brethren"), even when not explicitly delegated to do so. A certain amount of ambiguity (some of it perhaps calculated and functional) is thus associated with operational directives out of the bureaucracy.[1]

The bishops and other local officers are recruited from the grass roots, and each echelon of the priesthood leadership is recruited from the lower ones. Thus even the general authorities are men of worldly experience who have usually had careers in business or in the professions before "retiring" (usually in middle age) to accept calls to full-time work as general authorities. A fair number of these appointments come out of the professional church bureaucracy itself, especially out of the administration of the Church Education System (CES). In many other cases, a new general authority gives up a promising career in midstream and at some personal sacrifice. One advantage of this recruitment from lay to official positions is that it minimizes the gap in education, culture, and experience so often found between the clergy and laity in other denominations. Another advantage is that it provides grass-roots aspirants with an alternative status ladder to which to devote themselves apart from their regular occupations (though, to be sure, "success" in lay church careers tends to be correlated with success in worldly occupations, especially in the settled areas of the church like Utah and the West Coast).

In such a system, it can be difficult to distinguish the grass roots from officialdom, especially in beliefs, attitudes, values, and peer networks. Yesterday's relatives and college roommates become tomorrow's church superiors at one echelon or another; but the terms of appointment are only temporary (except for the general authorities), so there is a fair amount of rotation both vertically and horizontally. To start with, then, the distinction between the official and the grass-roots levels must be made in operational roles at a given point in time.

In conventional sociological theory, it is the requirements of the role (more than personal traits) that most influence the posture and the behavior of the role occupant. Priesthood roles, of course, cover different jurisdictions and carry different prerogatives at the different levels. Officially, therefore, a leader's preferences and policies are valid only within his realm of authority, except as he is expressly carrying out directives from higher echelons. Intentionally or not, lower-level and midlevel priesthood leaders sometimes introduce ambiguity into a situation by failing to make clear when they are speaking for themselves instead of for their superiors.

Most general authorities recognize the potential hazard that the grass roots will tend to regard as "official" whatever "the Brethren" say. Accordingly, the leaders at these top echelons tend toward greater restraint than do those at lower levels in speaking or acting on their personal preferences, whether in doctrine or in policy. During the past few decades, furthermore, especially in fundamental policy matters, the general authorities have (with only a few exceptions) increasingly submitted to a collective norm of public action or expression only by consensus, in clear contrast to the period earlier in this century when some important public disagreements were tolerated among the general authorities. Today the Brethren thus present a public appearance of almost monolithic unanimity, despite the vigorous debates that certainly take place behind closed doors.

Grass-Roots Responsiveness to Official Retrenchment Efforts

Modern Prophets and Continuous Revelation

Despite a common perception that grass-roots Mormons are equally monolithic in following their prophets, church members actually interpret calls for obedience differently. As an encapsulation of that principle, "Follow the Brethren" is probably heard with greater frequency now than earlier in the century, when the church held a more assimilationist posture. In general conference addresses, at least, that theme began receiving much greater emphasis after 1950 than in the generation immediately preceding. To some, "follow the Brethren" implies unquestioning obedience, but the Mormon folk, as well as their leaders, differ considerably in the latitude they claim for themselves in interpreting the mandates of the prophets, whether living or not (Ludlow, 1992:520). Such latitude is made possible, indeed, by the various sources of ambiguity about what is "official" and therefore binding upon truly faithful Latter-day Saints. Two incidents will illustrate.

In the midforties, an article was published in the "official" church magazine, then called the *Improvement Era*, on the subject of sustaining and obeying church leaders. The article ended with a ringing endorsement of blind obedience: "When our leaders speak, the thinking has been done." The authorship of the article was not given, and the implication was left that it had come from the First Presidency. In actuality, it was probably written by one or more of the anonymous civil service staff at the magazine and given cursory or tacit approval by one or two of the general authorities. In any case, the article (and surely the dictum on which it ended) marked one of the first salvos in the new retrenchment campaign then only in its inception.

When the article came to the attention of the Unitarian minister in Salt Lake City, he reacted somewhat sternly in a letter to the president of the Mormon church, George Albert Smith, pointing to the implications of such counsel for the autonomy and conscience of the individual church member. Thereupon President Smith wrote a most conciliatory letter to the minister, in which he explicitly repudiated such counsel and cited the long Mormon tradition of freedom of conscience, starting with the well-known dictum of Joseph Smith, "I teach them correct principles, and they govern themselves" (see Editors of *Dialogue*, 1986).[2]

Under the circumstances, it appears that the president himself had not been aware of what had been published, with the presumption of his approval, in the church magazine. Had the article not been so publicly called to the president's attention, it almost certainly would have stood indefinitely as "official" church teaching, when in fact it represented the views only of those leaders and staff members involved in publishing it. Obviously, "follow the Brethren" meant something different to them from what it meant to him who was then chief among "the Brethren" themselves.

A more recent example is the pair of stern sermons by President Ezra Taft Benson (1987a, 1987b) drawing the line between male and female gender roles in strict traditional terms. Some Mormon "working mothers" apparently quit their jobs immediately, despite the prospect of severe financial hardship without the second salary in the home. They felt thus obliged, in the name of "following the Brethren," to obey the prophet's counsel (Anderson, 1988).

At the time of these sermons, ironically, scores of "working mothers," all on church salaries, could already be found among the prophet's civil service bureaucracy, including some of the female faculty at BYU. Many of these women had children still of school age. Some families at the grass roots apparently interpreted "follow the Brethren" more strictly than did the personnel departments presumably responsible to the Brethren themselves. Furthermore, a year after President Benson's stern instructions, his first counselor, Elder Gordon Hinckley (1988), delivered instructions to Mormon girls in the *Ensign* magazine emphasizing the reconciliation of domestic and extradomestic roles for Mormon women. Thus, in this instance, as in others, "official" church policy, as distinguished from the personal preferences of powerful leaders, can be somewhat ambiguous (perhaps functionally so).[3]

Some survey data support this variety of interpretations as well (see table 8.1). One of the questions asked of the respondents in the Utah and San Francisco surveys of the 1960s was: "What do you think an LDS church member ought to do when faced with a certain church policy or program with which he does not fully agree?" The respondent was then given five alternatives. A similar question was asked twenty years later of a very different sample, namely the readers of *Dialogue*, the privately published scholarly journal for Mormons (and others) of an intellectual bent.

The differing populations and time periods do not permit definitive generalizations from the figures, but some of them are at least suggestive and are consistent with theoretical expectations. For example, the distributions for the first, "blind obedience," option are about what we would expect, even if the surveys had all occurred at the same time: The Utah Saints, long ensconced in the entrenched stage of church development, were the most conservative, the most likely to accept on faith whatever they thought the Utah church establishment required. The San Francisco

TABLE 8.1. Estimated Reactions to Disagreement with Church Leaders (percentages)

Course of Action When Faced with Disagreement	SLC 1967	SF 1969	*Dialogue* Readers (1987)
Accept it on faith and carry it out	42	27	10
Refuse to go along as a matter of conscience	7	19	*
Dissent privately but avoid open conflict	*	*	24
Express self frankly to leaders but then comply even if no change	40	37	37
Gather support for one's position and petition church leaders	3	10	4
Other and miscellaneous	7	8	26
N (100%)	958	296	1,779

SOURCES: My 1967–68 and 1968–69 samples and *Dialogue* 20, no. 1 (1987): 27–53.

NOTE: The *Dialogue* sample cannot, of course, be compared directly with others given the time lapse and given that *Dialogue* subscribers are almost by definition independent thinkers, whereas the earlier SLC and SF samples were more like representative cross sections of their respective populations.

* = This alternative was not offered in the applicable questionnaire.

Saints, still in the settlement stage of development, were much less likely to respond in that way.

The *Dialogue* readers, rather independent thinkers almost by definition, were by far the least likely to give such a response, and it seems quite probable that they would have responded in very much the same way even if they had been asked twenty years earlier. Indicative of the same independent thinking is the relatively large proportion of *Dialogue* readers who gave "miscellaneous" responses not classifiable in any of the categories provided in the questionnaire (though these responses tended to reflect combinations of those categories).

In some ways, the most telling figures are those for the fourth option, reflecting what could fairly be called the modal Mormon response. The similarity of these three figures across time, space, and varied samples is especially noteworthy: Approximately 40% of all three samples would obey their leaders, not blindly, but only after insisting that the leaders first consider their dissenting views. Even the conservative Utah Saints were as likely to choose that response as to choose "blind obedience." In any case, the data in table 8.1 at least illustrate the variety in the grass-roots Mormon understanding of what it means to "follow the Brethren." Of course, we cannot draw any conclusions from this table about changes across time in grass-roots Mormon attitudes, but we get at least one strong indication of such change from the BYU surveys of Christensen and Cannon (see chapter 11), who found that BYU students were more than twice as likely in 1973 as in 1935 to place obedience to church authority above their own preferences (Christensen and Cannon, 1978).

Genealogy and Temple Work

Official responses and grass-roots responses toward temple work mirror each other quite closely. In one generation the number of temples has gone from eight to fifty. Concomitantly, Iannaccone and Miles (1990) showed that temple work, whether for the living or for the dead, had increased tenfold from 1950 to 1985, compared with only a fivefold increase in church membership. Given the increase in the sheer number of temples, and their geographic diffusion in North America and in the world, it is almost certain that grass-roots participation in temple rituals has increased greatly during the past generation.

The same appears to be true of the genealogical research that makes most of the temple work possible. Nearly every stake center in the church now has a computerized genealogical library (recently renamed Family History Library). Regular delivery of data disks to the stake centers from the central genealogical files in Salt Lake City makes it possible for amateur researchers of all kinds to have immediate local access to hundreds of thousands of verified names of deceased ancestors and others, which can then be organized into family trees and family group files. There have always been a few genealogical specialists among the Mormons at the grass roots, but until recent years they had to travel to Salt Lake City to work in the central library.

Now that advanced computer technology and small, compact disks have made it possible for Mormons to work with their genealogies in their local stake centers, are they heeding the call of their leaders to participate in this uniquely and authentically Mormon avocation? An initial look at the patrons of the various stake centers would not be encouraging (at least outside of Utah), since most of them turn out to be non-Mormon genealogy buffs delighted to find such resources in their neighborhoods! More systematic data, however, indicate increasing grass-roots participation by

Mormons in genealogical research: During the eighties, there was a 25% increase in the number of Mormons submitting names of the deceased to temples for vicarious religious ordinances and a 250% increase in the number of those ordinances ("endowments") actually done (*Church News*, Feb. 9, 1991, 11). The "name extraction" program of the church (in which amateur volunteers glean from public records the names of deceased individuals irrespective of family ties) had yielded a total of more than 20 million new names for vicarious temple rituals by 1990. Two-thirds of these had been extracted during only the previous five years (*Ensign*, Jan. 1992, 79; *Church News*, Sept. 25, 1993, 3, 7).

Missions and Missionary Work

The full-time missionary corps of the Mormon church in 1993 stood at almost 50,000, the overwhelming majority of whom are young men between the ages of nineteen and twenty-five, serving at their own expense for two years. Young women are encouraged also to consider missions, but not as strenuously as the men are; furthermore, the women are not permitted to serve until they reach twenty-one years of age. The reasons for that are not entirely clear, but they seem to stem from patriarchal traditions that favor a longer period of parental guidance and protection for young women and an expectation that they should first be given a chance for an early marriage in place of a mission. Young women thus comprise only about 10% of the missionary corps. Older couples are also being encouraged increasingly to enter missionary service of varying lengths after retirement.

Colleagues on the professional research staff of the church have indicated that about a third of the Mormon males between nineteen and twenty-five years of age serve missions for the prescribed two-year period. This same level of participation has obtained since 1960, except for a temporary decline during the Vietnam war era, when the military draft was in force. In assessing how much compliance with the church program is represented by this level of missionary participation, one wonders what to use as a standard of comparison. On the one hand, participation by a third leaves two-thirds who are not complying with the regular appeals of the church leaders for all young men to prepare for missions. On the other hand, for a third of these youth to be thus engaged at a time in life when their non-Mormon peers are in college or working seems extraordinary by comparison with what is expected in other denominations. Also, this level of missionary service is probably greater by at least half than that which obtained before 1960.

However satisfactory this level of compliance might seem to church leaders, it has certainly played a major role in the rapid membership growth that the Mormon church has enjoyed, especially since 1960, from 1.5 million to 8.5 million (*Ensign*, May 1993, 98; Ludlow, 1992:1518–26). Beyond its impact on the church institutionally, missionary service has always served as a powerful means of religious socialization for the individual missionary. Data from my surveys of Mormons in the sixties indicated that missionary service was second only to family background as the chief predictor of adult religious commitment, and therefore more important than formal religious education. Missionary service thus represents also a powerful assertion and a particularly intensive cultivation of the special Mormon identity. One is reminded here of the finding by Shaffir (1978) that "witnessing" had a corresponding function for individual Hassidic Jews. In a generation when Mormons, like Jews, have been subjected to decades of American assimilation, the identity-maintaining function of proselytizing assumes a special importance.

Family Solidarity

So much emphasis is placed on family life, both within Mormon congregations and in outside proselytizing efforts, that Mormons sometimes leave the impression that they regard wholesome family life as a Mormon invention. There is little doubt that the contemporary program of Mormon family retrenchment, including the oft-mentioned family home evening beginning in the early sixties, anticipated the more recent motif of family renewal that has since become fashionable in the nation (Ludlow, 1992:495–97). What is much less certain is whether this institutional emphasis has made a difference in the ways that Mormons actually live their family lives. Twenty-five years ago, when my surveys in Utah and San Francisco were conducted, only about half of the Mormon families in those samples were holding the prescribed weekly family home evening with appreciable regularity. There are no subsequent data indicating any higher levels of compliance. Furthermore, given the increasing proportions in the church of both single people and older couples beyond child-rearing years (Heaton, 1987b), it is not realistic to expect anything near total compliance at the grass roots.

The evidence from recent studies of Mormon family life indicates that

Mormons are both similar to and different from other Americans in family relationships. This topic might deserve a separate chapter in its own right, except that so much about it is already in print (e.g., Campbell and Campbell, 1981; Heaton, 1986, 1987a, 1987b, 1992; Heaton and Calkins, 1983; Heaton and Goodman, 1985; Thomas, 1983; and Ludlow, 1992:488–92). The research indicates that Mormons differ from others primarily in a greater tendency toward marriage, both first and subsequent marriages (after widowhood or divorce); and in a preference for relatively large families.

Although Mormons do marry at a relatively high rate (Heaton and Goodman, 1985), a noteworthy fraction (perhaps a third) of Mormons between twenty and thirty years of age are unmarried (single, divorced, separated, or widowed). This situation is not uncommon in other denominations, but it is a relatively new feature of Mormon life that has received some scholarly commentary (e.g., Cornwall, 1987b; Oswald, 1990; Rees, 1991; Young, 1990).

Among the married, the relatively large Mormon family size cannot be attributed to a general reluctance to use artificial contraceptives, for the Mormon resort to such devices is on a par with that of other Americans (Heaton and Calkins, 1983; Ludlow, 1992:1522–36). We must credit instead a relatively strong prochild sentiment among Mormons: Babies are simply good things to have (Ludlow, 1992:486–88).

We can see from table 8.2 that Mormons, compared with other Americans, not only aspire to have larger families but actually do so, which is consistent with earlier findings in the sixties (see table 4.8). Indeed, throughout recent decades, Mormon family size has remained close to twice the national average, though it has tended to follow the same pattern of peaks and valleys as have the national figures in North America (Heaton, 1986; Thornton, 1979); the same has been true generally for Mormons in other developed countries, too, but not in the less developed ones (Heaton, 1989).

Although Mormons have big families, spouses don't always stay together despite the teachings of their church leaders. The Mormon church does not have a theological position on divorce per se, but its teachings about the eternal nature of family bonds (especially when solemnized in a temple marriage) certainly encourage strong marital and family commitments and discourage divorce (Ludlow, 1992:486–88). Yet divorce (even of temple marriages) has always been permitted for due cause. Indeed, during the polygamous nineteenth century, a fair amount of fluidity was

TABLE 8.2. Family Size Preferences (percentages)

Family Size	Mormons	Non-Mormons
Ideal		
No children	1	1
1–2 children	22	52
3–5 children	56	37
6 or more children	18	6
N (100%)	235	6,292
Actual		
No children[1]	21	27
1–2 children	26	39
3–5 children	41	28
6 or more children	12	5
N (100%)	343	9,292

SOURCE: Based on cumulative data, 1972–90, from the annual General Social Surveys of the National Opinion Research Corporation. See Davis and Smith (1990) and the Appendix herein.

NOTE: Mormon *N* includes all available cases; Non-Mormon *N* is a random subsample of all cases. See the Appendix. The question about ideal family size was not included in every annual survey. The differences between Mormons and others are statistically significant at or below the .000 probability level.

1. Includes people never married.

permitted both in divorce and in the changing of spouses in cases of manifest marital incompatibility (Ludlow, 1992:391–93; Van Wagoner, 1986). With the assimilationist thrust of early twentieth-century Mormonism, however, Mormon marriage and divorce norms came to resemble closely the Victorian and post-Victorian ideals of the nation as a whole. Thus, monogamy was required and divorce was strongly discouraged.

The turbulence of the sixties and seventies wreaked its havoc on Mormons as it did on the rest of the nation. Almost any Mormon bishop will admit that marital problems in his flock are the most endemic, prevalent, and vexing problems of his calling. They often involve sexual transgression, which is an even more serious sin for Mormons than for many other denominations. In any case, and for whatever reasons, the divorce rate for Mormons is close to (or only slightly below) the national average, even in Utah (though the Utah figure is not high compared with the mountain and western states generally). Church leaders can take some comfort from the additional fact that temple marriages are much less likely to break up than nontemple marriages: The divorce rate for nontemple marriages is six times that for temple marriages (Howard M. Bahr, 1981; Heaton and Goodman, 1985; Ludlow, 1992:391–93; Martin, Heaton, and Bahr, 1986).

Yet, the relatively low divorce rate among temple-married couples must be small comfort to Mormon leaders when they realize that most Mormon marriages are not performed in temples (Ludlow, 1992:857–59, 1532). Furthermore, the traditional Mormon preference for early marriage combined with the early start on a family means that when Mormons get married they do so at higher risk of divorce, by virtue of those factors alone, than do non-Mormons who marry later, start their families later, and have fewer children (Christensen, 1968; Christensen and Cannon, 1964). Compliance with traditional Mormon family norms is obviously a mixed blessing, but for those who comply with the injunction to prepare spiritually for a temple marriage, the prospects for a stable and satisfying family life are obviously enhanced.[4]

Furthermore, women especially are expected to uphold this stable family life by following traditional gender roles. Despite some ambiguity in official statements, lesson manuals disseminated throughout the church typically carry strong injunctions for Mormon women, and especially mothers, to give highest priority to their domestic responsibilities. In table 8.3, we can see evidence of considerable grass-roots compliance with these church teachings, at least at the level of attitudes.

While the preferences in gender roles expressed by Mormons in this table are certainly conservative and family oriented in comparison to those expressed by non-Mormons, it is worth noting that even the Mormons are split in half on the first two statements (only 48% and 52%, respectively, in agreement). Furthermore, the question remains as to how well actual behavior reflects the attitudes expressed in this table. Reliable data from other studies indicate that while Mormons use a great deal of traditional patriarchal rhetoric, relationships between husbands and wives are in actual practice as egalitarian as in non-Mormon families.

Indeed, Mormon wives and mothers in North America are gainfully employed outside the home at about the same rates as in the rest of the nation, on average (around 50%), although the Mormon women might feel more guilt about it (Albrecht, Bahr, and Chadwick, 1979; Howard M. Bahr, 1979, 1982; Bluhm, Spendlove, and West, 1986; Ludlow, 1992: 1535). Mormon women in Britain are in the labor force at about the same rate as Mormon women in North America, but at a lower rate than are British women generally. In both Mexico and Japan (especially the latter), Mormon women participate in the labor force actually at higher rates than

TABLE 8.3. Attitudes toward Women's Roles (percentages)

Agree with the Statement	Mormons	Non-Mormons
Working mothers' relationships with children can be as warm and secure as nonworking mothers have.	48	60
It is more important for a wife to help with her husband's career than to have one of her own.	52	35
A preschool child is likely to suffer if the mother works.	68	52
It is much better for all involved if the man is the achiever outside and the woman takes care of the home.	68	47
N (100%)	141	3,187

SOURCE: Based on cumulative data, 1972–90, from the annual General Social Surveys of the National Opinion Research Corporation. See Davis and Smith (1990) and the Appendix herein.

NOTE: The percentages refer to respondents answering "agree" or "strongly agree." All comparisons between Mormons and non-Mormons are significant statistically at probabilities between .000 and .034.

do other women in those countries (Ludlow, 1992:1535). Recent data on Mormon women in the United States indicate that their extradomestic employment is associated with reduced church activity (Heaton, 1992), although the causal direction of that relationship is not clear.

Religious Education

As part of the Americanization of Utah, the Mormon church gradually relinquished earlier control over public education. In an effort to integrate religious education with the new state school curriculum, the church began in 1912 a system of high school "seminaries" (Bennion, 1922). In Utah and adjoining states, where Mormon numbers are large, these seminaries meet during the school day in church-owned seminary buildings close to the local high schools. Despite periodic political controversy (Buchanan, 1993), Mormon students are permitted by local school boards to integrate seminary classes into their school programs on a released-time basis, and about 70% of the eligible students do so (Ludlow, 1992: 274–76, 1295–96).

Elsewhere in North America, where Mormon numbers do not justify separate seminary buildings or full-time teachers, the students take seminary classes instead on an early-morning basis, rather than on released time during the day. These classes usually meet in the Mormon church building nearest the high school, and the teachers are usually nonprofessional volunteers. The parents are responsible for organizing transportation arrangements to get students to seminary and then from seminary to school. Since these seminaries usually begin at about 6:30 A.M., students and their parents must arise quite early, the more so the farther away they live from the church. These distances can amount to twenty-five miles or more in areas where Mormon numbers are sparse.[5]

Early-morning seminary often precludes participation in extracurricular school activities. All things considered, most Mormon youth and their parents make noteworthy sacrifices for participation in early-morning seminary, so it is not surprising that these participation rates drop to about half of the eligible students (Ludlow, 1992:1295–96). In truly peripheral areas of the church, the official expectation of seminary participation for all Mormon youth requires sacrifices that members who are otherwise quite faithful consider unreasonable (Lambert, 1985). Nevertheless, in 1990 the seminary program was operating in all U.S. states and in at least ninety other countries.

At the college level, religious instruction takes place at one of the 1,200 institutes of religion operated by the church. In many ways, these are the Mormon equivalent of the Roman Catholic Newman centers and the Jewish Hillel centers. They are usually located adjacent to, or very near, the campuses of colleges and universities of all kinds. The program began in 1926 with the establishment of the first institutes at the University of Idaho and at Utah State Agricultural College (now Utah State University). The first institutes outside of North America were established in Australia during 1969, and institutes are now found in more than sixty other countries. Since participation in institutes of religion is much more voluntary for college students living away from home than seminary is for high school students, institute enrollments are understandably much smaller, but still comprise more than 125,000 college students internationally (Ludlow, 1992:684–85).

Simple numbers and percentages about seminary and institute participation do not tell the whole story, however. Access to such religious education differs considerably according to which stage of church growth and development obtains where one happens to live. In Utah and neighboring states high school seminaries are readily available, and institutes of religion are found near every college and junior college. The full-time CES instructors are professionally trained and earn reasonably good salaries and benefits. High school students need only run across the street to the seminary building during an open school period. Until recent legal pressures brought by the American Civil Liberties Union, moreover, students could receive high school credit for some of their religion classes at seminary, and seminary grades were included with their school report cards. In such an environment, church leaders and parents have found it relatively easy to get their youth to comply with the expectation for seminary attendance.

For locales in the pioneering and settlement stages, seminary classes are much harder to get to, and institutes are provided only near the major colleges and universities. Pressure to participate from parents, peers, and church leaders is somewhat less effective, of course, the more sparse the Mormon population and the older the students in question. The teachers, for their part, are typically volunteers from a local congregation who have to rush off either for work or for home at the end of class, just as the students must rush off to school.

For the teacher of early-morning seminary, daily classes mean relentless lesson preparation on top of all other daily duties for a stipend of only about six hundred dollars per year. For the student, seminary means at least an hour a day less of sleep than other students get and the forfeiting of any extracurricular activities that conflict with seminary. For the parents, seminary means extra-early rising, early-morning shuttling of one's own and the neighbors' children to the seminary class, and then on to school, sometimes over considerable distances, in all kinds of weather. In this situation, grass-roots "compliance" with the religious education program takes on an altogether different meaning in most of the world from what it has in Utah.

The wonder is that the institutional and family resources of the Mormons continue to flow so freely into a church program with so little demonstrable impact. As the data in table 5.4 indicated, religious education (especially high school seminary) has little independent impact on adult religious commitment, at least when home influence is taken into account. Even the more recent and more systematic data reported by Cornwall (1987a) makes the same point, though with the important qualification that seminary participation does help indirectly by channeling Mormon youth into religiously supportive peer groups.

The continuing grass-roots support for the church education system has depended in large part upon the widespread impression that it makes a strong contribution to a youngster's later religious commitment. What parents, after all, would not want that kind of backing for their efforts at home? In its recruiting appeals over the years, the CES has routinely made the claim that Mormon students who attend seminary or institute are much more likely (than those who do not attend) to go on missions and to have temple marriages as adults (see, e.g., *Church News*, Nov. 14, 1992, 6). While that claim is surely made in good faith, and is even true (as far as it goes), it is also spurious; for the full truth is that Mormon youth from strongly religious homes are most likely to go to seminary *and* to go on missions *and* to get married in the temple. In other words, the home, not the seminary instruction, is the chief determinant of all such outcomes.

In recent years, the church research office has been asked to undertake a comprehensive empirical evaluation of the religious education program of the church. The results of such an evaluation, if indeed it has been undertaken, would not be made publicly available, in any case. Whatever the outcome of that research, it is unlikely that the resources or scope of the CES will ever be seriously reduced. Today there are literally thousands of religious educators and administrators whose entire careers depend upon the perpetuation (if not the expansion) of CES, and several of them in recent years have been recruited to the ranks of the general authorities of the church. Here it is necessary only to recognize what scholars and students of large, complex organizations have always known: Entrenched bureaucracies die hard, even if their usefulness is open to question. A careful cost-benefit analysis of CES, therefore, whatever its outcome, might matter but little.

Summary

In this chapter, we have reviewed the evidence for grass-roots compliance with the five retrenchment thrusts initiated by the church leadership after midcentury. In general, an appreciable degree of compliance is apparent. Rank-and-file Mormons are inclined to uphold the principle of continuous revelation by following their prophets, even when they have certain reservations, but they also vary considerably in the latitude they allow themselves in this obedience. In genealogy and temple work, a relatively small proportion of all the members do most of the work, but overall activity in these unique Mormon preoccupations has increased greatly in recent decades.

The continuing Mormon commitment to missionary work has enlisted a large minority of the young men of the church, and a smaller minority of the women, in a very effective missionary corps mainly responsible for the rapid church growth. The family life picture is somewhat more mixed. Mormons appear fairly traditional in their rhetoric about spousal roles but in practice are about as egalitarian as other Americans. They have their share of family difficulties, but their divorce rate is relatively low if they marry in the temple, as the church prescribes; and they have larger families than most other Americans have. Their efforts to rear children as faithful Mormons are bolstered by an extensive program of religious education and indoctrination, in which probably a majority of the high school students are involved. In at least these five respects, then, the church appears to have arrested, if not reversed, the erosion of distinctive Mormon ways that might have been anticipated in the sixties.

Notes

1. This LDS civil service bureaucracy thus resembles the "agency" bureaucracies in other denominations. As Chaves (1993) demonstrates, such a bureaucracy is potentially a rival in power and resources to the priesthood hierarchy itself. The LDS "correlation movement" can be seen in part as a means of maintaining priesthood control in this situation. Yet communication and mutual influence are fostered informally through regular recruitment to priesthood leadership from the civil service bureaucracy ranks.

2. This dictum has been attributed to Joseph Smith by (among others) his associate and eventual successor as president, John Taylor, in the *Millennial Star*, 15 Nov. 1851, 339.

3. For additional discussions of the aftermath and implications of the 1987 pair of sermons by President Benson, see Lavina F. Anderson (1988), Oswald (1990), and Young (1990).

4. An analysis by Heaton (1992) of a recent national sample of women has compared Mormon women with those of other major denominations in some of these same key respects. In general, this latest analysis confirms the earlier findings summarized here. However, Heaton found that rates of premarital sex and divorce appear to be increasing for Mormon women. Religious activity and participation also seem to have a greater impact on Mormon women than on other women with regard to premarital sex, divorce, early marriage, family size, and employment outside the home. Church influence thus appears especially important in the lives of Mormon women. An interesting convergence appeared generally between Mormon women and fundamentalist women in matters of sex, marriage, divorce, extradomestic employment, and certain other characteristics. Contrary to the anecdotal evidence sometimes presented in the mass media, however, Mormon women are not especially susceptible to depression (Bluhm, Spendlove, and West, 1986).

5. In areas where Mormon population is especially sparse, seminary is administered on a home study basis, without formal daily instruction.

CHAPTER NINE

Modern Mormon Religiosity and Its Consequences

Although the data so far appear to support the retrenchment hypothesis, we have looked only at the grass-roots response to the five main initiatives of the church leadership. Here we consider Mormon religiosity more generally. Belief, however, is only one way of assessing the religiosity of a people. Stark and Glock (1968), in a pioneering analysis of the different ways of being religious, identified and provided empirical validation for five different dimensions of religiosity: belief, experience, practice, knowledge, and consequences. Nationwide survey data collected by the National Opinion Research Corporation (NORC) will make possible a few comparisons between the Mormons of the sixties and Mormons of the eighties in addition to comparisons between contemporary Mormons and other Americans. Yet such comparisons will of necessity be limited because of certain basic differences in sampling and strategy between the recent NORC surveys and mine from the sixties.

Under a grant from the National Science Foundation, the NORC, in collaboration with other professional organizations, has conducted an annual General Social Survey (GSS) each spring from 1972 to the present (except for 1979 and 1981). The sample each year has totaled about 1,500, which is a common size for the national samples drawn by Gallup and other polling organizations. An elaborate and sophisticated sampling technology makes it possible to produce data representing the entire nation with a high degree of accuracy, despite the relatively small sample sizes. The data come from interviews of more than an hour each with noninstitutionalized adults. The interview schedule differs somewhat from year to year: Some questions are asked every year, some only every second or third year, and others have been added only very recently, as public and scientific interest have required (see Davis and Smith, 1990).

Since Mormons in recent decades have represented only 2% or 3% of the population of the United States, any one annual national sample could be expected to include only a handful of Mormons. Furthermore, since Mormons are not evenly distributed throughout the country but are found disproportionately in the sparsely settled Mountain West, their proportion in a national sample would be even smaller. To compensate partially for such regional underrepresentation generally, the GSS has in recent years deliberately oversampled the mountain states, so the Mormon subsamples have become a little larger. However, even at their largest, the Mormon samples in any one year are too small for meaningful analysis. Only by aggregating the annual Mormon samples across a number of years can we obtain a total Mormon sample of reasonable size. Through 1990, that size totals 343, the great majority of which comes from the 1980s.

The national (non-Mormon) sample, if similarly aggregated across the years, would total more than 26,000, which is much larger than necessary. Accordingly, a random sample of that sample ($N = 9292$) was drawn by computer in such a way as to give greater weight to the eighties (25% samples in the earlier years and 50% samples in the more recent years). Both the Mormon and the national samples, therefore, are especially representative of the eighties (one would be reluctant to drop the pre-1980 samples altogether, since we need all the Mormon cases we can get to achieve statistical significance). More information about the NORC-GSS can be obtained by consulting Davis and Smith (1990).

Scientific squeamishness about asking religious questions in federally supported surveys has served to minimize the number of questions on religious beliefs included in the GSS in any one year. In the seventies, especially, there were very few such questions. In more recent years, however, religion questions have proliferated (though they still do not include such basic Christian items as whether one believes in God or in the divinity of Jesus).

General Mormon Religiosity

Beliefs

Such data as we have from other sources give us every reason to assume that Mormon beliefs in God, Christ, the mission of Joseph Smith, and all

TABLE 9.1. Selected Religious Beliefs

Belief	Mormons %	Mormons *N*	Non-Mormons %	Non-Mormons *N*
Strong or somewhat strong belief in one's own religion.	62	322	41	7,925
Belief in life after death.	93	256	71	6,598
Belief Bible should be taken literally as God's word.	27	127	35	3,091
Belief Bible is God's inspired word but shouldn't be taken literally.	67	127	45	3,091
Belief Bible is book of fables.	6	127	19	3,091

SOURCE: Based on cumulative data, 1972–90, from the annual General Social Surveys of the National Opinion Research Corporation.

NOTE: All Mormon/Non-Mormon comparisons are statistically significant at the .000 level. *N* varies in size because not all questions were asked in every year of the GSS surveys.

other traditional Mormon ideas would rank Mormons in the eighties at least as high in orthodoxy as they were in the sixties (cf. Cornwall et al., 1986). Unfortunately, the GSS data do not include affirmations about God or Christ in particular or (naturally) about Joseph Smith. They do include questions about belief in life after death, in the Bible, and certain other relevant matters (see table 9.1).

Although the questions in table 9.1 provide a limited range of comparison between Mormons and others, it is apparent that levels of belief are notably higher for Mormons. They tend to believe in Mormonism more strongly than other Americans believe in their religions. Given some historical ambivalence about the Bible, Mormons at this time are still less likely than others to take the Bible literally; yet modal Mormon belief in the Bible does represent a considerable commitment to it as divinely inspired: Two-thirds of the Mormons take that position as compared with fewer than half of the other Americans.

We can further compare the level of belief in life after death with data collected in the sixties. During that period, on average Mormons believed in life after death at about the same rate as did Protestants and Catholics, within about ten points (see table 3.3). In table 9.1, however, the gap has widened to more than twenty points (Mormons 93% versus non-Mormons 71%). To the extent that we can consider the sixties data comparable to the those from the GSS, this widened gap in belief would be consistent with the retrenchment motif.[1]

Differences between Mormons and others are to be found not only in the percentage levels of belief, however, but potentially, at least, in the *kinds* of belief about life after death. The GSS interviews presented three conceptualizations of afterlife, in particular, that seemed to distinguish Mormons from others: "People picture life after death in many different ways. We'd like to know how you think of life after death." Then the respondent was presented with a seven-point scale for each of three different sets of polar opposites:

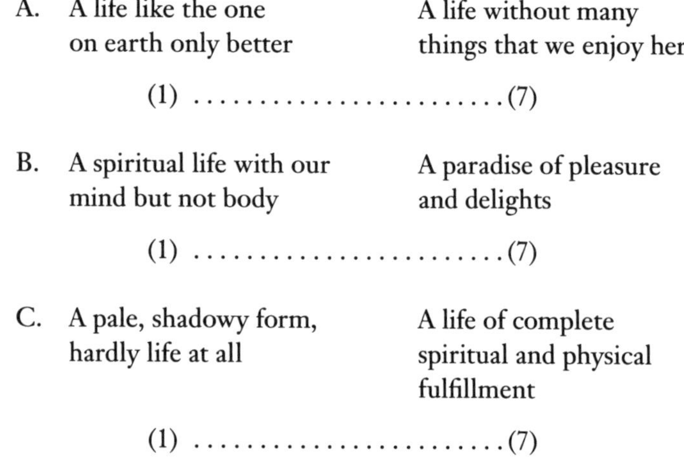

A. A life like the one on earth only better — A life without many things that we enjoy here

(1) . . . . (7)

B. A spiritual life with our mind but not body — A paradise of pleasure and delights

(1) . . . . (7)

C. A pale, shadowy form, hardly life at all — A life of complete spiritual and physical fulfillment

(1) . . . . (7)

It is apparent from table 9.2 that although the overwhelming majority of Mormons believe in a life after death, they tend to believe in quite a

TABLE 9.2. Conceptions about Afterlife (percentages)

Conceptions about Afterlife[1]	Mormons	Non-Mormons
A. Life like the one here on earth[1]	81	60
B. Paradise of pleasure, delights	32	19
C. Life of complete fulfillment[2]	92	71
N (100%)	118	2,600

SOURCE: Based on cumulative data, 1972–90, from the annual General Social Surveys of the National Opinion Research Corporation.

NOTE: Percentages represent the combined responses of 1–3 on the 7-point scale for A and 5–7 on the 7-point scale for B and for C. All three comparisons are significant at .000.

1. At point 1 alone the Mormons had 64% versus 40% for the others.

2. At point 7 alone, the Mormons had 74% versus 46% for the others.

different kind of afterlife from that anticipated by most other Americans. This discovery will not be particularly surprising to anyone who knows traditional Mormon theology. Since the earliest teachings of the Prophet Joseph Smith, Mormon theology has rejected the traditional Christian dualism between spirit and matter and has tended to project onto the next world marriage and family relationships, as well as other "worldly" features of existence (McMurrin, 1969). While we do not have data available to trace any changes across time in such conceptions, grass-roots Mormons appear to be maintaining their distinctive beliefs in life after death.

Experience

In recent years, the GSS has included questions about a number of religious experiences people might claim to have had. For three of these, one finds some meaningful comparisons between the Mormon and the non-Mormon responses:

> "How often have you . . . ?"
>
> A. Felt as though you were really in touch with someone who had died (Choices: never in my life, once or twice, several times, often, and no answer).
>
> B. Felt as though you were very close to a powerful spiritual force that seemed to lift you out of yourself (same choices) and . . .
>
> C. How close do you feel to God most of the time? (Choices: extremely close, somewhat close, not very close, not close at all, don't believe in God).

Although the third claim takes on the nature of a platitude, all three of the claims to spiritual experiences are considerably more frequent among Mormons than among others, on the average (see table 9.3). Mormon religiosity thus contains a noteworthy element of spiritual experience, as well as belief. This might be a relatively recent development, judging from some of the data in the sixties. One of the questions in those surveys asked, "Since you were an adult, have you ever had a feeling that you were being visited by a departed relative or other personage from the spirit world?" The responses of "yes, I'm sure I have," and "yes, I think that I have," when combined, yielded 32% for the Utah Mormons and 28% for the California Mormons, both well below the 57% claiming contact with the dead in table 9.3.

The surveys in the sixties also asked whether (as adults) the respondents

TABLE 9.3. Spiritual Experiences

	Mormons	Non-Mormons
Felt in touch with someone dead:		
Never	43%	59%
Once/twice/more often	57%	40%
N (100%)	86	2,370
Felt close to spiritual force:		
Never	39%	59%
Once/twice/more often	59%	39%
N (100%)	118	3,141
Feel extremely or somewhat close to God most of the time.	93%	82%
N (100%)	178	3,141

SOURCE: Based on cumulative data, 1972–90, from the annual General Social Surveys of the National Opinion Research Corporation.

NOTE: $p < .019$ for A, .000 for B, and .001 for C.

had ever felt that they were "somehow in the presence of God," and this time the same question was asked in the Glock and Stark survey of California Protestants and Catholics. With the responses "yes, I'm sure," and "yes, I think so" combined, almost twice as many Protestants and Catholics as Mormons felt they had ever been in the presence of God (72% versus 36%). Of course this question, while worded identically, might still have had a somewhat different meaning for the Mormons from what it had for others; yet the Mormon claim to this kind of spiritual experience was only half as frequent as it was for the Catholics and Protestants (on average) in the sixties, and there was a strong convergence between the two samples of Mormons on this question just as there was on the item about contact with the dead. This question is only roughly comparable with "feeling close to God" (table 9.3), but it might be significant that the affirmative Mormon responses to such questions were well below those from other denominations in the sixties, while now they are considerably above those of the others.

It must be conceded that at least much of the difference found between the responses in the sixties and those in the more recent GSS data could be a result of asking different questions during the two periods. Yet the kinds of questions, especially the one about feeling in touch with the dead, do not differ greatly. On balance, we have some basis for at least a strong suspicion that Mormons today are claiming more spiritual experiences (especially by comparison with others) than they did in the sixties, which again would be very compatible with the retrenchment thesis.

Practice

The third dimension we can consider with the GSS data is religious practice. Stark and Glock (1968) distinguished between private, personal devotions (such as individual prayer) and public ritual activity (such as church attendance). Their data and mine from the sixties (see table 3.5) indicated levels of personal prayer "at least once a week" ranging from 76% to 83% for Mormons, Catholics, and the Protestant average (though considerably lower for California Mormons). The GSS survey asked the comparable question in categories that included daily, as well as weekly, personal prayer (see table 9.4); but if we were to use the weekly category (not included in the table) for comparison with the format of the question in the sixties, the more recent Mormon figure from the GSS would be 86%, a notable increase over the 76% (Utah) and 61% (California) in table 3.5, while the non-Mormon figure now would be 77%, nearly the same as in the sixties (the Catholic-Protestant average then). With the *daily or more* category in table 9.4, the gap between Mormons and others is even greater (74% versus 55%).

A similar picture emerges when we compare figures for church attendance then and now. Weekly (or greater) attendance for Protestants in the sixties averaged 36% and for the Catholics 70% (see table 3.4). The comparable Mormon figures were a modest 37% (Utah) and 26% (California). In the more recent GSS data (table 9.4), the gap has widened greatly in favor of the Mormons (58% versus 29%). The compliance of Mormons with the emphasis of their church on the principle of tithing is also ap-

TABLE 9.4. Religious Practices

	Mormons		Non-Mormons	
Practice	%	*N*	%	*N*
Personal prayer daily/more often	74	197	55	4,796
Church attendance weekly or more	58	343	29	9,292
Contributions of $1,000/yr. or more	41	86	8	2,531

SOURCE: Based on cumulative data, 1972–90, from the annual General Social Surveys of the National Opinion Research Corporation.

NOTE: All comparisons are statistically significant at the .000 probability level.

parent: Mormons are five times as likely as others to contribute as much as one thousand dollars a year to the church (here comparisons with the sixties are not very appropriate, for neither the dollar categories nor the dollar values were at all the same in the corresponding questions).

Knowledge

No recent data are available on Mormon religious knowledge, the fourth of the "dimensions of religiosity" posited by Stark and Glock. In the sixties, Mormon respondents were asked two of the same Bible questions that Glock and Stark put to their Catholics and Protestants. One question asked whether the Book of Acts is "an eyewitness account of the ministry of Jesus." The correct answer (no) was profferred by 27% of the Mormons (combined) and 36% of the Protestants and Catholics (combined). The other question required the respondents to choose from a list of Jesus' disciples the one who "denied him three times." This question was answered correctly (Peter) by 70% of the Mormons and 76% of the Protestants and Catholics. In other words, in the sixties the Mormons were somewhat less knowledgeable than the non-Mormons on these two Bible questions, despite the lack of encouragement for Bible study common to the Catholicism of that day.

Comparable data of that kind are not available for the contemporary period, so we cannot tell whether the gap between the Mormons and others in Bible knowledge has grown larger or smaller. On the one hand, we might be tempted to predict an increase in Bible knowledge for today's Mormons, since the church recently began emphasizing use of the scriptures as the basic "textbooks" for all church classes. On the other hand, the interpretive commentary in the lesson manuals represents a narrow, didactic, proof-texting approach to scripture study. Furthermore, between the sixties and the eighties the Bible-reading conservative Protestant denominations increased their share of total Protestant membership, while the Catholics became a much more Bible-reading denomination than before Vatican II. With all of these variables, current biblical knowledge cannot be compared across denominations with our data.

Consequences

Stark and Glock called their fifth and final dimension of religiosity "consequences," meaning primarily the consequences of one's religious commitments for living in the world outside the church. We saw some of these consequences already in chapter 8, where family life comparisons, some of them across time, were made for Mormons and others (also Albrecht, 1989). An abundance of literature indicates, furthermore, that Mormons have remained much more conservative than most others in sexual behavior, whether premarital or extramarital (e.g., Heaton, 1987a, 1992; Roof and McKinney, 1987).

Another well-known consequence of Mormon religiosity is the tendency toward abstinence from alcohol, tobacco, and certain other substances. In the recent GSS data 27% of the Mormons (N = 224) and 72% of the national sample (N = 5,546) confessed to any use of alcoholic beverages. For smoking, the corresponding figures were 13% (Mormons) and 37% (others). Clearly most Mormons are complying with their religious teachings (embodied in a revelation entitled the "Word of Wisdom"), especially where tobacco use is concerned. Yet one might argue that for a fourth to use alcohol is rather a large proportion among a people ostensibly "abstinent." More recent research by Stephen Bahr (1994), based on quite other data, also indicates relatively high abstinence rates for Mormons, not only from alcohol and tobacco but also from all the other drugs so problematic for modern societies.

Politics is not ordinarily considered a religious topic in itself, of course, but the increasing prominence of religious motivation in American political ideology and behavior has given greater salience lately to religious differences in political orientation. It is widely believed that Mormons tend toward more conservative political preferences than do most other Americans. In many respects, this common perception is accurate. The GSS data indicate that 32% of Mormons consider themselves to be conservative compared with only 15% of others. Most Mormons, though, like most others, consider themselves moderate, with nearly two-thirds falling into this category. Political party preference reveals even larger differences between Mormons and others. Only 32% of Mormons tend toward Democratic preference, while more than half of all others do. Republicans make up 60% of the Mormon population, but only 33% of the rest of the nation, which certainly verifies the public perception of Mormons as more conservative in general than the rest of the country.

This overwhelming conservatism has not always been the case. The Mormon rank and file, and many of the leaders as well, tended to vote Democratic until at least the fifties (Croft, 1985). The Mormon distribution by political party, indeed, remained close to that of the nation as a whole into the seventies, and even as Utah began to vote more heavily Republican, it was not so different from its neighboring mountain states (Olson and Beck, 1990). Recall that the survey data from the late sixties also revealed how close the Mormon party breakdown was to that of its neighbors (see table 4.4).

The gap between Mormons and others has grown since the sixties, but this is not just because of increased Republican preference among Mormons. During the sixties around 15% of Utah and California Mormons considered themselves independent, while only 6% do now. Furthermore, the proportion of Republicans among Protestants and Catholics has decreased dramatically from 53% to 33%. Mormon Democratic loyalty, meanwhile, has remained quite constant at about 30% of the population (32% according to the GSS compared with an average of 28% in the sixties). Thus, the increased Republican complexion of the Mormons seems to have come mainly from a switch of Independents to the Republican side.

Party preference, though, does not tell the whole story either. Aside from party loyalties, Mormons, like others, have views on contemporary social issues, such as civil rights and sex education in the schools. Mormon views on such matters are by no means always predictable from their generally conservative political orientation. On many issues, Mormons have always held strong libertarian views, especially where First Amendment rights are concerned (owing, no doubt, to the Mormons' own experience with religious persecution). On still other issues, the Mormons' views are not so different from those of their neighbors, on the average. Such was the case in the sixties, at least, from the data we saw in chapter 4, where Mormons did not differ greatly from others in attitudes about the national issues of the day. Table 9.5 shows us a sampling of contemporary Mormon attitudes, compared with those of the nation, on certain issues where the differences were statistically significant in the recent GSS.

Data from the GSS survey are highly congruent with the answers given by Mormons and others in the sixties on freedom of expression. Only around 20% of the different Mormon samples at that time (see table 4.7) would have denied atheists the right to preach their beliefs, which reciprocates well with the 80% in the GSS survey who would allow people to preach against religion. A similar reciprocal pattern occurs for the non-Mormon samples here and in the sixties. In both, the Mormons appear somewhat more libertarian than others on freedom of speech for atheists, and their relative position has not changed much.

Mormons also are obviously more libertarian than others about manda-

TABLE 9.5. Attitudes on Selected Social Issues

	Mormons		Non-Mormons	
Belief	%	*N*	%	*N*
People against religion and churches should be allowed to express their beliefs.	80	222	66	6,397
School prayers should not be required.	52	181	37	4,619
Schools should teach sex education.	69	201	82	5,167

SOURCE: Based on cumulative data, 1972–90, from the annual General Social Surveys of the National Opinion Research Corporation.

tory school prayer on average (52% versus 37%), again owing probably to the history of Mormon-establishmentarian conflict. A question about school prayer was asked also in the sixties surveys although it was worded rather differently from that in the GSS poll. Only about a third of the Mormons at that time agreed that "public schools should not conduct prayers for children," a figure quite close to the Protestant and Catholic average of 29%. In the meantime, of course, growing pressure from Protestant evangelicals has made the school prayer issue more salient, but the Mormon reaction (much more so than that of the others) has apparently become more libertarian, rather than less so, for in the GSS somewhat less than half thought school prayer should be required.

However, Mormons are apparently somewhat more conservative than others about sex education in public schools, but still more than two-thirds of them (69%) agree schools should teach the subject. They would thus probably be far less resistant to the idea than are most other conservative religious denominations, though they still rank far behind the country as a whole, where over 80% agree that sex education should be mandatory.

All in all, contemporary Mormons present quite a mixed picture in their opinions on today's social and political issues, just as they did in the sixties. In general, Mormons seem more conservative than others in politics and in some social issues, particularly those relating to family, sex, and drugs. Otherwise Mormon social outlooks are not notably conservative. This is abundantly clear also from the comparisons provided in a recent and very comprehensive study of American religious denominations, also based on the NORC General Social Surveys (Roof and McKinney, 1987). Chapter 6 of that work demonstrates that Mormons rate higher on a general scale of civil libertarianism than any but the most liberal Protestant

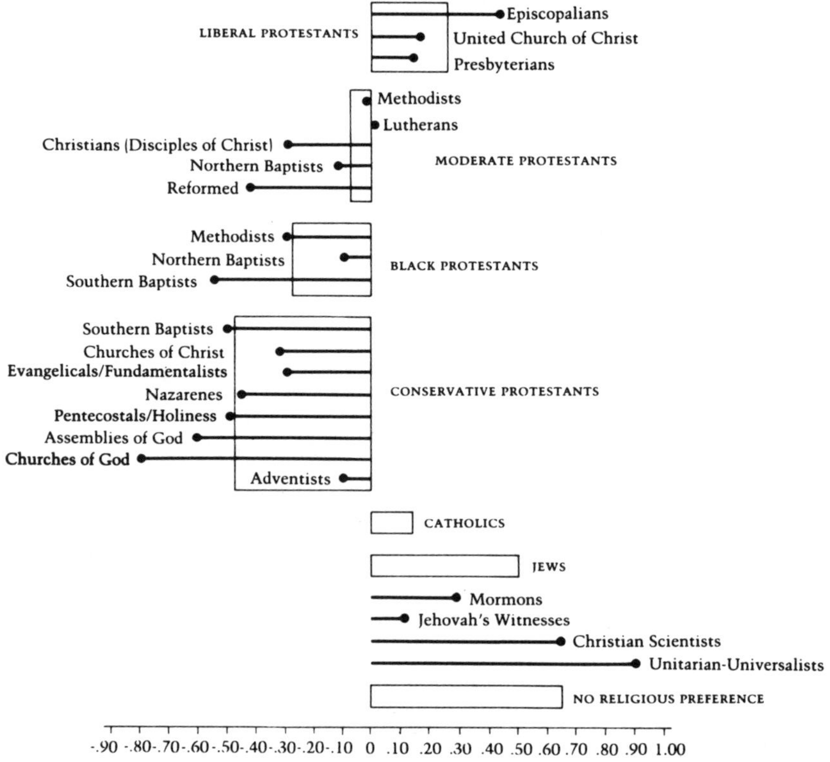

FIGURE 9.1. Comparison of Mormons with Other Denominations in Attitudes toward Civil Liberties. Reproduced with permission from *American Mainline Religion: Its Changing Shape and Future* by W. Clark Roof and William McKinney, figure 6–1, p. 195. Copyright © 1987 by Rutgers, the State University.

denominations, along with Unitarians and Christian Scientists. Figure 9.1 summarizes the Roof and McKinney findings.

The same pattern is apparent on the scale of racial justice developed by Roof and McKinney, where again the Mormon figures go in the opposite direction from those of other conservative denominations, placing the Mormons nationwide in the liberal camp, contrary to the racist image that has been attached to Mormons since the sixties (see fig. 9.2).

Even more surprising, and more strongly at odds with the Mormon public image, is the Mormon position on the women's rights scale developed by Roof and McKinney (see fig. 9.3). This scale is a composite measure based upon the average responses to a series of questions on women's

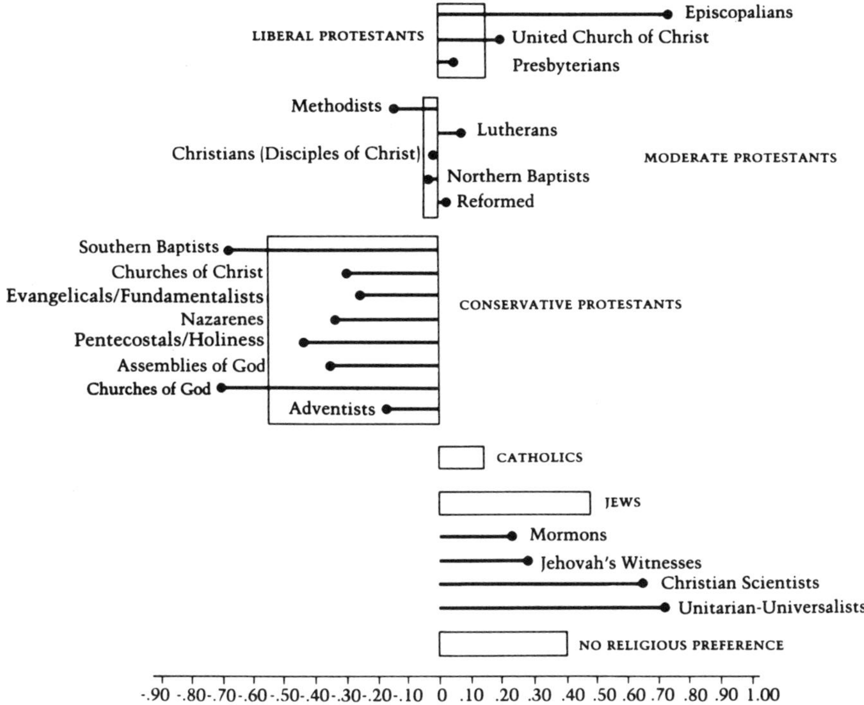

FIGURE 9.2. Comparison of Mormons with Other Denominations in Attitudes toward Racial Justice. Reproduced with permission from *American Mainline Religion: Its Changing Shape and Future* by W. Clark Roof and William McKinney, figure 6–2, p. 200. Copyright © 1987 by Rutgers, the State University.

obligations in the home, women's emotional fitness for politics, women's careers despite husbands' available support, acceptance of a woman as a presidential candidate, and abortion under various circumstances. On this composite scale, Mormons once again stand on the liberal side, along with Episcopalians, Presbyterians, Unitarians, and Jews, and very much at odds with the various conservative Protestant denominations. Apparently the Mormon reluctance about women's rights, which we saw in chapter 8, arises only in cases where the issue of child care is paramount, an issue not raised directly by the Roof and McKinney scale.

In life-style matters, though, we see the same Mormon conservatism that was apparent in the sixties (see chap. 4). Roof and McKinney developed a "new morality" scale based on questions about abortion for any

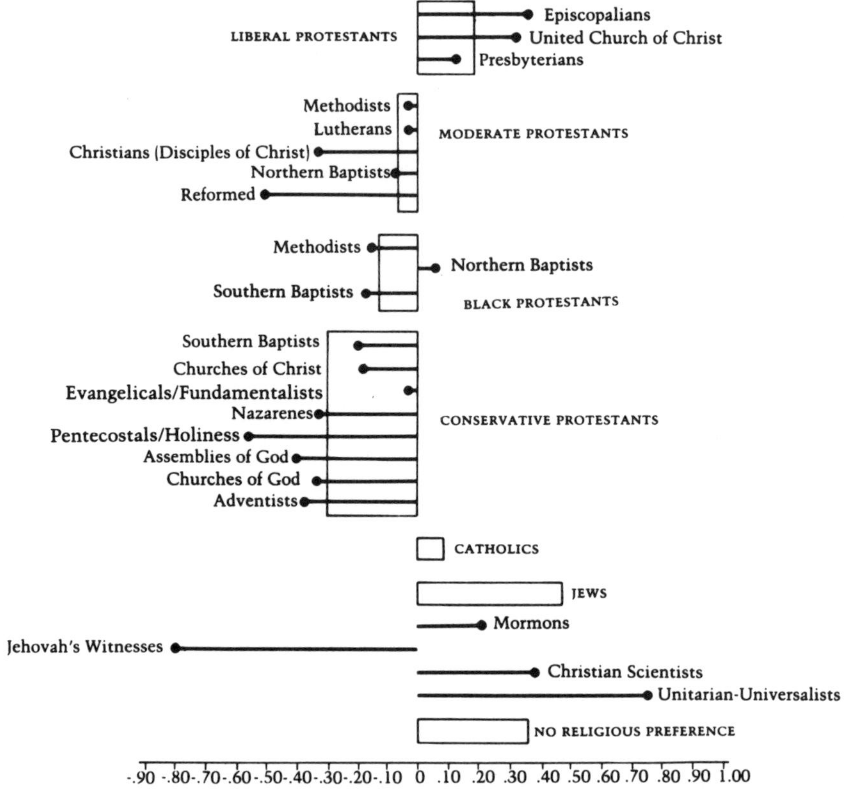

FIGURE 9.3. Comparison of Mormons with Other Denominations in Attitudes toward Women's Rights. Reproduced with permission from *American Mainline Religion: Its Changing Shape and Future* by W. Clark Roof and William McKinney, figure 6–3, p. 209. Copyright © 1987 by Rutgers, the State University.

reason, extramarital and premarital sex, homosexuality, divorce, and marijuana legalization (see fig. 9.4). As we would expect, Mormons left the liberal side of this scale and joined the Southern Baptists, Assemblies of God, and other fundamentalist denominations well over on the conservative side. Since Mormon views on sexuality have diverged significantly from those of the rest of the country for many decades, it is difficult to say whether those differences have widened since the sixties. What is suggested, though, from figure 9.4 is that Mormons today are at least as conservative in these life-style matters as they are liberal in civil liberties, racial justice, and women's rights.

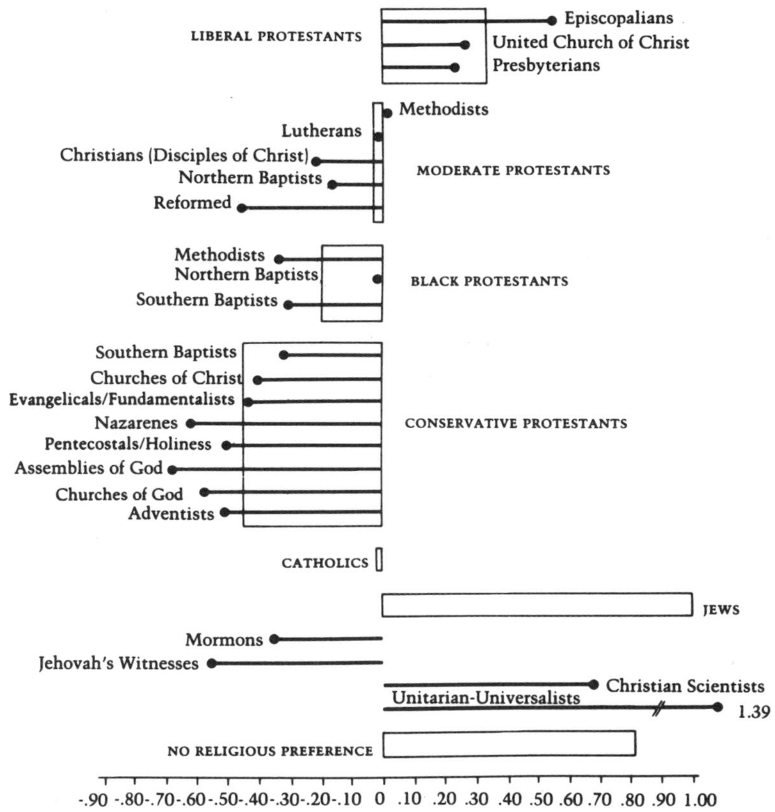

FIGURE 9.4. Comparison of Mormons with Other Denominations in the "New Morality." Reproduced with permission from *American Mainline Religion: Its Changing Shape and Future* by W. Clark Roof and William McKinney, figure 6–4, p. 214. Copyright © 1987 by Rutgers, the State University.

SUMMARY

In this chapter we have looked beyond the grass-roots Mormon compliance with the five general thrusts of the church retrenchment program to more general questions of how Mormons, in comparison with others, express their religiosity. A few of the questions from recent NORC-GSS surveys, when aligned with their counterparts from surveys in the sixties, made possible some rough comparisons between Mormons and others, then and now, in certain religious beliefs, practices, and experiences. These comparisons suggest that Mormons have grown somewhat more "religious" since the sixties, in comparison with non-Mormons, as we would expect from the generalized Mormon retrenchment motif.

With respect to certain presumptive behavioral consequences of their religious commitments, especially in comparison with others, Mormons remain at least as conservative as they were in the sixties. This is apparent in the Mormon rates of abstinence from alcohol, tobacco, and other substances, in their attitudes toward sexual issues, and in national politics. However, in partial contradiction to their public image, Mormons stand mostly on the liberal side of the continuum on certain other social and political issues, notably on civil rights, and even on women's rights, except where these seem to conflict with child-rearing roles.

Note

1. It must be conceded here that juxtaposing the sixties data with the eighties data might well exaggerate the widening gap between Mormons and others. The data from the sixties compare Mormons with the Protestant and Catholic *church members* who comprised the Glock-Stark samples. By contrast, the NORC-GSS respondents constitute a random sample of the entire (noninstitutionalized) adult population of the United States, church members or not. It was not possible to draw a subsample only of church members from the GSS data set, since respondents were not asked about actual membership (as opposed to denominational identification) except in the 1988 survey. However, it seems unlikely that this discrepancy in sampling would make a serious difference in the case being presented here, given that almost all respondents in the NORC-GSS claimed some kind of religious affiliation and that two-thirds of them claimed to attend church at least as often as "several times a year." For American Protestants, at least, and increasingly for Catholics too, the difference between formal church membership and an informal claim to affiliation is probably rather moot for most purposes.

CHAPTER TEN

Mormon Fundamentalism: The Institutional Matrix

Mormons and Mormonism have always participated to some extent in many of the developments that have occurred in the nation more generally, including religious developments. The very origins of Mormonism must be understood in the context of religious and other cultural developments that swept through the western frontier in Jacksonian America (Cross, 1950; Hill, 1989; O'Dea, 1957). Even during the relative isolation of the early Utah period, Mormons were by no means untouched by such national developments as feminism, spiritualism, and evangelism. During the first part of the twentieth century, the new state of Utah participated increasingly in such national issues and controversies as Prohibition, the League of Nations, the social gospel movement, and scriptural higher criticism (Alexander, 1986b; Barlow, 1991). We should not be surprised, then, that religious fundamentalism too has played its part in the development of Mormon religious life and culture, as it has in other denominations.

Fundamentalism is not a specific creed but rather a certain way of thinking about religion, about deity, and about the other world. The general tendencies have been explored at some length in scholarly works devoted to the fundamentalist tradition in American Christianity (e.g., Ammerman, 1987; Marsden, 1980) and need not be discussed here at great length. Neither is fundamentalism a binary trait, such that a person either is or is not clearly a fundamentalist. Rather, people (and denominations) are more or less fundamentalist, on balance, compared with others. The categorical label *fundamentalist* tends to be attached to those persons, churches, outlooks, or life-styles that seem to reflect fundamentalist tendencies enough to make them conspicuous in comparison to some ill-defined but more moderate position. This chapter proceeds with that caveat in mind and with, one hopes, due regard for the hazards it implies.

In its fullest form, fundamentalism is characterized by such beliefs as scriptural inerrancy and literalism; salvation by grace (sometimes through a born-again experience); authoritarian leadership; and strict obedience to pastoral injunctions. Along with this general theological outlook there is also a certain austerity in dress and personal style, traditionalism in gender roles, prudery in sex, and hostility toward "modernist" influences like "secular humanism," biblical criticism, and scientific theories such as evolution (Ammerman, 1987; Marsden, 1980). While such an outlook might be most common at the folk level, among the unsophisticated, it certainly has its more sophisticated and articulate exponents at the professional level, as well, from William Jennings Bryan to Jerry Falwell and Pat Robertson.

Early in the twentieth century, Protestant Christianity underwent a kind of schism between those theologians (like Rauschenbusch) who represented the social gospel movement, a more secularized view of Christianity focused on the social and ethical tasks of the church, and those who preferred instead to stay with the "fundamentals" of the "old-time religion" more common to nineteenth-century Protestantism. Probably no historical episode epitomized this schism as well as the Scopes Trial ("Monkey Trial") of the 1920s. While the schism cut across denominational lines, a tendency developed in time for some of the denominations to be more heavily influenced than others by the social gospel movement.

These denominations, including Episcopalians, Methodists, Presbyterians, Congregationalists, American (northern) Baptists, and a few others, have come to be considered the mainline American denominations that now comprise a clear majority of Protestant church members in the United States and Canada (Bibby, 1987; Roof and McKinney, 1987). On the other hand, the Southern Baptists, the Assemblies of God, and many smaller sects have clung to the fundamentalist style and content, though the Southern Baptists themselves have had considerable contention in recent years between their own moderate and fundamentalist factions (Ammerman, 1990).

This necessarily superficial overview of the schism does not, of course, do justice to the complexity of the picture; nor does it take into account related topics like the "neo-orthodox" school of thought that developed in various denominations and seminaries toward midcentury (White, 1987), which has further complicated the religious scene. Nevertheless, it is fair to say that in American Protestantism generally during the twentieth century, entire denominations, as well as factions within denominations, have tended to sort themselves according to either a more liberal social gospel orientation or a more conservative fundamentalist one, with a kind of intermediate category sometimes called "evangelical" (though the differences between evangelicals and fundamentalists are more in the nature of intellectual style than of theological content).

Mormonism was not immune to this schism and in fact has always had its own fundamentalist tendencies.[1] A number of scholars have noted the paradox in which such tendencies have existed side by side in Mormonism with liberal, humanistic, and antinomian impulses (Ericksen [1922] 1975; McMurrin, 1969; O'Dea, 1957). There has always been a certain literalism running through Mormon scriptural hermeneutics and practical applications (Barlow, 1991; Cummings, 1982). This fundamentalist motif has ebbed and flowed in Mormon history. Leaders have at some times urged Mormons to think for themselves in interpreting and applying their religion, while at other times enjoining them strenuously to "follow the Brethren," almost in blind obedience. Mormon leaders, past and present, have also advocated roles for women that have been both egalitarian and Victorian (Foster, 1979, 1981); and they have both condoned and condemned multiple marriages and divorces, even into the twentieth century (Van Wagoner, 1986).

The evolution and higher criticism controversies of the twenties and thirties also found outspoken partisans on both sides among Mormon leaders, as well as among intellectuals (Barlow, 1991; Bergera and Priddis, 1985; Keller, 1982; Sherlock, 1979, 1980). Even as these controversies were going on, the church began bringing conspicuously social gospel elements into its program as part of its increasingly assimilationist posture toward the nation as a whole (Alexander, 1982, 1983, 1986b; Kenney, 1978, 1987; Lowry Nelson, 1985). These opposing tendencies have thus been alternately dominant, both at the folk and at the official levels, in response to internal and external developments.[2]

Institutional Developments Fostering Fundamentalism among Mormons

In addition to the ebbing and flowing of fundamentalist tendencies in the underlying Mormon culture, certain administrative and institutional developments in recent Mormon history have also contributed to a resurgence of fundamentalism. These developments have had understandable origins and rationales that do not derive from fundamentalism itself, or from any desire to foster fundamentalism. Yet some of their consequences have had that effect. While a number of such unintended contributors to the spread of Mormon fundamentalism could perhaps be identified, this chapter will focus on five: (1) the lay clergy; (2) the priesthood correlation movement; (3) frequent turnover in the First Presidency; (4) reaction to the rise of a new class of intellectuals; and (5) the disproportionate conversion of southerners.

The Lay Clergy and Folk Fundamentalism

One important feature of Mormonism that facilitates the spread of emergent trends is the blurred distinction between the folk and the official levels of religious expression. Any active church member, whether female or male, can potentially be made a teacher or a local leader at any time. On becoming teachers or leaders, members do not leave behind their accumulated religious ideas and understandings, including the folk wisdom that might have no basis in official doctrine. These leaders might later be rotated back among the membership and thereby bring back to the grass roots an added increment of credibility for their folk wisdom deriving from the prestige of recent office.

Once these leaders (almost always male) move up the ranks to the regional or general level, credibility for them among the folk naturally tends to increase, even when they are speaking or acting on their own personal preferences. This process of upward and downward circulation between the folk and leadership levels is usually considered one of the organizational assets of the Mormon tradition, for it does institutionalize an element of egalitarianism that bridges the gulf between the laity and the clergy (terms almost never used in Mormon parlance).

The same process, however, has also unintentionally institutionalized a means for circulating and validating folk wisdom, both at the grass roots and up and down the hierarchy. Recent illustrations of this tendency can be seen in the proliferation of Utah scams into which some church members have blindly followed their leaders and in the Paul H. Dunn episode.[3] Since Mormon leaders, furthermore, are not professionally trained or sophisticated in theology, this circulating folk wisdom often has a quaintly fundamentalist flavor. One is reminded here of the observation by Leone (1979) that there is a sense in which each Mormon is his or her own theologian.

Add to this the fact that there is in Mormonism no tradition of canon law and thus no a priori basis for assigning or denying legitimacy to many of the acts or statements of church leaders at any level. Most leaders are quite restrained in this situation, feeling some sense of responsibility to distinguish official from personal initiatives. (This seems the more true the higher the office.) Yet, in the final analysis, much leeway is left for powerful and assertive leaders to impose their individual doctrines and wills, at least within their areas of jurisdiction, but sometimes even without.[4] These impositions might include the most idiosyncratic interpretations of doctrine or scripture and even the most egregious superstitions (such as fourthhand stories of encounters with departed spirits); but these are rarely, if ever, questioned by higher authority, as long as they are, in some sense, "faith-promoting."[5]

In a period of retrenchment, that which is fundamentalist in nature easily converges with, and reinforces, that which is faith-promoting. Indeed, as Buerger (1985) and Hutchinson (1982) have shown, many of the books, articles, and tapes by church leaders (widely marketed through church outlets) are intended more as popular than as theologically sophisticated products. Since they sometimes rely on secondary sources from the Protestant evangelical world, they are apt to reflect as much traditional fundamentalism as authentic Mormonism (see also chapter 6 on changing themes in general conferences).

The career of the late apostle Bruce R. McConkie provides a good example of how fundamentalist thinking from the grass roots can be brought into the top leadership echelons and thereby given implicit legitimation back at the grass roots. Elder McConkie entered the ranks of the general authorities on the First Council of Seventy in 1946 at the age of only thirty-one, an appointment probably not unrelated to the fact that his father-in-law, Joseph Fielding Smith, was then a prominent senior apostle. Up to that point, Elder McConkie had had brief careers in law and in the military (during World War II). From 1972 until his untimely death in 1985 he was a member of the Quorum of the Twelve Apostles. During his career he was a key member (and, indeed, often chairman) of ecclesiastical committees charged with overseeing many activities crucial to the intellectual life of the church, including the church education curriculum, the BYU board of trustees, and the preparation of the new integrated LDS scriptures.

Elder McConkie's many sermons, books, and other writings represent a decidedly conservative theological viewpoint, in common with those of many of his colleagues in the leadership. He went considerably beyond most of his colleagues, however, in his animosity toward modern scholarship in religion, and particularly toward the theory of evolution and other theories relating to the age of the earth or of the human species. He also affected an extraordinarily authoritative style, allowing for but little, if any, doubt about the correctness of his own views. Indeed, he cited himself more often than he cited others in his later writings (Buerger, 1985). In his interactions with subordinates, especially intellectuals, he showed but little tolerance toward those who questioned any of his views.[6] Not surprisingly, those who worked under him in the church leadership, and especially in the professional bureaucracy, were inclined to be deferential. Accordingly, a special tendency can be seen in the lesson manuals prepared under his supervision in recent years to cite his published work. It is not necessary to assume that such citations were included on his own insistence, but one can assume that the curriculum writers he supervised would at least have sought to please him.

It seems reasonable to attribute to Elder McConkie a convergence in both content and style with Protestant fundamentalism, given (1) his anti-modernist and anti-intellectual understanding of Mormonism (McConkie, 1984); (2) his authoritarian expectation of unquestioning obedience by church members; (3) his readiness to label as "heresies" certain doctrines with which he disagreed, even though they had no settled canonical status in the church (McConkie, 1982; Robson, 1983); and (4) the admixture of traditional religious folklore with some of his doctrinal teachings, especially where racial issues were concerned. Indeed, he was the most visible and insistent modern Mormon exponent of discredited biblical folklore about racial differences (ideas, incidentally, drawn mainly from the writings of his father-in-law). These ideas can be found under various entries in McConkie's one-volume encyclopedia *Mormon Doctrine* (1966), and they were not all removed from the 1979 reprinting of that volume, even though the church itself had by then abandoned the last vestiges of its traditional racial policies (see discussion of this issue in Mauss, 1981, especially 32–35).

Mormon Doctrine, indeed, is probably the best known and most often cited of all of McConkie's works (Buerger, 1985). At the Mormon grass roots, it is considered authoritative, if not definitive, and easily ranks alongside the older *Articles of Faith* (by Talmage) in its importance as a quasicanonical source for popular reference. There is a tremendous irony in this fact, one that shows clearly how the persistence of one strong-willed leader with fundamentalist leanings can prevail against the preferences of other leaders, even some of the most powerful, in a lay ministry with ambiguous limits to legitimate authority. The irony is that when *Mormon Doctrine* first appeared in 1958, it drew the distinct displeasure of the First Presidency of the church and of many of the other general authorities, even some of the most conservative (Paul, 1992:chap. 8).

The records of First Presidency meetings during 1959 and 1960 make clear that the first edition of *Mormon Doctrine* was considered so problematic among the general authorities that Apostle Mark E. Petersen was asked to do a thorough study of the book. Several others among the presiding brethren did their own analyses. All reported serious concerns to the First Presidency about the doctrinal soundness of the book, and Elder Petersen (no flaming liberal) went so far as to claim that he had found at least a thousand "doctrinal errors" in it. Early in 1960, Elder McConkie was called in for a conference with the First Presidency and informed of their misgivings. In deference to his feelings and his public standing, the Presidency decided that no public repudiation of the book would be issued, but Elder McConkie was instructed in no uncertain terms that the book was never to be reprinted or republished, even in revised form. In an uncharacteristically docile response, he accepted the judgment of the Presidency and agreed not to reissue the book. However, he did so anyway a few years later, and the second edition of the book (revised and enlarged) went on to become a popular classic.[7]

The career of that book, like the career of its author himself, is a convincing illustration of the manner in which the lay ministry of the Mormon church is open to the infusion of fundamentalist and even non-Mormon ideas simply from the natural circulation and recruitment of leaders from the grass roots. Such circulation and infusion are, of course, even easier and more common at the lower and more local echelons of the lay leadership. Nor is Elder McConkie's case the only such illustration: It is evident from the public statements of Apostle Boyd K. Packer that he shares some of the fundamentalist positions that Elder McConkie had.

Priesthood Correlation and Centralized Management

The rationale and motivation for the correlation movement instituted by Harold B. Lee in the sixties included the necessity to bring under centralized control the various semi-autonomous auxiliaries and church programs that had become increasingly unwieldy with the rapid growth of the church after World War II (Allen and Leonard, 1992:chap. 20; Chandler,

1992). This growth, especially in the Third World, had inevitably been accompanied by the complications of increased cultural diversification and an increased drain on church resources, all of which had kept the church from getting out of debt even by the early sixties. Correlation thus also included a deliberate strategy of standardization, simplification, and reduction in programs.

Whatever the original motives for the correlation movement, it has had many consequences for the basic nature of the Mormon subculture and quality of community life, not all of which, surely, were intended. These include the importation of corporate management practices and the recruitment of church leaders experienced in those practices. Given the already hierarchical nature of the Mormon ecclesiastical polity traditionally, the addition of correlation has indeed enhanced the centralization of control at increasingly higher levels or echelons of the hierarchy.

One concomitant, of course, has been an erosion in the autonomy not only of local bishops and other priesthood leaders but also of local auxiliary leaders and even teachers in church classes, all of whom are expected to use the same standard program manuals and lesson materials throughout the entire church. Traditionally each auxiliary of the church had had its own curriculum committee, but in 1973 all of these were subsumed under a general churchwide Curriculum Department that correlates all planning, development, sequencing, and publication of lesson materials for all auxiliaries and all age groups. The perfectly defensible rationale for this correlation is to produce and maintain such reduced and simplified curricula as "can be used anywhere in the world, under any cultural or political circumstance, so that the only culture we're bound by is the culture of the gospel" (*Church News*, Dec. 29, 1990, 6, 10).

The earlier diffusion of auxiliary curriculum and leadership responsibilities, as well as the greater local autonomy in general ecclesiastical operations, once represented a charismatic realm in which local leaders and teachers were deliberately left to lead or to teach "by the Spirit." This made control more difficult, of course, but it also left more room for the development of a truly spiritual element in the work of the church at the grass roots. Theoretically, leaders and teachers are still supposed to work "by the Spirit," though this charismatic element has now been highly routinized and channeled by correlation.

Ideally, on the one hand, the simplified manuals and lesson materials would seem to leave more room than ever for the individual teacher or leader to invoke the Spirit as a guide in his or her work. On the other hand, ironically, the control imperative in correlation seems to leave little such room in actual practice. Local teachers and leaders are regularly reminded by their priesthood leaders to stick to the manual in their work. Occasional injunctions from church headquarters reinforce the exclusion of outside ideas or materials. In 1990, for example, one of the general authorities serving in the Curriculum Department of the church gave this instruction: "Don't use extraneous sources when teaching courses in the Church. When you do, you have just said, 'I'm thankful for what the Lord has given me, but it's not good enough. I have a better idea'" (*Church News*, Dec. 29, 1990, 6, 10).

Nor must classes permit too much free-ranging discussion, if one takes seriously a recent *Church News* editorial decrying the "contention" that occurs when class members are permitted too much discussion of varied doctrinal viewpoints (June 20, 1992). To the extent that correlation implies operationally a cut-and-dried approach to church teaching and leadership, it reinforces, however unintentionally, the classical fundamentalist tendency toward unquestioning obedience, rote learning, and indoctrination in preference to understanding and informed commitment.

Even if unintended, one of the most profound consequences of correlation has been its impact on the power and autonomy of the traditionally female auxiliaries (Relief Society and Primary) and derivatively for individual female church members. Traditionally the Relief Society, for example, had almost total autonomy, with its own program, its own curriculum, its own publications, and (perhaps most important) its own budget. However, when it was correlated along with all the other auxiliaries, the Relief Society was placed under the total control of the priesthood. Since by definition this meant control by men only, the consequence was to reduce drastically the power and visibility of women even in matters that had traditionally been their own province (Cornwall, 1994; Derr et al., 1992; Iannaccone and Miles, 1990; Mangum and Blumell, 1993).

Ironically, this process coincided with the rise and increasing stridency of the feminist movement in the surrounding society. This change has thus reinforced within an already patriarchal Mormonism the rigid gender roles usually associated with Protestant fundamentalism and fostered a strong and growing feminist reaction among the better-educated Mormon women. In recent years, the priesthood leaders have undertaken to reverse somewhat this reduction in women's prestige with certain concessions at the margins, but the internal pressures to restore the ecclesiastical power and visibility of Mormon women are likely to increase with time.

Not all of the implications and consequences of correlation have been as noticeable as in the examples discussed so far. Some of them have occurred more subtly at the level of "organizational culture." Much has already been written about the gradual displacement of the earlier pastoral and prophetic leadership style in Mormon church life (apparent even at midcentury) with the current correlated managerial style associated with modern corporations (Nibley, 1983; Tarjan, 1990; Woodworth, 1987). Tarjan (1992) has astutely observed the concomitant transition even in the metaphors of church organizational life, once familial in nature but now corporate and managerial.

Other subtle consequences of correlation have undermined the traditional Mormon sense of community and identity, thereby indirectly fostering a resort to fundamentalist extremes in an effort to recover an eroded Mormon identity. With the control of the church welfare program now more centralized and professionalized, church members are rarely called upon to exercise their cooperative spirit (once a Mormon hallmark) through volunteer labor at church welfare farms and canneries. Church buildings are now designed by formula, built and maintained by hired professionals, and funded entirely from general church headquarters. No longer do local Mormons hold fund-raising projects or turn out with their hammers and saws to help erect a new building for which they have sacrificed their time and treasure. However rational and efficient these changes have been, they have also meant lost opportunities for the fostering of community bonds and a sense of shared Mormon identity.

The same can be said about the consequences of the consolidated meeting schedule, a somewhat later expression of correlation implemented in the early eighties. Until then, Mormons typically had two or three meetings each Sunday (morning and then afternoon or evening). The various auxiliaries for women, youth, and children then met again during the week. With the new schedule, virtually all meetings are crowded into a three-hour block on Sunday (with additional planning meetings for leaders either before or after this block). It is no doubt more efficient, both in time and in material costs, to get almost all the meetings over with on one day and thereby leave more time for individual families to have to themselves. Such, indeed, has been the rationale offered for the consolidated meeting schedule.

Yet an unintended side effect has again been a drastic reduction in opportunities for communication and bonding among church members. No time is left for informal visiting in the foyer or in the back of the chapel as members are hustled through the short breaks from one meeting to the next. Most Mormons (at least outside of Utah) never see or hear from each other between Sundays, for their auxiliaries now meet on Sunday instead of during the week, again reducing opportunities outside of church proper for association with Mormon peers and the sharing of a common Mormon identity (especially where children are concerned).

So what has all this discussion of correlation to do with facilitating fundamentalism among the Mormons? The answer to this question has two aspects, one direct and one indirect. The centralized, standardized, and top-down managerial control associated with correlation has produced a structure and a mentality that fosters conformity, unquestioning obedience, and a proof-texting approach to religion that we have typically seen in Protestant fundamentalism. That is a direct (though surely unintended) consequence of correlation. An indirect consequence (via reduced communal contacts and activities) has been a further undermining of the very sense of Mormon identity already under attack from the assimilation process of the early twentieth century. This can only encourage the recently noticeable tendency for Mormons as individuals to resort to fundamentalist extremes in the search for the boundaries that are supposed to make the Mormon identity distinctive.

As the boundary between Mormons and others has been maintained less and less from the outside by geography, politics, or social distance, many Mormons have found it necessary to draw their own boundaries from the inside. In the name of Mormonism, some have adopted especially austere religious styles, fleeing from ambiguity to the seeming safety of the most conservative extremes in doctrine, gender roles, health practices, and other observances, in order to claim identities as "real Mormons." The more they do so, ironically, the more they resemble Protestant fundamentalists rather than traditional Mormons. Also ironically, this tendency is only heightened when correlation on the one hand fosters conformity to *vertical* leadership, while, on the other hand, reducing mechanisms and opportunities for the strengthening of *horizontal* community and identity.

Recurrent Instability in the First Presidency

The spread of fundamentalism in recent years can also be attributed in part to the seniority system for succession to the office of president of the church (Ludlow, 1992:1420–21). By tradition, now long institutionalized, the president is the Lord's ultimate and exclusive prophet to the world as long as he lives, no matter how incapacitated he might become. Only when he finally dies is he succeeded, and then by the apostle next in seniority of service (usually the president of the Quorum of the Twelve Apostles), no matter how old that successor himself might be! Especially with the improved medical technology of recent decades, some Mormon presidents have lived for several years beyond the time that they have been strong and lucid enough to carry out the responsibilities of office. During these interim years, the power of the president is always exercised in his name by one or both of his counselors in the three-man First Presidency. This arrangement suffices well enough for day-to-day ecclesiastical operations, but it weakens the First Presidency politically in its relations with the Twelve, who ultimately retain the exclusive power to reconstitute that presidency at the moment of the prophet's death.

This situation has apparently made it easier for powerful and assertive individuals in the hierarchy, or even in the civil service bureaucracy, to take initiatives of their own at certain times without much restraint from the top. While these initiatives have represented a variety of interests and agendas, some of them have had the effect of promoting the fundamentalist commitments of their sponsors. Indeed, there have been times in even recent Mormon history when the church leadership has seemed to have less control over its own eccentrics than over the membership at large.

One need not go back even as far as B. H. Roberts and Moses Thatcher for illustrations (Lyman, 1985). Recent examples can be seen in Elder Bruce R. McConkie's controversial book and in Apostle Ezra Taft Benson's persistence in promoting the John Birch Society for several years against the wishes of the president and most of the other general authorities (Quinn, 1993). Both of these episodes occurred late in the presidency of David O. McKay, who was not only noncombative by nature, and somewhat ambivalent about the cases, but was also enfeebled by advanced age; so the de facto leadership of the church was largely in the hands of his counselors. How can such things happen in a presumably monolithic hierarchy?

The answer, of course, is that the hierarchy has never been as monolithic as generally assumed and that control from the top has certainly been looser at some times than at others. Frequent incapacitation of the church president has, however, contributed to this loosened presidential control. J. Reuben Clark was First Counselor to President Heber J. Grant, one of the longest serving presidents in Mormon history (1918–45). By the time

President Grant finally died at eighty-eight, he had not been able to function meaningfully in his office for several years, perhaps even a decade, so President Clark functioned as de facto president during those years.

Grant's successor as president, George Albert Smith, was not in very good health himself and served only six years (to 1951) until his death at eighty-one. During his brief term, President Smith retained Clark in the First Presidency. The latter was always appropriately deferential to the presidents under whom he served, but he was a strong-willed leader who was hard to restrain, especially by presidents in ill health. Accordingly, he took many initiatives on his own, exerted great influence over appointments of new general authorities in the thirties and forties, and formed personal alliances among certain authorities collectively called "Clark men" (Quinn, 1983).

Similar situations have marked the terms of more recent church presidents, too, and still other presidents have died in office only a year or two after ordination. Indeed, if we consider such very brief terms as interregna and recognize the de facto incapacitation of the very old presidents during their final years in office, then it would be fair to say that at least half of the time since 1940 the presidency of the church has been either in "temporary" hands (of short-term presidents) or in "acting" hands (of counselors in the First Presidency).

Another observation that some might find astonishing is that the Mormon church (as of late 1993) has never had a president born in the twentieth century, even though that century is now almost over. None of this is meant to imply any incompetence or failure in the church leadership collectively; the growth and prosperity of the church during these years is ample evidence of the strength and success of that leadership, with or without a strong president. A successful "backup system," as President Hinckley called it (*Ensign*, Nov. 1992, 53), has clearly been operating. The issue, rather, is one of internal processes and politics.

Such a political situation suggests a power vacuum at the top, putting First Presidencies with acting or enfeebled presidents in an awkward position to exercise restraints on assertive individual apostles, especially senior apostles, when the latter are inclined to take questionable initiatives, or to deliver controversial sermons, on their own authority. One side effect of this situation is that strong-willed, conservative apostles are freer than they might otherwise be to promote fundamentalist ideas and interpretations in their sermons and writings or even to insert the same in church curriculum materials. They are also freer to harass church intellectuals whom they regard as disloyal.[8]

Reaction to the Mobilization of Mormon Intellectuals

Of all the developments in recent Mormon history that have fortuitously fostered the resurgence of fundamentalism, surely the most ironic is the rise and mobilization of a large corps of intellectuals. For at least a hundred years, until the middle of the twentieth century, intellectuals were prominent in the topmost leadership of the church and others were part of the founding faculty of the Church Education System (CES). Still others, particularly in literature and in the social sciences, found it difficult to reconcile church life with worldly learning in those early years and left Utah or the church (or both), constituting Mormonism's "lost generation" of intellectuals (Bringhurst, 1990; Geary, 1977).

Since midcentury the presence of intellectuals among the general authorities has been quite rare, at least by the usual definition of "intellectual." At the same time, however, the Mormon penchant for education, combined with the greatly enhanced educational opportunities following World War II, produced the most visible grass-roots generation of intellectuals that Mormonism had ever seen. Furthermore, the children of that generation, now young adults, show signs of constituting an even larger (and perhaps somewhat more strident) intellectual contingent, including, for the first time, many feminist intellectuals.

This postwar generation of Mormon intellectuals, now in their mature years, has differed from intellectuals of earlier generations in at least the following respects: (1) it is much larger in both relative and absolute terms; (2) it represents a continuous range of religious commitment, rather than being bifurcated into defectors versus apologists, as was the tendency earlier; (3) it is not as well represented in CES (proportionately) as it once was (though it is well represented at BYU itself); (4) it is well connected, through professional societies and communications, to non-Mormon peers and enjoys considerable intellectual credibility outside of Mormondom; and (5) it has its own publication outlets, scholarly meetings, and informal communication networks outside of church control.

As this generation of intellectuals began to reach its professional maturity, the church itself took the unprecedented step of appointing one of their number, Leonard J. Arrington, as official church historian in 1972;

and Arrington proceeded to recruit professional colleagues and apprentices from among these intellectuals to assist him in the production of a dazzling and distinguished array of special and general studies in Mormon history (see, e.g., Arrington, 1992; Bitton, 1983; Bitton and Arrington, 1988; and Quinn, 1992b).

It is not entirely clear what sort of political context within the church leadership made possible at just that juncture such an unexpected ecclesiastical embrace of the intellectual enterprise and its approach to writing history. It is certainly clear in retrospect, however, that the political context was a shifting one; for several powerful apostles began to regret the decision almost as soon as it had been made, applying strenuous efforts to close down the operation. After a troubled decade, a political compromise removed Arrington and his colleagues from church headquarters to a new and less visible academic institute at BYU (Arrington, 1992; Quinn, 1992a).

Perhaps even more important, in some ways, than the scholarly historical literature produced during the Arrington era, however, was a more sociological development: The new corps of sponsored historians constituted a focal point or nucleus around which the entire postwar generation of Mormon intellectuals could mobilize into a "critical mass" (no pun intended), which has thrived and persisted even after the attenuation of the Arrington enterprise. The energies and products of these new historians and social scientists have provided crucial nourishment to private, unsponsored organizations like the Mormon History Association and the Sunstone Symposia and to publications like *Dialogue*, *Sunstone*, and the *Journal of Mormon History*, which otherwise would have remained rather anemic if, indeed, they would even have survived.

During the past twenty-five years, these intellectuals and their publications have become increasingly worrisome to church leaders and especially irritating to those general authorities of a fundamentalist bent. It is in that sense that the intellectuals and their work have made an unintentional contribution to the fundamentalist reaction so often linked with the retrenchment motif in contemporary Mormonism. The writings and conferences of today's Mormon intellectuals have elicited an unusually public critical response from certain quarters of the church leadership. That response has had some support even among Mormon scholars of a conservative bent.

An unfortunate rift has accordingly developed in the ranks of Mormon scholars. On the one side are those most closely associated with unsponsored publications like *Dialogue* and *Sunstone*, and on the other side are those most closely associated with the CES, the intellectual center of which is at BYU in the department of church history and doctrine. As their writings make clear (e.g., Millett, 1987), many of these religious educators are disdainful of an intellectual (as opposed to a faith-promoting) approach to Mormon studies and have advocated the primacy of submission to church leaders over intellectual independence.[9]

On the other side, *Dialogue* scholars and other such intellectuals (including many in academic departments at BYU) sometimes feel resentful that their religious commitments and sincerity seem to be called into question by their critics in church education, whom they tend to see simply as obsequious allies of certain fundamentalist church leaders. At times the exchange between the two sides becomes quite acrimonious (e.g., Alexander, 1986a; Bohn, 1983, 1990; Bradford, 1988; Hill, 1993). It is not a totally polarized situation, of course, for there is an entire spectrum, and everywhere along that spectrum there are some intellectuals who fit comfortably. Nevertheless, it is true that the pressure from certain powerful church leaders in recent years has promoted a tendency among Mormon intellectuals to feel that they must choose sides.

Selective Conversion and Folk Fundamentalism

North American converts to Mormonism (like converts to most proselytizing religions) come disproportionately from the young and the unsophisticated, especially where, as in Mormonism, the missionaries themselves are so young. This does not, of course, mean that the converts are simple-minded but only that they are modestly educated (partly because they are still young), taken from the middle (or lower middle) of the social class ladder, often looking for security in a new and coherent meaning system, and with prospects of more to gain than to lose from such a basic life change (see Mauss, 1989:38). Converts rarely have any theological sophistication and are quite susceptible to remonstrances of a fundamentalist kind, especially if received as part of a new "plausibility structure" in a network of new young friends with fundamentalist leanings.

Age and social status, however, are not the only factors acting selectively on new Mormon converts. A third of them (31%) are recruited from religious backgrounds that are already conservative (see table 10.1). Mormon converts do not come disproportionately from such back-

TABLE 10.1. Religious Affiliations in Mormon Convert Backgrounds and in the Nation as a Whole (percentages)

Denominational Type	Mormon Converts	Others
Fundamentalist	31	31
Moderate	38	45
Liberal	25	21
No affiliation	6	3
N (100%)	108	9,292

SOURCE: Based on cumulative data, 1972–90, from the annual General Social Surveys of the National Opinion Research Corporation.

NOTE: The distribution of the Mormon converts is based on a question asking religious affiliation at age sixteen. The distribution of the others is what they reported as their present affiliations. "Fundamentalist" is more or less synonymous with "conservative," and the Catholics are included with the "moderates." The classification of denominations into these larger categories follows that of Tom W. Smith (1986, 1990) of NORC.

grounds, for all four religious categories contribute Mormon converts approximately in proportion to their numbers in the American population. Nevertheless, this still means that a third of the converts have been reared in conservative contexts to begin with.

Region is another selection factor. Mormon converts come disproportionately from the West, where Mormon communities and friendship networks are the most common. The traditional Mormon heartland of the Mountain West still is home to 62% of all U.S. Mormons (although the area accounts for only 4% of the total U.S. population), and the Pacific Coast comprises another 20% (versus 12% of the nation). Not surprisingly, then, most American converts to Mormonism also are found in those same regions (Davis and Smith, 1990). What is noteworthy is the recent disproportion of Mormon converts coming from the Bible Belt of the southeast (20%).

Only 13% of the general U.S. Mormon membership is found in the South at present; but when we compare the current locations and the origins (age sixteen) of lifelong members with those of converts, as in table 10.2, we see that converts are almost twice as likely as lifers to be southerners, especially in origin, i.e., up to age sixteen (20% versus 10%). That a fifth of the Mormon converts in the United States now come from the South puts one in mind of the "southernization" thesis discussed in chapter 8 (Egerton, 1974; Shibley, 1991). It is not clear what part migration has played in the southern susceptibility to Mormonism in recent years, but clearly the southern contingent is now an important minority of

TABLE 10.2. Regional Distributions of Mormon Converts and Lifers at Present and before Conversion (percentages)

	At Present		Up to Age 16	
Region	Lifers	Converts	Lifers	Converts
Mountain West	71	44	62	33
Pacific Coast	16	27	21	25
Southeast	11	18	10	20
All other regions	2	11	7	22
N (100%)	220	123	220	123

SOURCE: Based on cumulative data, 1972–90, from the annual General Social Surveys of the National Opinion Research Corporation.

the Mormon converts and correspondingly an important potential source of fundamentalist thinking in contemporary Mormonism.

SUMMARY

A kind of fundamentalism seems to have emerged more prominently among the Mormon grass roots in recent decades. This trend complements but goes considerably beyond the general tendency toward retrenchment and conservatism seen in earlier chapters. This chapter has explained how five institutional features of contemporary church life have had the unintended effect of fostering the spread of fundamentalism. This discussion has set the stage, as it were, for the examination, in the next chapter, of certain specific forms this fundamentalism has taken.

NOTES

1. In Mormon parlance, "fundamentalism" usually refers to the "polygamy holdouts"—that is, to those schismatics who have broken with mainstream Mormonism over abandonment of nineteenth-century polygamy and have continued to practice it, either surreptitiously in Salt Lake City or openly in more secluded sites like Colorado City (formerly Short Creek), Arizona. In this book, however, "fundamentalism" has the more common Protestant meaning.

2. These two tendencies seem somewhat parallel to the two different cognitive styles identified by Richard Poll (1967) with the Book of Mormon symbols Liahona and Iron Rod. The Iron Rod symbolizes a style (somewhat analogous to fundamentalism) that is more comfortable with answers than with questions, with unambiguous prescriptions from church leaders than with general principles, and with literal rather than figurative or relativistic interpretations of the scriptures. By contrast, the Liahona (a kind of mystical compass in the Book of Mormon)

represents just the opposite set of cognitive preferences. The two symbols, for Poll, do not represent differences in either sincerity or in compliance with church teachings but rather in how one understands the function of orthodoxy in one's life—i.e., whether truth is to be understood as an iron rod leading those who grasp it back to God's presence or as a spiritual compass that only points in general directions and leaves specific paths up to individuals. Like other ideal types, this distinction has been criticized for (among other things) oversimplifying reality (see, e.g., Jacob, 1989), but it continues to be cited regularly in the writings of Mormon intellectuals.

3. Elder Hugh Pinnock of the First Quorum of Seventy in a 1982 address at the BYU School of Management deplored this pernicious side effect of blind obedience in a "church where many leadership positions are held in awe" and thus many members have been susceptible to business scams on the mistaken assumption that "just because someone is in a leadership position . . . he can talk about a stock proposal." See *Sunstone Review* 2, no. 9 (1982): 10. There is a certain prescient irony in this warning, for Elder Pinnock himself was among those later victimized by forgery artist Mark Hofmann (Sillitoe and Roberts, 1988; Turley, 1992). For the story on the Paul H. Dunn case, see the lengthy exploration and discussion by the panel of commentators in *Sunstone* 15, no. 3 (1991): 28–57.

4. D. Michael Quinn (1993) has compiled a detailed history of the largely unsuccessful efforts even of the First Presidency of the church to restrain Apostle Ezra Taft Benson's campaign on behalf of the John Birch Society during the sixties.

5. In visiting various stakes around the United States and Canada during the past several decades, I have often heard sermons and testimonies from the pulpit in sacrament meetings, or even in stake conferences, that have promoted blind obedience to church authority, extreme interpretations of the Word of Wisdom, confinement of women to strictly domestic roles, condemnations of the theory of evolution, and other such fundamentalist remonstrances, none of which is any more "doctrinal" or "official" than their more liberal opposites would be. Yet I have never heard a word of subsequent "correction" or disclaimer about such teachings from the presiding church authority sitting behind the pulpit on such occasions. On the other hand, where a sermon or testimony is questionably "liberal" in its purport, the speaker might well subsequently be gently chided from the pulpit by the presiding officer or the audience might be reminded that the speaker's comments did not necessarily represent "church doctrine." Elsewhere I have suggested that the statements and writings of church authorities, whether local or general, can best be understood has having one of four types of ecclesiastical status: canonical, official, authoritative, or folk doctrine (1981:32–34). Only the first two are obligatory upon the membership, but all four are regularly used and cited in Mormon meetings.

6. Elder McConkie's seeming intolerance can be seen, for example, in an incident of a decade or so ago, well known in CES circles, where he publicly chastised a CES faculty member for writing a book promoting a personal relationship with Christ (which Elder McConkie regarded as a heterodox distraction from the more important personal relationship with God the Father). Another such incident can

be found in a 1984 letter to BYU Professor Eugene England (copy in my files), who had questioned some of Elder McConkie's ideas. Among the comments with which Elder McConkie responded was that "it is my province to instruct and your [England's] province to obey or to remain silent." As a more public expression, one might cite his address (1982) on "seven deadly heresies," which attached the heresy label to certain doctrines widely believed even by other general authorities of the church (living and dead).

7. This description of the *Mormon Doctrine* episode is found also in Paul (1992: chap. 8) and is based on a widely circulated set of daily summaries of the meetings and appointments of President David O. McKay during parts of 1959 and 1960 (copy in my files). By the time McConkie published the second edition of his controversial book, the members of the First Presidency who had chastised him (and had insisted on no republication) were either deceased or (like President McKay himself) in feeble health. The incident is somewhat reminiscent of an earlier one involving McConkie's father-in-law, Apostle Joseph Fielding Smith, who was instructed by President Heber J. Grant in the twenties to cease and desist from further argument over the theory of evolution but who nevertheless reintroduced the controversy through the 1954 publication of his *Man: His Origin and Destiny* after President Grant and all the other principals from the twenties had passed on (see Sherlock, 1980).

8. This kind of organizational conduciveness to irregular apostolic initiatives can be seen in a well-publicized campaign against several highly visible Utah intellectuals who were excommunicated during September and October 1993 for their critical writings and public comments. Secondary fallout consisted of a fair amount of bad publicity and the voluntary resignations of church membership by a number of sympathetic colleagues, including Pulitzer Prize–winning cartoonist Steve Benson, grandson of the church president. It appears from the press coverage that the First Presidency played no part in the excommunications and that the campaign was controversial even among the apostles, despite an effort to maintain a united front publicly. (See, e.g., *Salt Lake Tribune*, Oct. 2, 11, 16, 17, 20, 1993, and *New York Times*, Sept. 19, Oct. 2, 1993.)

9. See, for example, the presentations at the 1992 BYU Sperry Symposium by L. G. Otten ("Protection against Deception") and by R. G. Anderson ("Being Valiant by Following the Lords's Anointed"). This viewpoint tends to receive support in some of the BYU academic departments, too, especially political science, as well as in church history and doctrine. Note, however, that this rift in the ranks of the intellectuals is not so much between defectors and apologists, as earlier in the century, but rather occurs over the relative priority of intellectual independence.

CHAPTER ELEVEN

Expressions of Folk Fundamentalism

Whatever the conditions that might have facilitated the spread of fundamentalist thinking among the Mormons, what evidence do we have that such thinking has actually increased in recent decades? The evidence here cannot be conclusive, for there are no systematic studies of Mormon fundamentalist attitudes across time. Yet, there is some evidence, and it is persuasive. It can be seen in doctrinal trends and intellectual style; in an obedience and control mentality; in a susceptibility to fundamentalist scare scenarios; and in certain exaggerated forms of social conservatism.

Trends in Doctrine and Belief

The doctrinal content of Mormon folk fundamentalism has been explored at some length, and with convincing documentation, by O. Kendall White (1987) in his work on Mormon neo-orthodoxy.[1] White discusses three tendencies in particular: (1) a redefinition of God in the infinite, incomprehensible terms associated with traditional Christianity, rather than in the more contingent and finite terms used by Joseph Smith; (2) a redefinition of human nature in the pessimistic terms associated with the traditional dogmas of original sin and human depravity, rather than in the more optimistic and perfectible terms found in early Mormonism; and (3) a redefinition of salvation more in terms of grace than of works. As exponents of this neo-orthodoxy, White identified a number of authors connected with BYU's religion faculty.

These authors are not general authorities of the church, but because of their BYU connection, they would be regarded as authoritative by most Mormons. Through their writings, class lectures, participation in the churchwide lecture circuit (Know Your Religion series), and the like, they have been able to articulate doctrinal ideas that lend credence to folk fundamentalism among their audiences. Occasional speeches in a similar vein by general authorities themselves have had the same effect, of course, even when not strictly "official" in nature. Examples would include President Benson's talks on the primacy of obedience to prophets now living (1980) and on the appropriate roles of fathers and mothers (1987a, 1987b); the late apostle Bruce R. McConkie's "Seven Deadly Heresies" (1982); and the more recent public excoriation of the theory of evolution by Apostle Boyd K. Packer.[2] The convergence of all this Mormon neo-orthodoxy with conservative Protestantism, incidentally, has been duly noted in the pages of *Christianity Today*, an evangelical Protestant publication (Mouw, 1991).

It is hard to determine just how much influence such neo-orthodox teaching has had on the membership generally, but at the very least it would give aid and comfort to fundamentalist thinking at the grass roots (Crapo, 1987; Leone, 1979). Some evidence for an increase in fundamentalism, at least among Mormon youth, can be found in the surveys of Christensen and colleagues at BYU (see table 11.1).

While the two surveys summarized in table 11.1 were probably representative of student opinion at BYU at the two points in time, it is also probable that much of the drastic change in opinion between the two surveys can be attributed to a strong selective recruitment bias in the 1973 data. Unlike the students in the thirties, recent aspirants to BYU have had to obtain recommendations from their local bishops testifying to their "worthiness." In other words, only the most orthodox and conforming Mormon youth are permitted to attend BYU, and bishops (including some of a fundamentalist bent) are the final arbiters of worthiness. Of course, some of the statements in table 11.1 reflect only general (Mormon) orthodoxy, but others, especially those in the lower half of the table, indicate a mentality going well beyond orthodoxy to fundamentalism. BYU students thus do not represent Mormon youth generally but probably do represent a major proportion of future church leaders (including many from the 1973 cohort who would by now already be bishops, stake presidents, and even higher authorities).

Somewhat more compelling evidence of increased levels of fundamentalist thinking can be found in a study recently completed of Mormon scientists. The scientist Richard Wooten sent surveys in 1955 to all Utah-

TABLE 11.1. BYU Student Opinions (percentages)

Belief	1935	1973
Joseph Smith was a true prophet.	88	99
Mormon authorities get revelation today.	76	99
Mormon church more divine than others.	81	98
Prayers answered by divine intervention.	75	95
There is a personal devil.	38	95
Creation did not involve evolution.	36	81
Creation did not take millions of years.	5	27
Obedience to authority comes above one's own personal preferences.	41	88
Rejects any form of birth control.	11	42
Holds to strict Sabbath observances.	14	54
N (100%)	1,159	1,056

SOURCE: Compiled from Christensen and Cannon (1978), table 1.

born scientists listed in the 1949 edition of *American Men of Science* and again in 1992 to all those listed in the 1990 edition of *American Men and Women of Science*. In the surveys that were returned (more than 60% in both years), he first identified those Mormons whom he considered "strong believers" by their affirmative responses to a question about belief in the divinity of Jesus. Then he compared the responses of the 1955 devout believers with their 1992 counterparts on a variety of questions indicative of orthodoxy or of fundamentalism. Almost without exception, the results showed drifts toward fundamentalist belief among the Utah Mormon scientists during the four decades between the two surveys.

For example, in 1955, 40% of the devout Mormon scientists believed that evolution was the means by which God had created humans, but by 1992 even that relatively small percentage had declined to 37%. In 1955, 68% believed that the earth had taken hundreds of millions of years to create, but in 1992 that percentage had dropped to 57%. In the earlier survey, only 23% believed that God "often" intervenes in human affairs, a figure that rose to 85% in the later survey. When asked what part they thought scientific reasoning and logical thinking should play as a basis for religious convictions, those advocating only a "minor role, if any" rose from 16% to 45% between the two surveys, while those in favor of a "major role" declined from 58% to 36%.

An increasing belief in scriptural inerrancy can be seen in the decrease from 86% to 70% between the two surveys in those who would admit that the scriptures, though generally inspired, might be subject to some error. Similarly, the increase from 14% to 30% of those believing that the scriptures contain the words of the Lord without error would indicate a growing belief in scriptural inerrancy and perhaps of literalism as well. If we keep in mind that the data in these surveys came from Mormon scientists, most of whom probably had advanced degrees, we would be justified in assuming at least comparable changes at the Mormon grass roots more generally.

Indeed, a recent article comparing grass-roots Mormons in Missouri with their Catholic and Protestant counterparts found evidence in the same general direction (Johnson and Mullins, 1992). Although this study might have some biases from sampling and from response attrition, it did show the Mormons to have strong fundamentalist leanings in their basic beliefs. The scores of the Mormons on measures of "modernist theology" were consistently the lowest, even lower than those of the Southern Baptists; and in almost all indicators of fundamentalism the Mormons were consistently closer to the Southern Baptists than to any other denomination.

On an indicator of biblical literalism, for example, the average Mormon score was 4.17 (on a scale of 5.0) compared with the Southern Baptist score of 3.84. On measures indicative of conservative personal values, the Mormons were consistently high, but consistently low on indicators of humane social values, again very much like the Southern Baptists. On specific points of theology, of course, the Mormons showed a lot less similarity to the Southern Baptists, but the general convergence in fundamentalist thinking was consistent.

A similar convergence of local Mormon ecclesiastical leaders (bishops and stake presidents) with their Southern Baptist and fundamentalist counterparts can be seen in a national study on the prospects for a political coalition of the Mormons with the New Christian Right (NCR). Given the specific theological differences between Mormons and these conservative Protestant groups, such a coalition was deemed unlikely from this study, but the data clearly indicated a strong similarity between the Mormon and the NCR local leaders in religious particularism or exclusivism and in attitudes toward abortion, women's roles, school prayer, and several other current social and political issues.[3]

Aside from doctrinal content per se, a certain intellectual style is also indicative of fundamentalism. This style is uncomfortable with open questions and ambiguous answers. It strives for closure and certainty. It tends to attribute inerrancy to scriptures and to prefer literal interpretations (Ammerman, 1987). In the Mormon setting, it is reminiscent of the kind of thinking Poll (1967, 1983) has symbolized by the Iron Rod. This intellectual style is familiar to anyone who has regularly attended classes in Mormon Sunday schools or other auxiliaries and witnessed the consistent press for doctrinal closure, even if based only on what some church leader once said or on "what it says in the manual." Editors of the weekly *Church News* (e.g., June 20, 1992) occasionally support such a cut-and-dried approach to the study of religion by decrying doctrinal disagreements in church classes (called "contention") and by urging teachers not to stray from the contents of the official manual (*Church News*, Dec. 29, 1990).

The Control and Obedience Mentality

Both the scriptures and various authoritative statements in Mormonism celebrate the intellectual and moral freedom of the individual and condemn any attempt to constrain conscience or to impose "unrighteous dominion" by virtue of church authority (Doctrine and Covenants 121: 41–46; Ludlow, 1992—see, e.g., "Agency" and "Obedience"). Yet, an unintended consequence of the centralization, standardization, and correlation has been to make hierarchical control both easier and more attractive to leaders at all levels (Shipps, 1994). As long as such control is limited simply to the routine administration of church policies and programs, it does not raise questions of unrighteous dominion or require blind obedience. However, in the Mormon lay ministry, as explained earlier, much latitude remains for individual church leaders at all levels to assert personal control, in accordance with their own preferences, over the activities of church members. Most do not take advantage of this situation, but some do. Lavina Fielding Anderson (1993) has made an extensive compilation of such questionable initiatives, many of them very recent, at both the local and general levels of church leadership. Their sheer number, if not their gravity, certainly seems surprising.

Grass-Roots Illustrations

Illustrative anecdotes are actually not hard to come by, even on a firsthand basis. In my experience, for example, local church authorities, as far back as two decades ago and as recently as 1990, have forbidden otherwise eligible young men to participate in priesthood ordinances because of long hair; demanded that they shave beards as a condition of serving in leadership positions; chastised couples for using birth control methods; and disciplined otherwise loyal and active members for having "unauthorized discussion groups" on church topics, even in their own homes.

None of these actions would be called for by church doctrine or policy, but local and regional leaders are left free to carry them out. The justification given by these leaders in each case is the obligation for "obedience" on the parts of the church members affected. One stake president even cited Abraham's unquestioning obedience to God's commanded sacrifice of Isaac as precedent and justification for such arbitrary demands by some of today's church leaders.

The willingness on the parts of many grass-roots Mormons to accept whatever priesthood leaders say arises from a tendency to make a virtue out of blind obedience. For such church members, "follow the Brethren" means obedience for the sake of obedience, apart from rational, individual thought, study, or prayer. Such a mentality is a regular feature of Protestant fundamentalism, where strict obedience to pastors, even in nonreligious matters, is considered obligatory for the "true Christian" (Ammerman, 1987). Again, it is difficult to know just how widespread this mentality is among Mormons, either at the grass roots or in the leadership, but on the basis of the data in table 8.1 it might be attributable to at least a third of the membership, as of the late sixties anyway, and to as many as a tenth of even the relatively independent thinkers who subscribed to *Dialogue* in the eighties.

Controlling the Intellectuals

Assertions of control over the speaking and writing of church intellectuals has become more common in recent years, especially on the parts of individual general authorities of the church (Quinn, 1992b). Again, however, it is not always clear to what extent these assertions of control represent an official and coordinated policy of the hierarchy collectively and to what extent they are simply questionable initiatives on the parts of powerful individuals in the hierarchy. Some of these individuals are well known for their suspicion of intellectuals and their desire to control any public discussion of church matters among the membership.

A case in point occurred during the spring of 1983 when the late Elder

Mark E. Petersen, a senior member of the Quorum of Twelve Apostles, became deeply concerned about certain controversial articles published by church intellectuals in private scholarly journals like *Dialogue* and *Sunstone.* Some of the articles had aired publicly certain historical and doctrinal issues that Elder Petersen (and no doubt some of his colleagues) would rather had been left untouched. He telephoned the local priesthood leaders (usually stake presidents) of the offending authors and asked that the leaders interview these authors and express his concerns about their association with "apostate" publications.

Subsequent consultations among the many authors so favored (including me) revealed that different stake presidents had reacted in different ways. Some took their charge from the apostle rather lightly and were clearly uncomfortable about being in the middle of such a process. Others were quite heavy-handed and intimidating. The authors too reacted in various ways. Some of us shrugged off the incident, regarding it (probably correctly) as an unofficial initiative with no real consequences; others were deeply offended and took the story to the local newspapers. Ultimately the First Presidency itself called a halt to Elder Petersen's personal campaign, which, as it turns out, had been launched without their knowledge.

D. Michael Quinn (1992a) has published a particularly detailed account of such initiatives taken against him by church leaders for some of his controversial publications while he was a member of the BYU faculty. Such a move through the university board or administration, to punish or constrain a professor for his legitimate scholarly work, would certainly jeopardize the accreditation of any university. Therefore, Quinn claims, his critics in the hierarchy (some of whom, in fact, serve on the BYU governing board) instead used ecclesiastical channels to discipline him, demanding (for example) that his local stake president revoke his access to the temple. Such intrusions by general authorities into local relationships between church leaders and members are particularly irregular and questionable, since they occur outside of the established channels for church discipline: It is clear from the 1989 official *General Handbook of Instructions* for church leaders (section 10) that all church discipline properly originates at the local level.[4]

Many other Mormon scholars and intellectuals, including recent and current editors of *Dialogue* and *Sunstone*, have had similar experiences with both local and general church leaders. Some of these accounts have been published (Lavina Fielding Anderson, 1993), but others have not. Nor was it reassuring to Mormon intellectuals for church spokesmen to admit under questioning from the press that in church headquarters there is a committee for "strengthening church members." This committee's charge includes keeping files on those members regarded by certain leaders or staff bureaucrats as critics or apostates. In such practices, church leaders risk leaving the public impression that they are more interested in compliance than in conversion, in control than in compassion.[5]

Yet there is much ambiguity in the relations between Mormon intellectuals and the church leadership. It is difficult to determine when there is a concerted and deliberate campaign, as a matter of official policy, intended to control what the intellectuals publish about their church and religion, and when the efforts at control come from the initiative of individuals or small cliques within the hierarchy. After the 1991 Sunstone Symposium in Salt Lake City, the First Presidency and the Twelve issued to all church leaders a joint letter deploring some "(though admittedly not all)" of the topics that had been discussed at that symposium (First Presidency, 1991). The statement later appeared both in the *Church News* and in the official *Ensign* magazine. It was a carefully worded statement, which, as read by people knowledgeable about the symposium, singled out only a small proportion of the scores of sessions comprising that symposium.

However, less knowledgeable people, especially local and regional leaders with no firsthand experience in such symposia, often interpreted the First Presidency statement in the most conservative possible way and criticized symposium participants generally as undermining the church. Such was the interpretation, indeed, given the First Presidency statement by the administration of the CES to its faculty (CES, 1992). Whatever the intention of the church hierarchy, then, the issue tended to get construed at the grass roots as one of control and obedience of the participants in such symposia.

By contrast, however, the new *Encyclopedia of Mormonism* (Ludlow, 1992:1387–89) treats intellectual enterprises like *Dialogue*, *Sunstone* (both the symposium and the periodical), and other such unsponsored activities in rather a favorable way, suggesting several useful functions or purposes that they serve in the Mormon community. This encyclopedia has authoritative and not official status, but it is very unlikely that anything would have been included in it that would evoke the displeasure of the collective hierarchy. Furthermore, the great majority of authors, readers, and participants in these intellectual enterprises certainly define themselves as active and loyal members of the church, a fact almost certainly understood by the leadership. Thus one wonders whether the initiatives taken so far against the church intellectuals might not be understood as expressions of the fundamentalist preferences of certain church leaders, rather than as general church policy. For their part, the intellectuals have often reacted with pain, confusion, and alienation (e.g., Lavina Fielding Anderson, 1993; Capener, 1984; Newell, 1986; Toscano, 1988, 1993).[6]

Susceptibility to Fundamentalist Scare Scenarios

Whether embodied by certain church leaders or expressed at the grass roots, folk fundamentalism sometimes takes dramatic forms. Two recent episodes from Utah will serve to illustrate this point.

Satanic Conspiracies

Different worldviews carry different susceptibilities to different kinds of credulity. For example, a person who looks upon the world as an essentially user-friendly place with well-intentioned people might be more trusting about human nature than would be a person whose belief in original sin carried with it an implicit suspicion about others' motives. Depending on a given scenario, each of those worldviews might have either benign or disastrous consequences, but both obviously carry different implications for interpreting what one sees and hears in the surrounding world. To the extent that one has a fundamentalist worldview, for example, one is more likely to see both divine and diabolical forces as explanations for what happens in the world. This does not mean that fundamentalists are more likely than others to believe in God or in Satan. Many religious traditions teach of a god and of a devil, and some (including Mormonism) even regard them as actual persons. It is what one believes *about* God or Satan that is of special interest here.

During the past decade or so, the press has reported various rumors and allegations of "satanic" cult activities, including animal mutilations and killings or even human ritual murders and sexual perversions, sometimes involving children (Richardson, Best, and Bromley, 1991; Victor, 1993). A similar phenomenon has occurred in Britain (Jenkins, 1992). Many of these stories, even on a prima facie basis, have been so bizarre and unlikely as to tax the credulity even of the most sympathetic hearers. Furthermore, when solid, firsthand empirical corroboration has been sought, it has proved very elusive; and even much of the firsthand testimony has been demonstrably the product of retrospective reconstructions of personal "experience" under the influence of well-meaning therapists or counselors, themselves already convinced that such "satanic" experiences are widespread. Even when animal mutilations, murders, and unusual sexual practices have been proved, there has been little or no evidence of their connection with any organized movement, cult, or conspiracy, satanic or otherwise. After all, any perpetrator can invoke the name of Satan or leave behind symbolic "clues" associated with satanism in the public mind.

To most social scientists, these stories are familiar examples of urban legends or other expressions of collective rumor and delusion, somewhat reminiscent of the seventeenth-century outbreak of witchcraft in Salem. Most social scientists, and most police officers who have taken the trouble to follow such rumors to their ultimate, ostensible "sources," have come to the conclusion that few, if any, of these satanic scare stories have a factual foundation (Jenkins, 1992; Richardson, Best, and Bromley, 1991; Victor, 1993). Nevertheless, these accounts have continued to circulate, and certain individual "victims" have periodically come forward with "long-suppressed recollections" of "satanic" outrages perpetrated against them, or in their presence, sometimes in remote childhood. A growth industry has arisen among certain therapists in the helping professions, who have become specialists in dealing with such victims, and among certain law enforcement experts in "satanic cult practices," who have been able to command healthy lecture and consulting fees for sharing their expertise with community groups and law enforcement agencies.

The "discoveries" of satanic crimes and their victims have tended to occur most frequently precisely in those areas where the experts and specialists have been the most enterprising and energetic. Such a correlation suggests to most sociologists that the "discoveries" are as likely to *result* from the intervention of "experts" as to require it. One of the more ironic aspects of this satanism phenomenon has been the unlikely convergence of interests (and sometimes even an alliance) between religious fundamentalists and these experts from the helping professions, who have made common cause in an effort to expose and punish the satanic perpetrators. It was perhaps inevitable that this community of interests between therapists and fundamentalists should eventually find expression among the Mormons as well.

In mid-July 1990, one of the Mormon general authorities sent a confidential memo to the church committee charged with the responsibility for investigating instances of apostasy among church members. Apparently this church leader had received numerous reports from church members, and from Mormon therapists in various helping professions, to the effect that satanic sexual and other rituals had been practiced for many years in certain Mormon homes. Many of these reports were based upon incidents recalled, through therapy, by clients who had been victims or witnesses of such rituals in their early childhood, recollections in some cases "triggered" somehow by participation as adults in the special Mormon temple rituals. The church leader in question apparently found his informants credible enough that his memo called for a thorough investigation.

Whether such an investigation was ever actually conducted, how thorough it might have been, or with what results, is not clear at this writing. The episode became public only after a copy of the confidential memo was leaked to the press in October 1991. After obtaining confirmation of the story from a church spokesman, the Associated Press wire service carried the story across the nation, and the major Salt Lake City television channels publicized it during the evening of October 24, 1991. Eventually the memo was reprinted, with predictable partisan commentary, by the *Salt Lake City Messenger*, an anti-Mormon publication of the fundamentalist Utah Lighthouse Ministry.[7]

It seems highly unlikely that thorough research and investigation of an epidemic of satanic practices among the Mormons would provide any greater substantiation than has resulted from the same kind of research among others (cf. Jenkins, 1992; Richardson, Best, and Bromley, 1991; and Victor, 1993). Indeed, this episode is sadly reminiscent of a slightly earlier one in the local Mormon community of Lehi, Utah, where an "outbreak" of child sexual abuse supposedly occurred, eventually implicating not only the local bishop but even the father who had originally made the allegations against others. Upon thorough investigation by the civil authorities, the charges could not be corroborated, but meanwhile a number of marriages and families were seriously damaged, and the therapist in the middle of the controversy eventually moved on to greener pastures.[8]

The point is not, of course, that child sexual abuse or bizarre satanic cult practices could not occur among the Mormons. Nor is the point that the Satan doctrine in traditional Christianity (and shared by Mormonism) is embraced only by fundamentalists. It is a matter of what one believes about Satan. Folk fundamentalism, whether Mormon, Protestant, or Catholic, is more disposed than other religious expressions to credit accounts of satanic conspiracies and outbreaks of satanic practices in the society at large. That allegations of such practices, on such a large scale, should find credence all the way up to the level of the general authorities of the church is simply another illustration of how fundamentalist ideas can be carried from the grass roots well up into the Mormon lay leadership.[9]

Millennial Survivalism

Folk fundamentalism in the United States, especially in the West, has sometimes been mixed with a populist, right-wing political ideology. One recurrent expression of that mixture has been a kind of "millennial survivalism," which envisions an eventual Armageddon scenario with the hosts of evil arrayed against the true Christian patriots of America (see, e.g., Aho, 1990; and Lamy, 1992). The exact enemy identified in such scenarios varies from one version to another. During the cold war, the enemy always included communists, of course, both external and internal, and sometimes more shadowy collusions of communists, big business, and Jews, both foreign and domestic. In some versions of this scenario, the FBI and other law enforcement agencies have already been penetrated, or even taken over, by the enemy conspiracy. Most versions have also included racist elements long associated with the Ku Klux Klan; sometimes the KKK is even recognized as part of the broader patriotic alliance against the conspiracy.

Belief in such a scenario has often been expressed in the extensive stockpiling of food, arms, ammunition, medical supplies, and the like for survival in remote areas when the day of Armageddon arrives; also in gatherings for the study and discussion of doomsday literature (religious and political); in home schooling programs to keep the children from being exposed to the subversive curriculum of the liberal establishment; and in a certain amount of organization around the leadership of key figures, some of whom have only local notoriety while others are nationally known.[10] An example of a nationally visible figure would be James "Bo" Gritz, who helped to resolve the standoff and shoot-out in northern Idaho, during the summer of 1992, between the FBI and one of the families apparently acting on its millennial-survivalist beliefs. A distinguished Green Beret veteran and 1992 presidential candidate for the Populist party, Gritz is also a Mormon convert of ten years or so.

It is difficult to estimate just how influential this millennial survivalism has been among Mormons of fundamentalist leanings. One recent study of a related and overlapping phenomenon in Idaho (Aho, 1990) finds Mormons there represented in the Christian Identity movement approximately in proportion to their share of the total Idaho population, while in Utah Bo Gritz and his Populist party drew some 28,000 votes in the 1992 election. In any case, by the fall of 1992, Mormon millennial survivalists had become numerous and noisy enough to attract the serious attention of the church leaders, who apparently saw a potential for schism and decided on a crackdown. Accordingly, in the October 1992 general conference of the church a few of the general authorities included in their sermons some pointed criticisms of such millennialist thinking. The following month, at regional conferences of church leaders in central and southern Utah, certain forms of unacceptable millennialist behavior were spelled out, and subsequently some of those who persisted in such behavior were excommunicated from the church.[11]

There is no reason to believe that millennial survivalism has an especially large following among the Mormons. Despite a clear tendency toward conservatism in politics, especially in the western United States, most Mormons tend to avoid extremes and to look to their church leaders for guidance in such matters as how to prepare for the millennium. Nevertheless, the recent outbreak of millennial survivalism is indicative of a grass-roots layer of folk fundamentalism that remains available for mobilization by any kind of cultic fad that exploits fundamentalist traits like the need for certainty, the tendency toward scriptural literalism, and the preference for authoritarian leadership.

This particular episode illustrates also the potential which individual church leaders of fundamentalist bent can have, even unintentionally, of contributing to the susceptibility of grass-roots Mormons to fundamentalist extremism: The millennial survivalists criticized and disciplined by church leaders in 1992 defended themselves by drawing upon the sermons and writings of Apostle (now church president) Ezra Taft Benson from the sixties, when Elder Benson's preoccupations with communist conspiracies, and his public support for the John Birch Society, led to difficulties with his colleagues (Quinn, 1993).

Exaggerated Forms of Social Conservatism

We have seen in earlier chapters that Mormons have always exhibited a certain conservatism in family values, sexual norms, substance use, and other matters (see also Ludlow, 1992:1371–78, "Social Characteristics"). Given that general tendency, there is not much constraint, official or unofficial, upon those who carry this conservatism to fundamentalist extremes, whether for purposes of symbolic boundary maintenance or for other reasons. In the matter of chemical substances, this fundamentalism expresses itself in an elaborate checklist of things to avoid, including cola drinks, cocoa, white sugar, white bread, processed foods, and the like, going far beyond the official proscriptions in the Word of Wisdom against tobacco, alcohol, coffee, and tea.

Perhaps more conspicuous is an austere attitude in sexual matters, bordering at times on prudery, which is usually associated with Protestant fundamentalism (Mackelprang, 1992). One example is the indiscriminate hostility to rock music as conducive to sexual indulgence (e.g., De Azevedo, 1982). Another example is the preponderantly negative treatment of sex, even for married couples, in the main church sex education manual *A Parent's Guide* (Day, 1988), a book of lessons written and widely circulated specifically for church use, but never given official imprimatur. Still another example was a temporary effort by church leaders in 1982 to define and regulate sexual practices, even for married couples, by means of instructions through bishops during temple interviews, a practice quickly countermanded in a letter from the First Presidency (1982). Still another indication is a tendency on the parts of many Mormons to oppose not only school reading assignments that might contain salacious passages but also sex education itself, a tendency that drew critical comments about Utah in February 1988, even from the conservative Surgeon General C. Everett Koop.[12]

Sexual austerity is usually accompanied by rather rigid and traditional gender definitions in Protestant fundamentalism (Ammerman, 1987), and the same seems to be true of the Mormon fundamentalist mentality. The "cult of true womanhood," combining such sexual and gender attitudes, survives from Victorian times mainly in fundamentalist religion (Elliott, 1991; Foster, 1979, 1981; Welter, 1966); and an important dissertation (John R. Anderson, 1986) has demonstrated the convergence of such ideas between the Southern Baptists and the Mormons, as revealed in their respective women's magazines. For Mormons, BYU religion professor Rodney Turner (1972) has carried the Mormon position to the fundamentalist extreme of outlawing birth control and confining women to strictly domestic and child-bearing roles as a theological imperative, quite at odds with the models of politically and socially active Mormon ancestors expressed in the nineteenth-century *Women's Exponent.*

Officially, of course, while the Mormon church has always had a pro-child policy, it has never taken the anticontraceptive position of the Roman Catholic church or of some Protestant fundamentalists (Bush,

1976; Heaton, 1987a); and Mormon couples, despite relatively high fertility rates, use artificial contraceptives at about the same rates as do others in the nation (Heaton and Calkins, 1983). Yet the manifest hostility of authors and teachers like Turner (1972:213–42), and of a few individual church leaders, to contraception once again expresses a fundamentalist outlook on sex and women among the Mormon folk.

Summary

This chapter has reviewed the evidence for an increase during recent decades in certain expressions of folk fundamentalism among the Mormons, both leaders and laity. The argument is not that most Mormons have become Protestant fundamentalists but only that fundamentalist ways of thinking and acting seem to have become more common than earlier. As Mormons in the assimilationist period of the early twentieth century were more hospitable to secular scholarship, to the social gospel, and to other influences from the Protestant mainline, so today, as part of a retrenchment outlook, influences are being felt instead from the fundamentalist Protestant heritage. Both kinds of influence have parallels in the Mormon tradition, but neither is authentically Mormon.

There are two ironies in this recent Mormon opening to fundamentalism. One is that Protestant fundamentalists have always been the most vocal and vituperative of the anti-Mormons. The other irony is far more problematic for the Mormon future, and that is the increased susceptibility for defections. Some of these defections will be of the predictable kind, namely the departure of members, especially youth, who are basically loyal but intellectually expansive and curious and therefore increasingly uncomfortable in their encounters with fundamentalism at church. To some fundamentalists, these defectors can be dismissed with "good riddance." Yet there is another basis for defection that will prove much more painful to Mormon parents and leaders of a fundamentalist bent: the seeds of disillusionment that are unintentionally planted by fundamentalists themselves.

Mormons who are taught to take a literal, proof-texting approach to scripture study, and to believe that loyalty means blind acceptance of whatever leaders (past and present) have ever preached, are highly susceptible to disillusionment, either from anti-Mormon critics in other religions or from secular sources. For people taught to think in this way, each new anomaly discovered in church teachings or scriptures, each new disclosure of human frailty in church history becomes a crisis of faith. Especially in religion, if one's cognitive categories are limited to "either" and "or," and one's faith is undermined in the "either," then there is nowhere to go but the "or." Therefore, to the extent that a fundamentalist approach prevails in their religious education (especially in CES), Mormon youth will be more, not less, vulnerable to those who would undermine faith. After all, it does not take a professional muckraker to find anomalies and human frailties in the Mormon historical record. It is easy to discover that the Brethren have not always taught the same things, not always interpreted the scriptures literally, and not even always behaved honorably.

Thus, if young people of a fundamentalist bent are the de facto products of a Mormon upbringing, or are the most likely converts to Mormonism, they might also prove eventually to be the most vulnerable to defection. Of course many people, in and out of religion, find it possible to hold two contradictory premises at the same time, either by "compartmentalizing" faith from intellect or through some other kind of intellectual contortion. However, young people reared in the either/or style of fundamentalism, and also in a commitment to personal and intellectual honesty, will find such crises of faith very difficult to deal with, unlike the troublesome "intellectuals," who are by training and cognitive style actually better able to handle the relativity and ambiguities in religion. If the Mormon institutional pasture is not big enough for its intellectuals, then it will not likely be able ultimately to accommodate its disillusioned fundamentalists, either. That will leave an unquestioning and satisfied herd, to be sure, but one of a far different quality from the restless souls to whom the claims and teachings of Joseph Smith had such appeal. What may be at work, in other words, is a process of selective conversion and retention based on cognitive style, not on religious commitment per se; and what is at stake, especially in North America but eventually everywhere, is the very psychological composition of the future Mormon membership.

Notes

1. White, in fact (1987:xxi), noted that he would have preferred the term *fundamentalist* except for the idiosyncratic Mormon meaning of that term. See Robson (1983) for an analysis that supports some of White's contentions. O'Dea (1957: chap. 9) also sees some of the developments sketched in this chapter as expressions of fundamentalism in the usual (non-Mormon) meaning of the term. The point here is not that concepts like the omniscience of God and the part played by grace are by definition "fundamentalist" concepts. It depends on how they are ex-

plicated. Mormonism clearly leans towards the "works" side of any argument over the *relative* primacy of grace versus works in salvation. Yet there is much room for acceptance of a nonfundamentalist understanding of grace in Mormon soteriology. See, e.g., Silva (1992).

2. This address was given as part of the 1988 BYU Symposium on the Book of Mormon; see Packer (1990). Since the Book of Mormon itself contains no creation story and only a few passing allusions to the Genesis account, Elder Packer's attack on evolutionary theory as part of this symposium seems rather gratuitous, suggesting a special hostility toward the theory on the part of this apostle. In taking such a position, Elder Packer does not seem to be taking due account of the First Presidency statements of 1909, 1910, and 1925, the cumulative purport of which is to take no position on the evolution controversy itself. He is also apparently overlooking a contrasting treatment of the topic in the official church magazine (see Morris Petersen, 1987). Recall also in this connection the influence of Elder McConkie upon CES portrayals of the age of the earth (Paul, 1992:chap. 8) discussed at the end of chapter 6.

3. These data were presented in an unpublished study based on a national sample drawn from the Yellow Pages of telephone books by a professional polling agency (see Beatty and Walter, 1987). The total return rate for the questionnaires was 55%, including only eighty-five Mormon cases. One can only speculate about the biases introduced into the data from nonresponse. If we were to assume that religious conservatives are even less likely than moderates to respond to such questionnaires, the results reported might even underestimate the conservatism of the Mormon respondents. On the prospects for political coalition between Mormons and the NCR, see also White (1986) and Brinkerhoff, Jacob, and Mackie (1987a).

4. Of course any church leader or member (or even nonmember), in any jurisdiction, has the right to make a formal accusation, for cause, against any church member before the appropriate local leader. However, when such an accusation is made, the accused is entitled to know the source and to confront the accuser under the auspices of a local church court (recently renamed "disciplinary council"). Secretive accusations and summary judgments against members, without opportunity for defense or explanation by the accused, are simply not provided for in church discipline and must thus be regarded as irregular, if not indeed illegitimate, even when carried out by general authorities. Apostle Dallin Oaks, in fact, was quoted in an interview as acknowledging as much (*Salt Lake Tribune*, Oct. 11, 1993).

5. See stories in *Salt Lake Tribune*, "LDS Official Acknowledges Church Monitors Critics," Aug. 8, 1992, D-1; and "LDS Leaders Say Scripture Supports Secret Files on Members," Aug. 14, 1992, B-1.

6. Some of these intellectuals, much to their surprise and dismay, have recently been excommunicated (see chap. 10, note 8). The predicament for intellectuals is, of course, especially acute when they are faculty members at Brigham Young University or other church institutions with academic accreditation. Conflicts over academic freedom at BYU have occurred several times during the present century (Bergera and Priddis, 1985; Priddis and Bergera, 1993), most recently during 1992 and 1993 (see account in the news section of *Sunstone* 16, no. 1 [1992]: 62–

66). During 1992 and 1993, a number of campus controversies suggested the need for formalizing, to a greater degree than ever before, the academic freedom policy of the university. Accordingly, a series of committees representing the faculty, the administration, and the governing board worked together to produce two major documents, one a statement of philosophy and principles, and the other a set of operational "grounds and procedures" for the implementation of the basic principles. The first document seems generally unexceptionable, even fairly liberal, for a church-sponsored university, though not entirely without controversy. Most of the controversy, however, has focused on the second document, which provides, among other things, for consultation between university administrators and a given faculty member's bishop to ensure that the faculty member's "worthiness" is maintained. Since the effect of such an arrangement is to give local church leaders considerable influence over a person's professional position, it tends to compromise both the person's academic freedom and his or her pastoral relationships. See "BYU Continues to Debate Academic Freedom Issue," *Sunstone* 16, no. 4 (1993): 63–66. An early test of the new academic freedom framework came at the end of the 1992–93 school year, when two untenured professors, whose public statements had made them controversial, were fired after their three-year reviews. Since their professional publication records were not strong enough to suit some of their colleagues, the actual grounds for their dismissals remain questionable, but the cases have engendered considerable public comment, pro and con. Church-sponsored academic institutions cannot, of course, be expected to allow the same degree of latitude for academic freedom that is expected in secular colleges and universities. Yet the BYU crisis of the nineties clearly has its origins in the extraordinary efforts made in very recent years by some church leaders to extend their control beyond grass-roots intellectual expressions and into the professional lives of the academic faculties employed by the church. The most highly publicized (and arguably the most egregious) case of church discipline against a (now former) BYU faculty member is that of D. Michael Quinn, who was recently excommunicated for his continuing publications in church history, even five years after his resignation from the BYU faculty (see "Michael Quinn Investigated for Apostasy," *Sunstone* 16, no. 4 [1993]: 63, and Quinn 1992a; see also chap. 10, note 8).

7. Among other places, the stories can be found in the *Salt Lake Tribune* for October 25, 1991, in the *Chicago Tribune*, and even in the Waterbury, Connecticut, *Sunday Republican*, both for November 3, 1991. The *Salt Lake City Messenger* carried the story in its November 1991 issue, and then in its March 1992 issue it published a photocopy of the internal church memo with considerable discussion of the implications. The *Messenger*, of course, took the reports of satanic practices among the Mormons at face value, seeing in these reports only the latest expression of the diabolical tendencies already inherent in Mormonism from its sordid polygamous past. See also "Leaked Bishop's Memo Spotlights LDS Ritual Satanic Sexual Abuse," *Sunstone* 15, no. 5 (1991): 58.

8. This episode is recounted in some detail in (among other places) Shupe (1991:chap. 5). Even though the major theme of this book is the exposure of "corruption and scandal" in the Mormon church, the author was forced to conclude that the Lehi child-abuse scare had been groundless. For another account of satanic scares, sometimes involving children, see Wright (1992).

9. Before joining the ranks of the general authorities, the church leader in question was a professional CPA with B.A. and M.A. degrees in accounting from BYU. Such a background no doubt equipped him well to serve the church in a business capacity, and indeed his particular role in the presiding bishopric has traditionally specialized in the temporal affairs of the church. Yet there is little in such a background that would provide the theological or scientific sophistication to evaluate adequately the scare stories about satanism.

10. See, for example, printed program (copy in my files) of Preparedness Expo '92, a conference at the Seattle Center, Seattle, Wash., Oct. 2–4, 1992. Produced by the Preparedness Shows of Salt Lake City, the conference featured a few Mormon speakers, including "Bo" Gritz, who gave a series of three lectures on America's "secret combinations" and "advancing apocalypse." Many of the other lectures also featured conspiratorial themes but were interspersed among those on more mundane topics, such as family health, energy conservation, food storage, and the like.

11. This episode, the apparent implication of Bo Gritz as a leader of Mormon millennial survivalists, and their resort to the earlier writings of Elder Benson were covered quite extensively in the *Salt Lake Tribune* in late November and early December 1992. See, for example, "It's Judgment Day for the Far Right: LDS Church Purges Survivalists," Nov. 29, 1992, A-1, A-2; "Hero Turned Heretic?: Gritz May Be Leading LDS Flock into Wilderness," Nov. 29, 1992, A-2; "Mormons' End of the World Talk Could End LDS Membership," Dec. 2, 1992, B-1; and "LDS Church Disciplines Ultra-Conservative Survivalists," *Sunstone* 16, no. 4 (1993): 67–68. The episode was covered also in the February 1993 issue of *Religion Watch*, a newsletter published by Richard Cimino in North Bellmore, New York, which, in turn, was passing on a report from the *Christian News* out of New Haven, Missouri.

Besides a general distaste on the part of the Mormon leadership for political extremes, there is a special sensitivity about the potential for divided loyalty when church members join organizations that might offer alternatives to church leaders as guides in religious, social, or political decision-making. That is one reason that even the most conservative Mormon leaders (apart from Elder Benson) have always maintained a distance from the John Birch Society and from Cleon Skousen's Freemen Society. It is also probably the main reason that the KKK never took hold very strongly among the Mormons in Utah (Gerlach, 1982).

12. It should be noted that official church policy itself, while locating the responsibility for sex education squarely with the parents, does not oppose sex education in the schools per se. Parents are enjoined, however, to be sure that school sex education programs "in no way promote or encourage sexual promiscuity" but rather "advocate abstinence from sex before marriage" (Ludlow, 1992:1305).

CHAPTER TWELVE

The Angel and the Beehive: Present and Future

Since the symbols of the angel and the beehive were first introduced we have covered a lot of ground. In a general sense, the angel motif is expressed in the distinctively Mormon threads than run through this book (and, indeed, through the Mormon subculture itself). It symbolizes the historic claim of the Mormons that they are a peculiar people. The angel who appeared to Joseph Smith still appears in the unique spiritual claims of Mormonism: latter-day revelation through living prophets and new scriptures; the salvation and redemption of the dead, as well as the living, through vicarious temple ordinances; the eternal nature of family bonds, and thus the sacredness of the family even in mortality; the primacy of the responsibility upon all Mormons, not just the formal missionary corps, to proclaim the gospel and spread the faith to the ends of the earth.

These few claims do not, of course, constitute the sum total of all Mormon religious beliefs, but they come close to comprising the most distinctive ones. In proclaiming itself a Christian religion, Mormonism ostensibly shares also a number of beliefs and commitments with the larger Christian family. Yet, even here Mormonism has such a distinctive outlook on deity, theodicy, Christology, and soteriology that it is generally considered a stepchild, at best, in that family. To non-Mormons it seems ironic that the Mormon church continues to assert its Christian identity while still denying a common Christian descent and rejecting a number of major Christian dogmas. Yet that irony follows logically from the restorationism that is still another reflection of the angel motif. If Jan Shipps (1985) and others are correct in seeing in Mormonism the beginning of a new world religion, then sooner or later the Mormons will have to acknowledge their separateness from the Christian family, rather than merely their distinctiveness in that family.

Meanwhile, the Mormons as a people, and as an institution, must interact both with the other religions of the world (not only Christianity) and with the world's cultures more generally. This is where the beehive motif comes in. The beehive represents the borrowings from the outside world that have always been a part of the Mormon subculture (and, indeed, of all subcultures, religious or otherwise). The borrowings might have been less frequent or less important during times of isolation and reduced contact with the outside, but they have always occurred as a natural product of interaction and struggle with the surrounding world.

The beehive is a convenient and appropriate symbol for the cultural borrowings by Mormonism, because it is a traditional symbol of "the sweet results of [the] toil, union, and intelligent cooperation" of the Mormon people in the world (Ludlow, 1992:99); it is so pervasive and familiar among Mormons, especially in Utah, that it is (like cultural borrowings generally) appropriated by all kinds of causes and institutions, religious, educational, commercial, and others (Cannon, 1980); and it has become a kind of "communal coat of arms" linking the Mormon community across time and space (Ludlow, 1992:99). Like other coats of arms, though, it is a product of historical struggle in the world, a blend of ideals with experience.

Like all religions that have endured and spread, Mormonism has borrowed from its environment, so far mostly the American environment. That is neither a profound nor a novel observation, of course. Nor is it necessary (as some "faithful" historians seem to think) to choose between the two extremes of revelation or environmentalism in our effort to understand the essence and content of Mormonism. Any religion, at any point in time, is some sort of synthesis between its own novel inspiration and its borrowings from the outside. What is more interesting is to consider the *kinds* of borrowings and how these have changed across time in the successful Mormon effort to find and maintain the right kind and amount of cultural tension with the rest of America. Or, to carry our symbolism perhaps a little too far, the interesting question is what kinds of "nectar" from the environment have been sampled by the Mormon "bees" and why.

During the first half of the twentieth century, Mormons favored the nourishing nectar of nationalism. Both as individuals and as a church, they borrowed heavily from American institutions. Mormons embraced both major political parties and achieved leadership in both. They reared families in the monogamous, Victorian, and benignly patriarchal tradition so well epitomized by such fifties television shows as "Leave It to Beaver." They dreamt the American dream and realized it more fully than did most other Americans, achieving levels of education, income, and professional accomplishment that probably would have astonished their nineteenth-century grandparents. As a church (and no longer really a sect), the Mormons accumulated an extensive and diversified economic base, built their own internal civil service bureaucracy of experts, and brought into church governance the modern management practices learned so well by the new leaders trained in the best schools of business and finance.

Less well recognized, however, have been the influences on Mormons of mainstream American religion. The Mormon bees, after all, were not limited to the business world in what they brought into the hive. If, as the angel taught the Prophet Joseph, all the other religions had become worldly and apostate, then any nectar taken from them was just as surely a borrowing from the world as if it had come from General Motors or the Republican party. As we saw in chapter 2, certain Mormon leaders and educators deliberately reached out to the world of professional theologians for some of their ideas on Christology, higher criticism, and the King James Bible. Other concepts and practices from the social gospel movement are evident in the work of the Relief Society and the church social service programs of the twentieth century. By about 1960, Mormons from the grass roots on up shared most of their religious, political, and social beliefs with middle America and generally subscribed to what might be called the American civil religion. This, in sum, is the message of chapters 2, 3, 4, and 5.

The rest of the book, however, portrays a church and a people increasingly discontented with what the beehive had come to embody. The angel, it seemed, had been largely obscured or ignored in the preoccupation with Americanizing the hive. It was time to look to the angel once again for sustenance, for revitalizing the life of the spirit. A renewal of the distinctive, charismatic Mormon heritage has thus been apparent for the past few decades. This renewal has been part of a broader cultural trend toward retrenchment.

Inside the church, we have seen a new emphasis on the prophetic and revelatory claims of Mormonism, including the traditional claims to other-worldly efficacy for the temple work done in this world, vicariously or otherwise. We have seen also a new proselytizing thrust that not only recruits a larger proportion than ever of the youth in special missionary stints but also involves the grass-roots membership more systematically than ever. Meanwhile, a new focus during the past thirty years on strengthening the family and on indoctrinating the youth has sought to retain the members (and their children) already converted. This collection of initiatives has, indeed, been officially summarized in a new church mission statement (now ubiquitous in church literature) defining the three main objectives of the church as "perfecting the Saints, proclaiming the gospel, and redeeming the dead."

In relations with the outside world, the church has again been guided more by the inspiration of the angel, and less by the needs of the beehive, than earlier in the century. While the church clearly continues to care a great deal about its public image, it is more concerned now that this image should be clear, distinctive, and well represented than that it should simply mirror national trends and consensus. Partly because of the sheer size and resources it has recently acquired, but partly also because of its renewed self-image as a distinctive voice amongst the national babble of spiritual confusion, the Mormon church seems more willing now, and more secure also, in asserting itself politically on the national scene and not just in Utah.

So the angel is alive and well, and the church is anxious for the world to know it. The membership at large, for its part, has responded fairly well to the call of the angel issued through the church leaders. Some compliance at the grass roots with the renewal and retrenchment programs has been apparent, although probably not as much as the leaders would like. Partly because of these programs, but partly also because of changes in the religious world outside, Mormons today are relatively more "religious" than most others in the country, as measured by their declared beliefs, their religious practices, and other indicators of commitment. They are more distinctive than ever also in their proselytizing efforts and in their family norms and values. To that extent, then, the retrenchment program of the past few decades has had the net effect of resisting secularization and strengthening the institutional church.

Does this mean that the beehive motif has been abandoned as part of all this angel-inspired renewal and retrenchment? Certainly not. Neither the Mormons nor any other group living in the world can avoid borrowing from the surrounding culture, no matter how much inspiration they receive from their own unique spiritual heritage. The difference for the Mormon beehive between the present and the early twentieth century lies simply in the *changes* in the borrowings from the outside, the changes in the nature and mixture of the nectar.

Institutionally, we can see new or increased borrowing from the outside world in such modern features as the church's diversified financial empire; in its enormous mass media network; in its wholesale appropriation of computer technology; in the sophisticated political, legal, and public relations programs of its public affairs office; in its highly professional social research and evaluation office; in the large civil service bureaucracy hired to operate all such enterprises; in the management practices borrowed from the business world; and, not least, in the recruitment of the kinds of general authorities and other leaders with the competence to understand and oversee all of these borrowings. To speak of such things as "borrowings," however, is not in any way to discredit them. Many of them, including the more technological, simply enhance the church's ability to carry out its spiritual mission.

What are less obvious, and potentially more problematic, however, are the nonmaterial borrowings—the ideas, attitudes, and predispositions—that inevitably come along with the world's technologies, politics, management practices, and (not least) religions. Here is where the future struggle between the angel and the beehive is already taking place within the ecclesiastical structure, and to some extent among the grass roots as well. To the extent that these nonmaterial borrowings are especially American, they might also prove problematic when exported with church programs to other parts of the world.

Can the modern management practices, for example, reflected in centralization, standardization, and correlation be implemented without treating church members as employees? When these practices are combined with the Mormon tradition of prophetic leadership, can ordinary members and local leaders raise questions and make recommendations without the appearance of disloyalty or unbelief? Are these business practices themselves so characteristically American that they might actually undermine church growth in other cultures? Do these practices encourage a pastoral approach to church leadership, focusing on individual spiritual development, or do they deal with individuals mainly in categories and make cost-benefit calculations only in material terms? Recently church leaders have called for more ministering and less administering, but that is harder than ever in such a thoroughly correlated structure.

How about the inculcation of religious understanding at the grass roots? Do the standardization and rotation of the same lesson manuals year after year encourage the thoughtful and prayerful study of the scriptures, as the church leaders expect, or do they encourage instead a proof-texting and rote-learning approach to religious studies? As the mass-produced visuals and videotapes used for instruction in the churches and temples replace the preparations and presentations of live teachers and officiators, will the images in those visual materials (which are, after all, only artists' conceptions) come to be identified implicitly with the official teachings of the church and become the actual beliefs of the people? These are only a few of the interesting and problematic issues raised by the latest cultural borrowings in the beehive.

Perhaps even more problematic is the borrowing of ideas and practices characteristic of Protestant fundamentalism. In a sense, this resort is understandable. Just as there was a certain congruence earlier in the century between Mormon assimilationism and a resort to some mainstream Protestant thinking, so now there is a similar congruence between Mormon retrenchment and Protestant fundamentalism.

Yet, in the authentic and distinctive Mormonism of the angel, borrowing from one of the world's religious traditions is equivalent to borrowing from another. Both are from the realm of the beehive. It makes no difference that fundamentalism seems in some sense more strict or demanding. It is not, for that reason, any more Mormon. After all, a hostility toward scientific theories like evolution, a dependence on scriptural literalism and inerrancy, or a resort to unquestioning obedience are no more inherently Mormon than are a reliance on higher criticism, on liberation theology, or on the ACLU for legitimating one's beliefs. Nor is a family of twelve with a full-time mother any more authentically Mormon (for that fact) than a modern two-career couple with only two children, at least not from a doctrinal point of view.

A Glance Backward: O'Dea and Déjà Vu

It is important to emphasize that a tension—even struggle—within the church between countervailing tendencies is by no means a recent development. It has been present from the beginning, although the specific issues have varied across time with internal conditions and external influences. Many observers have noted that certain polarities seem to be inherent in the Mormon tradition and might never be resolved. Thomas O'Dea, in particular, devoted the concluding chapter of his now-classical *The Mormons* (1957) to "sources of strain and conflict." Some of these he saw as given in the nature of the religion, but most of them were products, in one way or another, of the Mormon encounter with "modern secular thought."

Writing at midcentury, near the apex of Mormon Americanization, O'Dea was clearly impressed with the success of the assimilation process, both from the Mormon side and from the national side. Yet, even then some of the Mormon reactions to this success were apparent in the conflicts between old and new values, between traditional and modern segments of both the leadership and the grass roots. Already he could see some of the handwriting on the wall of the temple. Some of the polarities he identified seem by now quaintly obsolescent: "progress vs. agrarianism" or even "patriotism vs. particularism."

Some of O'Dea's other polarities would have been more prescient had they been modified somewhat. For example, his "plural marriage and change of doctrine" would have been a more relevant harbinger of the sixties if "plural marriage" had been replaced by "the race issue" in his discussion of doctrinal change. In retrospect it seems almost incredible that O'Dea could have missed the Mormon racial struggle so close to its outbreak (an oversight that he fully, if belatedly, corrected in a 1972 essay). Of course, the larger issue of doctrinal change has, if anything, become even more crucial since O'Dea's 1957 book.

Most of O'Dea's other "sources of strain and conflict" are surprisingly contemporary four decades later: rationality versus charisma, consent versus coercion, authority and obedience versus democracy and individualism, family ideals versus equality of women, and political conservatism versus social idealism. It is clear from the evidence presented in this book that all of these polarities are still very relevant. What also seems clear from the evidence is that in each polarity one side has grown at the expense of the other since O'Dea wrote.

The charismatic call to follow the prophet, to accept the scriptures literally, and to save the dead has largely replaced the rationalism once found in the writings of science-oriented general authorities like Widtsoe, in scholarly lesson manuals, and in Book of Mormon archaeology (misguided though it often was). Institutionalized charisma through priesthood correlation and youth temple trips has also largely displaced the extensive youth programs for this world in sports, dance, drama, and speech once found in the old Mutual Improvement Association. The frequency of attempts by some church leaders in recent years to close down ad hoc discussion groups or symposia and to silence scholarly criticism suggests that authority, obedience, and even coercion have also gained in currency at the expense of individualism and consent.

The renewed emphasis on family ideals has certainly been accompanied by an erosion in the equality and power of women as far as ecclesiastical policy is concerned. There is a certain paradox here, since (1) there is no logical basis for an inverse relation between gender equality and strong family life; (2) there is a strong feminist strand in earlier Mormon history; and (3) equality for women in civil matters has strong grass-roots support among Mormons even today. Yet, ecclesiastical policy goes far beyond family supports (e.g., the family home evening program) to outright resistance against an Equal Rights Amendment in civil life; and the president of the church as recently as 1987 deplored the tendency of modern women to seek extradomestic careers (and the tendency of their husbands to condone it). The deliberate correlation of the women's Relief Society also had the effect of greatly reducing the power and autonomy of women in church governance.

Finally, the political conservatism which O'Dea saw forty years ago has clearly intensified by now. Whether or not this has been accompanied by a decline in social idealism is less clear. On the one hand, political conservatism implies a rather negative attitude toward public, government-funded programs based on social idealism, and that attitude is not hard to find among Mormons. On the other hand, organized expressions of social idealism from church headquarters do not seem to have diminished and might even have become more common in recent decades judging from recent church contributions to the amelioration of famine and misery around the world.

Although the church welfare program itself no longer involves the massive outlays of volunteer labor once required, one does see significant expressions of social idealism in the interdenominational celebration of Martin Luther King's birthday at the Interstake Center in Oakland (*Church News*, Jan. 1992) and the involvement of Mormon wards in the cleanup following the 1992 riots in Los Angeles (*Church News*, May 1992). Also in 1992, the church published a new public affairs handbook calling for increased Mormon cooperation with others for improving community life. In short, the social idealism of Mormons, both as a church and as individuals, does not appear to have been a casualty of increased political conservatism, though the latter has certainly grown.

All things considered, O'Dea's discussion of strains and conflicts was quite astute. He identified the main forms that are still important forty years later. He perhaps could not have predicted the retrenchment that has been so prominent a theme of this book or the effect of that retrenchment on the various polarities he identified. Indeed, his predictions about the future of Mormonism were generally very optimistic, given the adaptability that Mormons have shown throughout their history. As we stand on O'Dea's shoulders and look into the twenty-first century, how might we now assess the prospects for Mormons and their religion? What are the future forms of the struggle between the angel and the beehive?

A Look toward the Future

Both Jan Shipps (1985) and Rodney Stark (1984) have observed that we might well be witnessing in Mormonism the rise of the first new world religion since Islam. Shipps, in fact, suggests a comparison (or at least an analogy) whereby the origins of Christianity in Judaism are now being replicated in Mormonism's emergence from Christianity. In each case, the new religion begins by proclaiming itself a new dispensation of the old but eventually severs its umbilical tie and assumes a totally new identity. Obviously Mormonism has not yet reached this latest stage, but presumably it is only a matter of time. The analogy can be extended further: Just as Christianity was shaped and nurtured in the bosom of the Roman Empire, so Mormonism takes its strongly American cast (especially western American) into a multicultural world. That is to say, both the angel and the beehive go wherever the American LDS missionaries go.

What will happen to Mormonism, and particularly to its American complexion, as it is increasingly internationalized? To what extent is the historical Christian (specifically Roman Catholic) experience likely to be replicated by the Mormons? As Catholicism spread around the world, it brought its Roman ways along, but in time each cultural setting made the religion less Roman and more local in its complexion. This process has been described as "syncretism" by anthropologists and deplored as "corruption" or "apostasy" by religious purists. Yet, if it is to be truly catholic (in either the specific or the general sense), no religion can remain Roman. Nor can it remain American. Each cultural setting must both adopt and adapt to a "world religion." For Mormonism, that means that the angel will have to contend with a somewhat different beehive (and differently flavored nectar) in each part of the world where the hive is established.

O'Dea, if he were still with us, might well observe that the Mormon capacity for adaptation has been adequately demonstrated in its history so far. Yet, for an institution as for an individual, adapting to the culture of one's birth is far less problematic than adapting to the culture of one's migration; and Mormonism, for all its claims and aspirations about universality, has yet to rear a full second generation anywhere but in North America. The overwhelming majority of Mormon adults everywhere else are converts of the present generation. The socialization and retention of the second and third generations in each new country and culture will be as crucial as they are problematic. Information from knowledgeable church researchers indicates that such retention has proved very difficult so far. We simply won't know for several decades yet whether Mormonism can take root permanently in enough exotic locations to become truly a new world religion.[1]

We can expect, however, the same theoretical process to occur in each location as has occurred in North America. That is, Mormonism begins in each new setting as a sect (or cult in the terms of Stark and Bainbridge), in a condition of high tension with the cultural environment. Whether perceived locally as just another vulgar American import or as fundamentally subversive to the surrounding civil religion, Mormonism can expect to suffer the predicament of disrepute for a period of decades, at least, wherever it is imported. From the beginning, its popular image will likely be complicated also by whatever the local feelings are about the United States and its policies. The angel will reign supreme, drawing its devotion from a small band of converts so committed to the spiritual message of Mormonism (or already so marginal to their own culture) that disrepute and persecution will only strengthen their resolve.

To grow and prosper, however, the religion will have to resort to some degree and some forms of assimilation in each new culture, just as it did in North America during the early twentieth century. Just as surely as Mormonism was Americanized until it became respectable in the United States, it will have to be Japanized, Francized, and Argentinized (and so on around the world). Only through that process can Mormonism ever reduce the cultural tension in those other cultures enough to acquire a critical mass of membership, to retain succeeding generations, and thus to acquire a normal demographic profile in each locale. Lest the local beehive, however, overwhelm the angel, the church will then have to confront the predicament of respectability, just as it has recently done in the United States, and assimilation will have to be slowed or reversed by some degree of retrenchment.

The variety, complexity, and unevenness of this process in all of the cultures around the world will predictably defy the centralization, standardization, and correlation that have taken over Mormon ecclesiastical policy in recent years, especially where correlation is based on American (or even Utah) assumptions. Some of the consequences of the correlation policy in non-American settings have been ludicrous, even in quite recent years.[2] There are also many encouraging examples where sensitivity in Salt Lake City, as well as in the exotic mission field locales, has made possible the successful adaptation and implementation of church programs in perhaps some unlikely places.[3]

Certainly there is evidence that the general authorities of the church understand, at least in principle, the hazards of trying to impose a standardized and correlated church program on a worldwide basis. As recently as 1990, the regional leaders of the church were introduced to certain "course corrections" in church administration during a conference with the general authorities. These course corrections were motivated by an explicit recognition, clearly articulated by Apostle Boyd K. Packer, that the church had become overprogrammed and overregimented. Local ward communities, and even families themselves, had been left with too little autonomy and too little time of their own. The new administrative motto was to "reduce and simplify." The early dictum of Joseph Smith to teach correct principles and let the Saints govern themselves, which had been a casualty of the recent correlation movement, was to be rehabilitated.[4]

Yet in the actual implementation of such a sensible organizational course correction, at least three practical problems are already apparent. After an entire generation of centralization, correlation, and injunctions to "follow the Brethren," Mormons and their leaders at the grass roots have become accustomed to waiting for directions "from Salt Lake." Those directions continue to warn the Saints away from using any lesson material in their church classes that is "not approved," anything, in other words (except the scriptures), that comes from outside the highly simplified lesson manuals provided by the church, even when such "outside" material is written by Mormon authors.

In the name of simplification (and of churchwide equity), furthermore, local wards and stakes are now totally dependent upon the central church coffers for their budgets and are simply not permitted to raise any additional funds locally to support any activities outside those mandated by the newly simplified general church program. Such an arrangement reduces and simplifies, but it certainly does nothing to enhance local autonomy or to encourage the Saints to govern themselves in line with Joseph Smith's dictum.

A second practical problem arises from the impact of simplification upon the Mormon sense of community and identity. The simplification that has already occurred during the recent decades of correlation has deprived grass-roots Mormons of many of the natural opportunities for maintaining community ties that were once routine in the Mormon way of life (Allen, 1990; Cornwall, 1990; England, 1990).

Gone are the regular work projects for fund-raising or for the welfare program; gone are the speech and drama and dance competitions provided by the old Mutual Improvement Association; and gone are most of the meetings of the various auxiliaries during the week, at which the Saints were able to renew community ties with other Mormons outside of Sunday worship. The loss of these occasions for maintaining a sense of unique Mormon identity, through frequent participation in the life of the Mormon community, is likely to make that sense of identity increasingly problematic and thus only encourage the recent resort to fundamentalist extremes in search of the boundaries of Mormonness.

The third practical problem is that administrative simplification does not necessarily involve the kind of cultural and ideological simplification that might be even more necessary if Mormonism is to be adapted successfully to the various cultures of the world. Of course, one can hardly expect Mormonism to jettison the basic truth claims that have made it distinctive, but one wonders how "basic" are the Victorian patriarchal and sexual notions or the conservative political and economic biases that increasingly have come to characterize the Mormonism of the twentieth century.

Some appreciation for this more ideological kind of simplification can be found in the recent statement of Elder Richard P. Lindsay, a general authority of the church over Africa: "The answer to bridging different cultures is the gospel. What the Church is doing is building a gospel culture that transcends all boundaries and barriers. . . . Building a gospel culture doesn't mean the denial of everything in our separate heritages, although we must keep the doctrine pure and be willing to change certain traditions that aren't compatible with the gospel" (*Ensign*, Feb. 1993, 35).

Such an abstract understanding, however, again leaves the practical implications to be worked out, for it begs the question of exactly which doctrines have to be kept "pure" and which kinds of local traditions aren't "compatible" with the gospel. Thus, at an operational level, much remains to be worked out in order to make Mormonism a truly international and cross-cultural religion; and there remain many reasons for wondering about the prospects. One obvious reason for skepticism is the greater or lesser susceptibility of all people (including church leaders and bureaucrats) to ethnocentrism and cultural blinders. Another reason is the understandable tendency for American church leaders to recruit as local leaders, even in exotic locations, those who already seem most amenable and receptive to American ideas.

This is especially true when foreign regional representatives, stake presidents, and bishops are, as is often the case, recruited from the ranks of full-time employees of the CES or other church professional bureaucracies. There is a natural tendency, in other words, for recruitment to church leadership, at all levels, to have a selection bias in favor of those who are most likely to accept direction from the American hierarchy and least likely to express resistance to imported ideas.[5] This might make for smoother relationships between the American and the local leadership, but it will likely have the unintended consequence also of masking cumulative cultural strains and conflicts at the grass roots.

It is important to emphasize, however, that the cultural strains between the American church headquarters and the world's fledgling Mormon communities rarely involve the fundamental or distinctive doctrines of Mormonism. In France, for example (Derr, 1988; Jarvis, 1991), the problems of cultural adaptation do not arise from local resistance to the theology of the family as an eternal entity but rather from the programmatic demand that each family receive monthly visits from home teachers. (The home teaching program actually fits rather poorly in many different cultural settings.) Similarly, the Australian Mormons have no argument with the doctrine of continuous revelation and leadership by living prophets, but they take umbrage at the elitism and authoritarianism often perceived in the leadership style of the American hierarchy (Newton, 1991).

When we move from the programmatic level to the level of folk fundamentalism in tastes and styles, the cultural conflicts would seem to be even more avoidable. In French culture, for example, the bare human body does not evoke the same prudery that it does for religiously conservative Americans, and even active French Mormons have been known to spend holidays at nudist events (Jarvis, 1991). In such circumstances, one wonders what Utah definitions of modesty have to do with the essentials of the religion. Similarly, the tendency of American Mormons (De Azevedo, 1982) to identify drumming with sensuality has prevented Nigerian converts from using drums—their main musical instruments—in worship services (Boren, 1985). This cultural bias has required the wholesale (and quite unnecessary) importation of pianos for the Mormon wards and branches there (and the concomitant need for American missionaries to teach the African locals piano lessons). Examples of such cultural gaps between the locals and the Utah headquarters, even in quite recent years, can be multiplied almost endlessly.

The point of all this is not that the Mormon church is unique in facing such problems of adaptation to exotic cultures. The history of Christian missionizing is replete with exactly the same kinds of strains and problems between the traditions of the locals and the cultural biases of the missionizing churches. It is only that these predicaments are relatively new for the Mormons, at least on such a large scale. The other missionizing religions of history, whether Catholic, Protestant, Muslim, or even Buddhist, have all tended to find one of three forms of modus vivendi between the imported religion and the local culture: (1) they have settled for permanent status as a small, stable, or even declining fringe group (e.g., Buddhism in China); (2) they have made humanitarian projects, rather than religious proselytizing per se, their main thrust (e.g., mainline Protestants in the Third World); or (3) they have accepted large increments of local syncretism (e.g., Islam in Indonesia or Catholicism in Latin America).

These three postures are not, of course, mutually exclusive, and all of them are entirely defensible, or even commendable, depending on the circumstances. The Mormon church has dabbled in all three, but none of them has become the typical Mormon way. A fourth way (or perhaps it's a variant of the third) has been suggested by certain scholarly observers of the Mormon internationalization process (e.g., Allen, 1992; Firmage, 1989). This approach might be called a "minimalizing of Mormonism" to make it "maximally adaptable," or truly a "faith for all cultures" (Tullis, 1978).

Implied here is a process by which Mormonism would be reduced to a small number of basic and indispensable doctrines and principles—to the very essence of the angel, as it were. This spiritual core would link Mormon communities around the world into one universal religion, but it would also mean that each cultural community could adapt and embroider the core in accordance with its own needs. In light of the discussion above about the need for simplification, this would mean a simplification of a cultural and ideological kind, as well as of an administrative or programmatic kind.

Just what would be included in this kind of core Mormonism would have to be worked out by the church leaders (including, one hopes, many from outside North America) through a prophetic process that might be quite agonizing and time-consuming. It would not, however, be unprecedented, for exactly that process took place early in the twentieth century in the codification of the Mormon doctrines regarding mortals and deity, among others (Alexander, 1980). Of course, in each setting, too, vigilance would be required by the local leaders to ensure that the angel was not overwhelmed by the local beehive; i.e., that the adaptation, or syncretism, would not go too far.

The issue, in any case, is not whether such a process will occur, for sooner or later it will prove an indispensable concomitant of Mormon cross-cultural growth and development. The issue thus really becomes simply one of how the process will work itself out. Will it be consciously guided and directed by the leadership, in accordance with their prophetic mandates? Or will it take the form of hundreds and thousands of skirmishes around the globe as Mormons in each locale resist or evade the imposition of American cultural biases and traditions as part of their new religion? The answer, probably, is that both will prove important.

Will the particular church posture required to maintain optimum tension with the surrounding culture in North America determine the posture also in Indonesia and Finland? Or will Mormon leaders and members in those other locales be free to respond appropriately and constructively to local pressures for assimilation and repression? In the face of such questions, processes such as centralization, standardization, correlation, and even simplification become highly problematic. So do the worldly accretions represented by the North American beehive, whether in the form of corporate business practices or Protestant fundamentalism.

I think the Mormon church and its leaders will rise successfully to the challenge of cross-cultural growth and adaptation. In the process, the church and its culture will be transformed, even in North America. All of this will occur, however, in a very Mormon way, through the oft-cited principle of continuous revelation. Properly understood, this principle is not merely a ritual claim to divine guidance. It is actually a very pragmatic principle for governance and innovation. It does not imply that Mormon leaders and members sit around waiting for God to speak and give direction.

The Mormon way, rather, as set forth in such scriptures as the Doctrine and Covenants (9:7–9) and the Book of Mormon (Moroni 10:3–5), involves much human initiative (see also Ludlow, 1992:1225–27). The seeker must present a particular proposal, hypothesis, or similar question for divine confirmation or response. The model, of course, is the first epiphany of Joseph Smith himself, who began by thoughtfully formulating a specific question and then sought an answer through revelation. The same model was explicitly applied as recently as 1978, when then President Spencer W. Kimball explained how he and his colleagues had taken a specific proposal to deity for abolishing the long-standing denial of the lay priesthood to members of black African ancestry. In his announcement of the happy outcome of that encounter, President Kimball explained simply that the Lord had "confirmed" the proposition that the time had come to end the proscription (Doctrine and Covenants, Official Declaration 2; Ludlow, 1992:423–24).

This incident takes on added significance from an observation by Thomas O'Dea several years earlier (1972:155–67). By 1972 O'Dea recognized that the Mormon racial controversy presented a "diagnostic issue," or a crucial test of the ability of the Mormon church to respond successfully to modern secular thought. Presumably O'Dea would now say that the church eventually passed that particular test. Yet the entire process by which this policy was changed (and not just the policy change itself) has a significance that goes far beyond what O'Dea recognized: It is a case study of the influence that international Mormon communities can have upon the revelatory process in Utah. As such, it is also a harbinger of the future.

It seems clear from the historical record that President Kimball's quest for revelation in the racial matter was precipitated by events in Brazil (Grover, 1984, 1990; Mauss, 1981). For whatever reasons, but including, surely, the rapid church growth in South America, the church leaders decided in 1974 that Brazil would be the site of the first Mormon temple in Latin America. A large proportion of the Mormon community in Brazil had always had black African ancestry, and thus had been denied access to the lay priesthood, a prerequisite for participation in the main temple rites.

The spectacle of turning away thousands of faithful Mormon converts from a temple in their own country, just because of their partial African ancestry, apparently brought home to President Kimball and his colleagues, more forcefully than events in North America had ever done, the anguish connected with the traditional race policy. The same spectacle almost certainly would have brought the church into serious disrepute precisely in that part of the world where church growth was the greatest. Under these circumstances, President Kimball must have felt compelled, both for spiritual and for pragmatic reasons, to approach deity with the proposal for significant policy change, despite his awareness of continuing commitments to the traditional racial policy on the parts of several powerful colleagues in the hierarchy.

Such a revelatory process, with its fundamentally human elements, is thus well established in Mormon tradition and legitimated in recent Mormon practice. It will always be available for dealing with the issues that will inevitably arise as the church spreads around the world. The process will begin with the recognition of an international or cross-cultural predicament, followed by the framing of a pragmatic resolution to the predicament, which is then presented before deity for confirmation (or rejection) by spiritual means.[6] Notice, however, that the predicament or issue must first be recognized and characterized, and this is where the human qualities of the Mormon leaders themselves become so crucial. Only to the extent that they can divest themselves of their own cultural assumptions (which come, after all, from the beehive and not the angel) will they be free to frame properly the questions and propositions that they take to deity.

No doubt such cultural divestment is facilitated by the recruitment of leaders, including general authorities, from various parts of the world, which has already occurred to a considerable extent. Yet, if North American cultural biases are truly to be minimized, it will be increasingly important that a priori amenability to American ways of thinking not be a criterion for recruitment of international leaders. It is thus perhaps ironic that much of the value of a new leader from a different culture will lie precisely in his or her willingness to demur or even disagree with North American leaders on issues outside the spiritual core of the religion (Newton, 1991). It is not yet clear to what extent this quality can be reconciled with the present organizational emphasis on hierarchy, top-down management, correlation, standardization, harmony, and docility.

If the Mormon church is to become truly a new world religion in the twenty-first century, as some scholars have projected, the angel will have to be largely disengaged from the American beehive with which it has always contended, so that it will be freer to address other beehives elsewhere (Woodworth, 1990). The Mormon principle of continuous revelation, under the aegis of the angel, will play a major role in that liberation, but mainly as that principle is activated by the clashes among the varied Mormon beehives around the world, or, in other words, among the various versions of Mormonism, whether in America or abroad. These clashes, that is to say, will force Mormonism to define its minimal spiritual core as a condition of worldwide growth and adaptation. It is in that sense that the future of Mormonism will depend at least as much on the commitment, energy, and ingenuity of its Brazilian, Japanese, and Russian Saints as on its prophets in Salt Lake City.

Notes

1. Social scientists who study recruitment to new movements (usually termed "conversion" if the movement is religious) are well aware of the part played by "social availability" in the conversion process. Those who are most "socially available" for conversion in any society are those who have the least invested in conventional religious and other institutions, those, in other words, who have the least to lose by making such fundamental changes in their lives and in their social relationships. That is why conversions to new religions involve disproportionately those who are young, unattached, uninvolved in major career commitments, and separated from families and from earlier religious communities (or even alienated from them). This by no means implies any lack of intelligence or sincerity but only a certain kind of "marginality" that leaves them freer to act on their new commitments with a minimum of disruption in social and economic relationships.

When American religions like Mormonism are exported, additional kinds of "marginality" frequently characterize potential converts in foreign countries: They are more likely than their compatriots to be English-speaking (or interested in learning English); to be favorably disposed toward American ways and values; and to be alienated from their own local religions. They are often foreigners even in the lands where they are living (e.g., Africans in France and southern Europeans in Germany have proved more responsive to Mormon missionaries than have the native French or Germans, respectively). In Asia and Africa, furthermore, Mormon missionaries have been especially successful with people who had earlier already joined other Christian churches. All such characteristics make people "marginal" to their own environments and thus "socially available" for recruitment to new religions like Mormonism. Of course, in chaotic locations like the countries of the former Soviet bloc, social availability is at a very high level. A recent article in the official church magazine suggests that the importance of this availability is well understood (though in spiritualized terms) by Mormon leaders (Cowan, 1993).

Mormon converts outside of North America have so far come disproportionately from these socially available categories and probably always will. For Mormons this simply means "gathering the elect" wherever the "field is white and ready to harvest" (Doctrine and Covenants 33:3, 6; John 4:35). Conversion under these circumstances, however, can also be described as "skimming off the cream," which is mainly what Mormonism has been able to do in these countries in recent decades. However, a permanent and significant presence for Mormonism in such locations will depend on the ability of the church to hold the second and third generations of the convert families and to expand the appeal of the religion well below the level of the socially available "cream" in each country. Only then will it be meaningful to describe Mormonism as a new "world religion."

2. Examples of cross-cultural anomalies, conflicts, and other such predicaments among the world's Mormons can be found in Allen (1991, 1992), Barney and Chu (1976), Boren (1980), Derr (1988), Grover (1984, 1990), Haslam (1984), Jarvis (1991), Jones (1980, 1982, 1987), Knowlton (1988, 1989a, 1989b, 1992),

Lambert (1985), Lineham (1991), McMurrin (1979b), Newton (1991), Numano (1980), Seshachari (1980), and Tullis (1978).

3. Encouraging or relatively optimistic examples of Mormon transplantation to other cultures can be found in Allen (1991, 1992), Arrington (1987), Mabey and Allred (1984), Morrison (1990), Palmer (1970, 1978), Woodworth (1990), and Tullis (1978, 1987).

4. A copy of this address by Elder Packer is in my personal files. It was also reproduced, with a certain amount of commentary, in the Oct. 1990 issue of *Sunstone*. The same issue of that magazine contained a number of insightful discussions of the implications of the course corrections discussed by Elder Packer (see Allen, 1990; Cornwall, 1990; England, 1990; and Woodworth, 1990).

5. A rough count from announcements in the *Church News* during the summer months of 1992 revealed that about 20% of the new bishops and stake presidents appointed outside of North America were already church civil service employees (often CES) at the time of appointment. A previous career in CES is also very common among general authorities appointed during the past two or three decades, regardless of nationality.

6. According to the "formula" laid out in the Doctrine and Covenants (9:7–9), a quest for confirmation from deity can produce either a "burning in the bosom" (if the proposition is being confirmed) or a "stupor of thought" (if the proposition is being rejected or not confirmed).

APPENDIX

Survey Methods and Measurements

This book is offered as a work of social science. In the public arena, the term *social science* evokes feelings ranging from intimidation to scorn, partly because the term, and the craft to which it refers, are not well defined even by practitioners. Among academicians, the term connotes to some a tendency to belabor the obvious with new terms for old truisms; to others (even worse) an obfuscation of the obvious; and to still others a misguided effort to render "scientific" that which cannot, by its nature, ever be scientific, namely the study of unpredictable human beings. To be sure, the social science disciplines are arrayed along the border between those usually called "humanities" and those regarded as the "true" or "hard" sciences. It is perhaps to be expected, then, that social science is often seen as a stepchild (or even a hybrid) without a comfortable home in either the sciences or the humanities.

At its best, social science bridges these two camps and combines the logic and methods of each in productive and revealing ways. From the humanities come the inductive elements and methods of social science: key case studies, a probing of subjective human perceptions and feelings, and the quest for intuitive understanding and insight into human predicaments. From the sciences come the deductive approaches of social science: the systematic test of insights, sometimes rendered as hypotheses, to determine how widely they can be generalized; the search for regularities in human behavior that might permit some predictability; and the construction of theoretical or heuristic models that might provide explanation or meaning for those regularities.

Science as Method

The Importance of Comparison

Ultimately, of course, "science" is defined by what scientists do, whether in the "hard" or the "soft" sciences. Two crucial processes that define the scientific enterprise are comparison and quantification. We cannot generalize about a population (whether of humans or of molecules) in the abstract. We must have a basis for comparison. This necessity is expressed in the well-known experimental strategy of science, in which hypotheses are tested, and conclusions drawn, on the basis of comparisons between experimental and control groups. Social scientists, of course, face severe practical limitations in their ability to organize their research subjects ahead of time into experimental and control groups for ongoing study and analysis.

However, they are often able to make use of the same general logic through other kinds of meaningful comparisons. For example, some of the chapters in this book compare Mormons with other populations as the basis for generalizing that Mormons are more "religious" or more "conservative" in certain ways than are other denominational groups. It would be meaningless to assert that Mormons (or any people) are highly "religious" (or have any other quality) except by comparison with one or more other appropriate categories of people.

Some of the comparisons in this book are slightly more complex, contrasting well-educated Mormons with well-educated others, less-educated Mormons with less-educated others, and so on, since education, and not only denomination, might affect people's religious beliefs or practices. In this example, we are controlling for the variable of education, as well as for the variable of denomination. From part 2 of the book to part 3 there are also some implicit and explicit comparisons across time: The Mormon/non-Mormon differences (or lack of them) from the sixties are compared to the Mormon/non-Mormon differences of the eighties to determine whether the Mormons have changed and whether the gap between Mormons and others in certain attributes has widened or narrowed with the passage of time.

Of course, all such comparisons can be indefinitely complicated by the simultaneous addition of more variables, controls, and time periods. Such complications have necessitated the development and application of increasingly sophisticated quantitative and statistical techniques that permit simultaneous manipulation of all the variables contributing to a certain outcome (like religious belief) and even an assessment of their relative weights. In this book, however, the reader is spared such complicated statistical presentations.

Quantification and Measurement

Comparison, at least in science, implies quantification. If we want to determine whether the subjects in one group (or time) have more or less of a certain trait than those in another group, then we must find a way to determine and measure the varying amounts of that trait, whether it's radioactivity or religious belief. The simplest and most reliable kind of quantification consists of counting that which is already quantified in nature, such as the sheer number of atoms in a molecule. In social science, that kind of quantification is pretty well limited to demographic traits like the number of males versus females in a population, the number of babies born to the females in a certain age range, and so on. Science has also imposed its own systematic quantification on nature through more or less arbitrary and culturally variable measures of weight, length, time, speed, and the like. As long as these measuring systems have standard or constant intervals (inches, ounces, etc.), they are as reliable as those things already quantified in nature.

In social science, quantification can be quite difficult and even more arbitrary, for much of what must be measured cannot directly be observed. How does one observe and measure attitudes or beliefs, for example? Where in the brain can they be located, quantified, and counted? In popular or folk wisdom, we sometimes resort to informal and arbitrary ad hoc scales: "On a scale of 1 to 10, how do you like my new suit?" One can pose that question to six different friends and calculate an average score of (say) 4.5, but that would yield a very imprecise and unreliable measure of how much the new suit was appreciated. For one thing, each of the six friends might be using quite different criteria for their scales; for another thing, the interval between 2 and 3 might not be the same as that between 7 and 8 for any of the friends, to say nothing of differences in scale intervals from one friend to the next. Even if all six friends could agree on exactly the same criteria and the same score, it would be hard to know how standard the intervals would be. About the most that could be concluded would be that a 7 indicates more appreciation for the suit than a 3, but just how much more would be hard to say.

In their efforts to make quantification and measurement more precise and more meaningful than in this folk example, social scientists have developed a number of techniques that are laid out in any basic textbook on research methods. We recognize, to begin with, that we are dependent upon indirect and surrogate measures for assessing beliefs, feelings, and attitudes, since these can be inferred only from observed behavior, including verbal behavior (i.e., responses to questions in interviews or in questionnaires). The correspondence among attitudes, the verbal expression of those attitudes, and the actual behavior connected to the attitudes has always been highly problematic in social science. Will people tell researchers how they really feel about anything, especially on sensitive issues?

Even if they do report their real feelings or attitudes, will they act on those feelings in consistent and predictable ways? In wrestling with such methodological issues during the past few decades, social science has gained a great deal of sophistication in the techniques of constructing and asking effective questions in survey research, although not every survey, by any means, reflects that sophistication. Among the best examples are probably the preelection surveys of recent years, which typically produce results within two or three percentage points of the actual election outcomes, even with very small samples. Of course, success in such surveys depends as much upon sophisticated techniques of sampling as upon the construction of key questions, and that is another whole aspect of survey research in which great progress has been made.

Once beliefs or attitudes have been given surrogate quantification through respondents' verbal answers to questions, researchers must determine both how valid the answers are and how reliable they are. A question is regarded as valid to the extent that it indicates, or "measures," what it is supposed to measure. For example, an appropriately framed question about belief in God would probably be a more valid indicator of religiosity than would a question about how much a person likes her or his priest or minister. A question is regarded as reliable to the extent that it yields about the same responses from the same sample of persons each time it is used. For example, we would not consider a question about God very reliable if in one survey 60% of the sample thought of God primarily as compassionate and 40% as punitive, whereas those figures were reversed in a survey the very next week with exactly the same question and the same sample. We would wonder about both validity and reliability if the same sample in the same survey produced obviously inconsistent answers, such as agreeing overwhelmingly (in one question) that God is all powerful but denying overwhelmingly (in another question) that God could part the Red Sea.

Social scientists have developed various techniques for enhancing both validity and reliability. In some cases, a certain degree of "face validity" can be assumed. A question about whether (and to what extent) one believes in God, for example, would seem, on its face, to be one indicator of religiosity, at least for Christians. Yet reliability, and to some extent even validity, might be problematic when everything depends upon the answer to a single question, especially if the research interest is in a person's religious commitments as a Christian. A researcher is likely to feel more comfortable with multiple indicators of the same quality. Thus, for example, we would be more confident that a certain person held strongly Christian commitments if she or he affirmed beliefs in God and in the divinity of Jesus and in the truth of the Bible.

We would, of course, have to take into account different degrees of affirmation, too, since a respondent might believe in God more strongly than in the divinity of Jesus. Thus both the validity and the reliability of a question is likely to be enhanced if it allows for graduated responses, such as "agree strongly," "agree somewhat," "not sure," "disagree somewhat," and "disagree strongly" (although a certain research strategy might sometimes require a forced choice between agree and disagree). In this example, we have, in effect, a 5-point scale of agreement from none up to strong. This is obviously not a scale with standard and predictable intervals, as a 12-inch ruler would be, for we do not know if the "distance" between "agree strongly" and "agree somewhat" is the same as the distance between any other two points on the scale. Nor, indeed, can we be sure that these intervals would be the same "length" in a question about God as in a question about Jesus. We would be justified, however, in assuming that a person who agrees "strongly" with a statement of belief possesses "more" of that belief than does one who chooses one of the other options.

A putative measure of Christian belief, however, would be much more valid and reliable if somehow it could comprise simultaneously all three of these questions. Social scientists therefore tend to prefer composite scales for measuring global attitudes and cognitive systems like religiosity or conservatism. There are several different ways to construct such scales, but in this book, primarily in chapters 3, 4, and 5, two systems were used. They both begin by "validating" each question or indicator against a "criterion variable."

For example, if we assume that answers to a question on the divinity of Jesus are valid indicators of Christian commitment, then they should "predict" (or be highly correlated with) answers to other putative indicators of such commitment, which, for these purposes, would be called "criterion variables." In other words, the great majority of respondents answering "agree strongly" to the divinity of Jesus (if that is a valid indicator of Christian commitment) should also answer affirmatively to a criterion question about the actuality of Christ's miracles and to various similar criterion variables as well.

If several related questions or indicators are validated as more or less equally strong in correlation against criterion variables, then they might be combined into an additive scale. Suppose, for example, that we have four questions about traditional Christian belief, or orthodoxy: belief in God, belief in the divinity of Jesus, belief in a literal devil, and belief in the actuality of the biblical miracles. Suppose further that there were five options in answering each question and that we assign a graduating numerical score to each option: 0 = disbelieve strongly; 1 = disbelieve somewhat; 2 = don't know or not sure; 3 = believe somewhat; and 4 = believe strongly. If we then simply add together the scores of the four questions, then we get a composite scale ranging from 0 (belief in none of the questions) to 16 (strong belief in all four), with intermediate values determined by different levels of expressed belief (or disbelief) on the various questions. Such an additive scale still does not have standard intervals from one number to the next, but it is at least ordinal; that is, bigger numbers imply greater net or composite orthodoxy.

An alternative system of composite scaling is based upon the different "proportional effects" that the different questions have when tested against criterion variables. For example, if the responses about the divinity of Jesus are more strongly related (correlated) with one or more criterion variables than are the responses to the question about the devil, then the Jesus question will be given more statistical weight than the devil question in constructing the composite scale of orthodoxy. Factor analysis might also be used to estimate proportional effects, but with my scales it was used only in confirmatory ways. Any system of scaling requiring statistical manipulations is more complicated than are the simple additive scales (described above), which are thus often preferred unless the criterion variables indicate severe disparities in the relative importance of the component items.

In the chapters of this book that make use of scales both the simple additive and the proportional systems have been used, depending on the scale. All scales showed very strong validity against criterion variables, especially by comparison with any of their component items. Internal consistency in the scales was indicated by Cronbach alpha coefficients ranging from .67 to at least .90, which most social scientists would consider quite satisfactory. The alpha is a measure of how well the various components in the scale "hang together," as indicated by their intercorrelations with each other and with the entire scale.

In presenting the data from scales and from other variables, I have relied almost entirely on the use of tables, rather than on more sophisticated statistical presentations, partly in the interest of reader accessibility and partly because I am more comfortable with tabular presentations. The tables based on the NORC-GSS data include notations about statistical significance, which might not mean much to some readers but which become important especially with the relatively small Mormon samples in these tables. For the benefit of those unacquainted with this jargon, I will explain only that statistical significance does not refer to how important the tables' findings are in some general sense. That might instead be called "substantive significance."

Statistical significance, by contrast, refers only to the likelihood that a certain distribution in a table might have occurred by chance. This likelihood is usually indicated by a *p* figure (for probability). Since chance findings cannot provide much basis for making a case, the lower such probabilities the better. It is conventional in social science to consider a *p* of .05 or lower to be a safe level of statistical significance (i.e., five chances in a hundred of chance findings). In the tables based on my surveys from the sixties, the *p*s have not been noted, since the *p* sizes are largely a function of the sample sizes, which are reasonably large in those tables; thus probabilities of no more than .05 can usually be assumed.

Data and Evidence

The quantification and measurement procedures outlined above apply primarily to data gathered from surveys (with either questionnaires or interviews). Whether those procedures are the relatively simple ones described above or the more complex statistical manipulations often seen in the professional journals, their usefulness depends in large part upon the quality of the survey data. Some attention will be given next, therefore, to survey methods, with particular reference to the surveys on Mormons conducted in Utah and California in the 1960s. These provided much of the evidence presented especially in part 2 of the book.

Surveys

Until the church established its own department of social research in the midseventies (Cornwall and Cunningham, 1989), very few surveys had been conducted on Mormon populations. Earlier surveys were privately conducted and were thus limited by the resources, opportunities, and samples available to individual researchers. Accordingly, these early surveys relied on available samples that were small, unsystematic, and obtained through the goodwill and permission of local church leaders. Some of the surveys suffered noticeably from these limitations and even from the imposition of contraints or surveillance imposed by the cooperating church leaders. Although a number of graduate theses and dissertations were based upon these surveys, few publications in refereed journals appeared. Commendable pioneering examples can be found in the literature, however (e.g., Cline and Richards, 1965; Wilford E. Smith, 1959; and Vernon, 1955, 1956).

The first large-scale surveys on Mormons of which I am aware were conducted by myself between 1964 and 1969. Like the earlier ones, these were privately designed and financed and conducted originally for a Ph.D. dissertation. I had been active in the Mormon community in Walnut Creek, California, since the early fifties and had been part of a prominent East Bay Mormon family since 1936. Accordingly, in 1964 and 1965, when I undertook what I intended as a kind of "pilot study," the local Mormon bishops whose cooperation I sought were already acquainted with me or my family and therefore disposed to be trusting and cooperative. Without extracting any conditions or exercising any surveillance, the three bishops I approached each supplied me with a current roster of the names and addresses of all households in their respective wards and promised to inform their ward members that the surveys were being conducted with their knowledge and permission.

These three wards were chosen purposefully to comprise three different ecological settings: Oak Grove Ward was in an upscale suburban location in Concord; Pittsburg Ward was the sole Mormon congregation in that small industrial town (several miles east of Concord), and it had a large working-class population; still further east was the Antioch Ward, the only Mormon flock in that small town, still largely rural and agricultural in those days, very slightly touched as yet by the spreading suburban sprawl of the East Bay area.

The mailed questionnaire was a cumbersome, twenty-four-page mimeographed document adapted from the one then in use by Charles Y. Glock and Rodney Stark for their study of religion in American life at the Survey Research Center of the University of California (see their questionnaire in the appendix to Glock and Stark, 1966). Glock was the mentor for my doctoral dissertation, and Stark, also a graduate student, was his research assistant. Both were generous in sharing with me not only their questionnaire but considerable professional consultation and guidance as well.

This early pilot version of my questionnaire produced data of high enough quality to yield two professional publications (Mauss, 1966, 1968). Accordingly, I refined, modified, and tightened the document only somewhat and then produced a new one of similar length, professionally printed in pamphlet form, to be used for the subsequent surveys that would yield the actual data for the doctoral dissertation. For that purpose I wanted another California sample of the most highly urbanized kind and a large, representative sample of heartland Mormons from Salt Lake City itself. With data from both the pilot and the refined versions of my questionnaire, I reasoned, I would have samples from varied enough locales in Utah and California to permit findings and conclusions of a fairly generalized kind, at least for Mormons of the western United States. How was I to obtain the necessary data from these other locales?

At that juncture (1965–66) came a crucial intervention by Providence, serendipity, or both: The Presiding Bishop's Office (PBO) of the LDS Church was then in the process of evaluating and modifying two of its major programs, one for boys twelve to eighteen years of age (called Aaronic Priesthood Youth) and one for male adults of minimal church activity (called Aaronic Priesthood Adults). These studies were under the direction of Ray L. White, who at that time was a kind of chief of staff for the PBO. He had put together ad hoc committees to assist in these studies. A member of one of those committees was Richard Woolley, who happened to be living near me in California and had heard of my recent pilot survey. To make a long story short, Mr. Woolley and Mr. White installed me on both of the ad hoc PBO committees, and I helped to design and administer surveys for both their studies from 1965 to 1969. It was that association which opened the door for me then to conduct my own surveys with the backing of Mr. White.

The surveys which I needed to conduct for my purposes were much more extensive than anything needed by the PBO at that time, but Mr. White thought that his ecclesiastical superiors might welcome a chance to get more extensive data, especially on inactive church members, as a part of my surveys. He thought that they might even finance the surveys for me if we could agree on the terms of their access and my scholarly independence. As things turned out, however, the PBO was not willing to finance my surveys. However, Mr. White pledged his good offices in helping me gain the access I needed to conduct them with my own funds. Once I had chosen the sample wards in Salt Lake City and in California, I had only to refer the local ward bishops to Mr. White and his telephone number. All of the bishops did, indeed, call Mr. White, and all in due course gave me their ward rosters, their permission to survey their members, and their public approval of my efforts. None attempted in any way to exercise any restraint or surveillance over the process.

My first task was choosing the sample wards. For an urban California sample, it was fairly easy. I simply chose the Bay Ward and the Mission Ward, which between them constituted all of the Mormons then living in the most urbanized, downtown section of San Francisco (between Golden Gate Park and the Bay). For Salt Lake City, the process was somewhat more complex. Mr. White furnished me with the names and membership sizes of all the wards in greater Salt Lake City (from the state capitol on the north to the state penitentiary on the south), a total of more than four hundred wards comprising some 244,000 church members at that time. I then assigned successive blocks of numbers to each ward, corresponding with its membership size. For example, if the first ward had 603 members, I assigned it numbers 1 through 603. If the second ward had 587 members, I assigned it numbers 604 through 1,190, and so on through all the hundreds of wards in the greater Salt Lake City area. I then went to a table of random numbers and chose ten numbers. Each of the ten was located in a block of numbers assigned to one of the wards, and that ward then became part of the sample.

This sampling procedure, in effect, based a ward's chances of being selected on its membership size: the larger the membership, the greater the likelihood of being selected. The ten Salt Lake area wards chosen by this system were Colonial Hills Ward, Ensign Fourth Ward, Millcreek Sixth, Murray Third, Murray Fifth, Monument Park Fourteenth, Salt Lake City Nineteenth, Taylorsville Eleventh, Valley View Fourth, and Yalecrest Second. The proportions of each ward eventually comprising the sample of actual respondents ranged between 6% and 10% in most cases, but two wards (Murray Third and Yalecrest Second) had 13% and 14%, respectively. It should be noted that the intervening twenty-five years have brought many changes in both the names and the boundaries of these wards, but at the time of the survey, they were distributed around the Salt Lake City area in almost perfect accord with the distribution of the general population (i.e., the more populous the area, like the east side, the more wards from there appeared in the sample).

In all three surveys (California East Bay, San Francisco, and Salt Lake City), the same procedure was followed in obtaining the completed questionnaires: The questionnaire, with an appropriate cover letter assuring both anonymity and church permission, was mailed to each household in every sample ward, addressed alternately to the husband and to the wife in the case of married couples or otherwise to the one church member of record. The mailed packet contained a self-addressed, postage-paid envelope for returning the questionnaire; also included was a prepaid postcard to be returned separately by the respondent. The postcard contained simply the respondent's name, address, and the assertion that the questionnaire had been completed anonymously and mailed back separately.

The purpose of the postcard, of course, was to permit follow-up without compromising anonymity in the actual questionnaires. Respondents apparently understood and followed this system, for in every ward there were slightly more questionnaires returned than postcards (indicating a small likelihood of returned postcards falsely claiming completed questionnaires). After two or three weeks, those who had not returned postcards were sent follow-up letters with additional questionnaires. After another few weeks, nonrespondents were sent a remonstrating letter offering a duplicate questionnaire. The total response rate, after follow-up, ranged from 50% to 68%, depending on the ward, with an average return of almost 60%. This was essentially the same system used by Glock and Stark, though they claimed a higher response rate.

The total response rate for my surveys was actually somewhat better than Glock and Stark obtained, since my ward lists suffered from much less obsolescence than did their congregational lists. I was also able to learn more than they did about nonrespondents: After follow-up efforts were finished, I was able to review with each ward bishop or his clerk the cases of all nonrespondents. For each such case, the bishop provided data on gender, age, approximate education level, occupation, and level of church activity. As might have been anticipated, a comparison on these traits of respondents and nonrespondents indicated that the latter were somewhat more likely to be of working-class, male, elderly, and inactive in the church. The resulting demographic biases in the survey data had to be taken into account, of course, in generalizing the results; but the biases were not extreme, so the data could be considered reasonably representative of adult Mormons in the various locales.

Interestingly enough, these surveys were replicated (with the Utah and San Francisco questionnaire) about ten years later among Mormons in the U.S. Southeast (Alabama, Georgia, Florida, and Tennessee) under very similar circumstances, and with a similar return rate, for a doctoral dissertation on the relative influence of region and religion upon racial attitudes (Ainsworth, 1982).

The other principal source of survey data for this book, introduced mainly in the more recent comparisons of Mormons and non-Mormons (part 3), was the General Social Survey (GSS) conducted annually with federal funding under the auspices of the National Opinion Research Corporation (NORC). The reader is referred to the cumulative codebook for this data set (Davis and Smith, 1990), which is readily available in university libraries and contains detailed treatments of all the methods used, questions asked, and results obtained through the surveys from 1972 through 1990. Suffice it to say here that these GSS data are of a high quality rarely achieved in survey research. They come from skilled interviews (not mailed questionnaires) with meticulously drawn samples of all (noninstitutionalized) adult residents of the United States.

The GSS data were used primarily in chapters 8, 9, and 10. Chapter 9 contains an explanation of the number of Mormon cases available for analysis from the GSS samples and explains how the Mormon and non-Mormon cases were aggregated for appropriate comparisons. The tables in these chapters were compiled and designed especially for this book and are based upon Mormon samples that (depending upon the questions) reach a maximum of 343 cases drawn mainly from interviews during the eighties. Figures 9.1–9.4, however, while also based on GSS data, were appropriated from an earlier study (Roof and McKinney, 1987) using a somewhat smaller Mormon sample.

Secondary Sources

The surveys described above, plus brief and passing references to other original data sources (e.g., tabulations from almanacs and key church publications), constitute most of the primary sources used in this book. The rest of the evidence for the arguments presented here comes from secondary sources. This means that I have not only relied on the findings and judgments of other scholars but I have sometimes made interpretations of their work that they might or might not approve. In this process, I have tried to be fair. I have not deliberately made biased selections from their work, nor have I intentionally misrepresented their findings and conclusions. Yet the reader must remain alert to the differences between what others have written and the meanings that I have ascribed to what they have written. They are responsible only for the former; I am responsible for the latter.

I have used different secondary sources in different ways. Some of them, like the historical overviews of Allen and Leonard (1992), Alexander (1986b), Quinn (1983), and Shipps (1985), have provided me with valuable general information about key developments and changes of direction in the institutional history of the Mormon church. Others have been valuable to me primarily for having focused on specific aspects of Mormon history, such as the doctrinal shifts analyzed by O. Kendall White (1987) or the changing political relationships traced by E. Leo Lyman (1986). Still others, like the work of Shepherd and Shepherd (1984) on changing leadership rhetoric, have not only traced general trends but have provided important corroborative statistical data for the major thesis of this book.

Indeed, an especially persuasive kind of evidence for this thesis is to be found precisely in several works written entirely independently by other authors for other purposes. This book has presented, in broad brushstrokes, the general thesis that Mormon institutional life and culture passed through an assimilationist phase during the first half of the twentieth century; then, in reaction, as it were, to the very success of that assimilation, partially turned back toward retrenchment and particularism in its relationships with the surrounding American society. The evidence for this two-phase process is to be found in the comparison of the survey data and the historical descriptions found, respectively, in parts 2 and 3 of the book; but there is much evidence in the work of others, too.

The Barlow study (1991) of the changing uses of the King James Bible, written with a different theme entirely, converged so well in its findings with the thesis considered here that it served as a persuasive case study in chapter 7. The Shepherd and Shepherd (1984) study was not guided by the two-phase theoretical process advocated here; yet its meticulous analysis of rhetorical data was cited regularly in this book since it unintentionally offered surprisingly clear evidence in support of the same process. White's (1987) study, written to demonstrate a turn toward "crisis theology" in Mormonism, in effect also supports the main thesis of this book by documenting a new penchant for fundamentalism (neo-orthodoxy) in certain theological circles. Likewise Paul's (1992) study of Mormon relationships to science documents a recent retreat from a relatively modern outlook on scientific issues earlier in Mormonism to a more fundamentalist one now. Even Hicks's (1989) history of Mormon music indicates a turn from the fairly generic Christian hymnody of midcentury to a more particularistic Mormon hymnody in the eighties.

When so many scholars, with no indication of collaboration, produce specific studies that converge so well with an independently developed general thesis, that thesis perforce acquires a high degree of credibility. I am thus extraordinarily grateful to these colleagues, not only for what I have learned from them, which is considerable, but for the unintentional support that their fine work has given to my own efforts to explain the course of recent Mormon history.

References

Abrahamson, Harold J. 1973. *Ethnic Diversity in Catholic America.* New York: Wiley.

——. 1980. "Religion." In *Harvard Encyclopedia of American Ethnic Groups,* ed. Stephen Thernstrom, 869–75. Cambridge, Mass.: Harvard University Press.

Aho, James A. 1990. *The Politics of Righteousness: Idaho Christian Patriotism.* Seattle: University of Washington Press.

Ainsworth, Charles H. 1982. "Religious and Regional Sources of Attitudes toward Blacks among Southern Mormons." Ph.D. diss., Washington State University.

Albrecht, Stan L. 1989. "The Consequential Dimension of Mormon Religiosity." *BYU Studies* 29 (2): 57–108.

Albrecht, Stan L., and Howard M. Bahr. 1983. "Patterns of Religious Disaffiliation: A Study of Lifelong Mormons, Mormon Converts, and Former Mormons." *Journal for the Scientific Study of Religion* 22 (4): 366–79.

Albrecht, Stan L., and Tim Heaton. 1984. "Secularization, Higher Education, and Religiosity." *Review of Religious Research* 26 (1): 43–58.

Albrecht, Stan L., Howard M. Bahr, and Bruce A. Chadwick. 1979. "Changing Family and Sex Roles: An Assessment of Age Differences." *Journal of Marriage and the Family* 41 (1): 41–50.

Alexander, Thomas G. 1970. "An Experiment in Progressive Legislation: The Granting of Woman Suffrage in Utah in 1870." *Utah Historical Quarterly* 38 (1): 20–30.

——. 1980. "The Reconstruction of Mormon Doctrine: From Joseph Smith to Progressive Theology." *Sunstone* 5 (July–Aug.): 24–33.

——. 1981. "The Word of Wisdom: From Principle to Requirement." *Dialogue* 14 (3): 78–88.

——. 1982. " 'To Maintain Harmony': Adjusting to External and Internal Stress, 1890–1930." *Dialogue* 15 (4): 44–58.

——. 1983. "Between Revivalism and the Social Gospel: The Latter-day Saint Social Advisory Committee, 1916–1922." *Brigham Young University Studies* 23 (1): 19–39.

——. 1986a. "Historiography and the New Mormon History: A Historian's Perspective." *Dialogue* 19 (3): 25–49.

——. 1986b. *Mormonism in Transition: A History of the Latter-day Saints, 1890–1930.* Urbana: University of Illinois Press.

Allen, James B. 1973. "Personal Faith and Public Policy: Some Timely Observation on the League of Nations Controversy in Utah." *Brigham Young University Studies* 14 (1): 77–98.

——. 1990. "Course Corrections: Some Personal Reflections." *Sunstone* 14 (5): 34–40.

——. 1991. "Would-be Saints: West Africa before the 1978 Priesthood Revelation." *Journal of Mormon History* 17:207–47.

——. 1992. "On Becoming a Universal Church." *Dialogue* 25 (1): 13–36.

Allen, J. B., and Glen M. Leonard. 1992. *The Story of the Latter-day Saints.* 2d ed. Salt Lake City: Deseret Book.

Allen, James B., Ronald W. Walker, and David J. Whittaker, eds. n.d. "Studies in Mormon History: A Bibliography with Index and a Guide to Further Research." Ms.

Ammerman, Nancy T. 1987. *Bible Believers: Fundamentalists in the Modern World.* New Brunswick, N.J.: Rutgers University Press.

——. 1990. *Baptist Battles.* New Brunswick, N.J.: Rutgers University Press.

Anderson, John R. 1986. "American Women and Conservative Religion in the Post-war Decades: Southern Baptist and Mormon Women's Magazines, 1945–1975." Ph.D. diss., Washington State University.

Anderson, Lavina F. 1988. "A Voice from the Past: The Benson Instructions for Parents." *Dialogue* 21 (4): 103–13.

——. 1993. "The LDS Intellectual Community and Church Leadership: A Contemporary Chronology." *Dialogue* 26 (1): 7–64.

Arrington, Leonard J. 1958. *Great Basin Kingdom: An Economic History of the Latter-day Saints.* Cambridge, Mass.: Harvard University Press.

——. 1964. "Origins of the Welfare Plan of the Church of Jesus Christ of Latter-day Saints." *Brigham Young University Studies* 5 (1): 67–85.

——. 1967. "The Founding of the LDS Institutes of Religion." *Dialogue* 2 (1): 137–47.

——. 1968. "Intolerable Zion: The Image of Mormonism in Nineteenth Century American Literature." *Western Humanities Review* 22:243–60.

——. 1987. "Historical Development of International Mormonism." *Religious Studies and Theology* 7 (Jan.).

——. 1992. "The Founding of the LDS Church Historical Department, 1972." *Journal of Mormon History* 18:41–56.

Arrington, Leonard J., and Davis Bitton. 1979. *The Mormon Experience: A History of the Latter-day Saints.* New York: Alfred A. Knopf.

Arrington, Leonard J., Feramorz Y. Fox, and Dean L. May. 1992. *Building the City of God: Community and Cooperation among the Mormons.* 2d ed. Urbana: University of Illinois Press.

Ashment, Edward H. 1990. "Making the Scriptures 'Indeed One in Our Hands.'"

In *The Word of God: Essays on Mormon Scripture*, ed. Dan Vogel, 237–64. Salt Lake City: Signature Books.

Avant, Gerry. 1992. "Speaking Out on Moral Issues." *Church News*, June 6, 6.

Baer, Hans A. 1988. *Recreating Utopia in the Desert: A Sectarian Challenge to Modern Mormonism*. Albany: State University of New York Press.

Bahr, Howard M. 1979. "The Declining Distinctiveness of Utah's Working Women." *BYU Studies* 19 (4): 525–43.

——. 1981. "Religious Intermarriage and Divorce in Utah and the Mountain States." *Journal for the Scientific Study of Religion* 20 (3): 251–60.

——. 1982. "Religious Contrasts in Family Role Definitions and Performance: Utah Mormons, Catholics, Protestants, and Others." *Journal for the Scientific Study of Religion* 21 (3): 200–217.

Bahr, Howard M., and Stan L. Albrecht. 1989. "Strangers Once More: Patterns of Disaffiliation from Mormonism." *Journal for the Scientific Study of Religion* 28 (2): 180–200.

Bahr, Stephen J. 1994. "Religion and Adolescent Drug Use: A Comparison of the Mormons and Other Religions." In *Contemporary Mormonism: Social Science Perspectives*, ed. Marie Cornwall, Tim B. Heaton, and Lawrence A. Young. Urbana: University of Illinois Press.

Barlow, Philip L. 1991. *Mormons and the Bible: The Place of the Latter-day Saints in American Religion*. New York: Oxford University Press.

Barney, R. D., and G. G. Y. Chu. 1976. "Differences between Mormon Missionaries' Perceptions and Chinese Natives' Expectations in Intercultural Transactions." *Journal of Social Psychology* 98:135–36.

Bart, Peter. 1981. *Thy Kindgom Come*. New York: Linden Press.

Beatty, Kathleen M., and Oliver Walter. 1987. "Mormons and the New Christian Right: Reevaluating the Prospects for Political Coalitions." Paper presented at the annual meeting of the American Political Science Association, Chicago, Sept.

Beckford, James A. 1985. *Cult Controversies: The Societal Response to New Religious Movements*. New York: Tavistock.

Beecher, Maureen U. 1982. "The 'Leading Sisters': A Female Hierarchy in Nineteenth Century Mormon Society." *Journal of Mormon History* 9:25–39.

Beeton, B. 1978. "Woman Suffrage in Territorial Utah." *Utah Historical Quarterly* 46 (2): 100–120.

Bennion, Adam S. 1922. "The Utah Plan of Religious Education for High School Students." *Religious Education* 17:53–54.

Benson, Ezra Taft. 1980. "Fourteen Fundamentals in Following the Prophets." Address to the BYU Devotional Assembly, Feb. 26.

——. 1987a. *To the Fathers in Israel*. Salt Lake City: Corporation of the President of the Church of Jesus Christ of Latter-day Saints.

——. 1987b. *To the Mothers in Zion*. Salt Lake City: Corporation of the President of the Church of Jesus Christ of Latter-day Saints.

Berger, Peter, and Thomas Luckmann. 1966. *The Social Construction of Reality*. Garden City, N.Y.: Doubleday.

Bergera, Gary J. 1988. "What You Leave Behind: Six Years at the MTC." *Dialogue* 21 (1): 146–55.

——. 1991. "The New Mormon Anti-intellectualism." *Sunstone* 15 (2): 53–55.

Bergera, Gary J., and Ronald Priddis. 1985. *Brigham Young University: A House of Faith*. Salt Lake City: Signature Books.

Bibby, Reginald W. 1987. *Fragmented Gods: The Poverty and Potential of Religion in Canada*. Toronto: Irwin.

——. 1990. *Mosaic Madness: The Poverty and Potential of Life in Canada*. Toronto: Stoddart.

Bitton, Davis. 1983. "Ten Years in Camelot: A Personal Memoir." *Dialogue* 16 (3): 9–32.

Bitton, Davis, and Leonard J. Arrington. 1988. *Mormons and Their Historians*. Salt Lake City: University of Utah Press.

Bitton, Davis, and Gary L. Bunker. 1978. "Double Jeopardy: Visual Images of Mormon Women to 1914." *Utah Historical Quarterly* 46 (2): 184–202.

Blais, Pierre. 1984. "The Enduring Paradox: Mormon Attitudes toward War and Peace." *Dialogue* 17 (4): 61–73.

Blakely, Thomas A. 1985. "The Swearing Elders: The First Generation of Modern Mormon Intellectuals." *Sunstone* 10 (9): 8–13.

Bluhm, Harry P., David C. Spendlove, and Dee W. West. 1986. "Depression in Mormon Women." *Dialogue* 19 (2): 150–55.

Blumell, Bruce D. 1979. "Welfare before Welfare: The Twentieth Century LDS Church Charity before the Great Depression." *Journal of Mormon History* 6: 89–106.

Bohn, David E. 1983. "No Higher Ground: Objective History Is an Illusive Chimera." *Sunstone* 8 (1–2): 26–32.

——. 1990. "Our Own Agenda: A Critique of the Methodology of the New Mormon History." *Sunstone* 14 (3): 45–49.

Boren, Murray. 1980. "Worship through Music Nigerian Style." *Sunstone* 5 (6): 41–43.

Bradford, M. Gerald. 1988. "The Case for the New Mormon History: Thomas G. Alexander and His Critics." *Dialogue* 21 (4): 143–50.

Breitman, George, ed. 1965. *Malcolm X Speaks*. New York: Grove Press.

Bringhurst, Newell G. 1981. *Saints, Slaves, and Blacks: The Changing Place of Black People within Mormonism*. Westport, Conn.: Greenwood Press.

——. 1990. "Fawn M. Brodie, 'Mormonism's Lost Generation,' and *No Man Knows My History*." *Journal of Mormon History* 16:11–23.

Brinkerhoff, Merlin B., and Marlene M. Mackie. 1984. "Religious Denominations' Impact upon Gender Attitudes: Some Methodological Implications." *Review of Religious Research* 25 (4): 365–78.

——. 1986. "Applicability of Social Distance for Religious Research: An Exploration." *Review of Religious Research* 28 (2): 151–67.

Brinkerhoff, Merlin B., Jeffrey C. Jacob, and Marlene M. Mackie. 1987a. "Mormonism and the Moral Majority Make Strange Bedfellows?: An Exploratory Critique." *Review of Religious Research* 28 (3): 236–51.

——. 1987b. "Religious Tolerance: Mormons in the American Mainstream." *Dialogue* 20 (3): 90–95.

Brinkerhoff, Merlin B., Elaine Grandin, Irving Hexham, and Carson Pue. 1991. "The Perceptions of Mormons by Rural Canadian Youth." *Journal for the Scientific Study of Religion* 30 (4): 479–86.

Bruce, Steve. 1993. "Religion and Rational Choice: A Critique of Economic Explanations of Religious Behavior." *Sociology of Religion* 54 (2): 193–205.

Buchanan, Frederick S. 1993. "Masons and Mormons: Released-Time Politics in Salt Lake City, 1930–56." *Journal of Mormon History* 19 (1): 67–114.

Buerger, David J. 1982. "The Adam-God Doctrine." *Dialogue* 15 (1): 14–58.

——. 1983. " 'The Fullness of the Priesthood': The Second Anointing in Latter-day Saint Theology and Practice." *Dialogue* 16 (1): 10–44.

——. 1985. "Speaking with Authority: The Theological Influence of Elder Bruce R. McConkie." *Sunstone* 10 (3): 8–13.

——. 1987. "The Development of the Mormon Temple Endowment Ceremony." *Dialogue* 20 (4): 33–76.

Bunker, Gary L., and Davis Bitton. 1983. *The Mormon Graphic Image, 1934–1914.* Salt Lake City: University of Utah Press.

Bush, Lester E., Jr. 1976. "Birth Control among the Mormons: Introduction to an Insistent Question." *Dialogue* 10 (2): 12–44.

——. 1985. "Ethical Issues in Reproductive Medicine: A Mormon Perspective." *Dialogue* 18 (2): 40–66.

Bush, Lester E., Jr., and Armand L. Mauss. 1984. *Neither White nor Black: Mormon Scholars Encounter the Race Issue in a Universal Church.* Salt Lake City: Signature Books.

Campbell, Bruce L., and Eugene E. Campbell. 1981. "The Mormon Family." In *Ethnic Families in America,* ed. Charles H. Mindel and Robert W. Habenstein, 379–416. New York: Elsevier.

Cannon, Charles A. 1974. "The Awesome Power of Sex: The Polemical Campaign against Mormon Polygamy." *Pacific Historical Review* 43:61–82.

Cannon, Hal. 1980. *The Grand Beehive.* Salt Lake City: University of Utah Press.

Cannon, Mark, R. Bushman, Q. McKay, R. Wirthlin, and G. Magnum. 1962. "What Is the Proper Role of the Latter-day Saint with Respect to the Constitution?" *BYU Studies* 4 (2): 157–77.

Capener, Cole R. 1984. "How General the Authority?: Individual Conscience and De Facto Infallibility." *Sunstone* 9 (2): 26–30.

Chandler, Clay. 1992. "Correlation: The Boring of a Generation." Paper presented at the annual Sunstone Symposium, Salt Lake City, Aug.

Chaves, Mark. 1993. "Intraorganizational Power and Internal Secularization in Protestant Denominations." *American Journal of Sociology* 99 (1): 1–48.

Christensen, Harold T. 1960. "Cultural Relativism and Pre-marital Sex Norms." *American Sociological Review* 25 (1): 31–39.

——. 1968. "Children in the Family: Relationship of Number and Spacing to Marital Success." *Journal of Marriage and the Family* 30 (2): 283–89.

——. 1973. "Attitudes toward Marital Infidelity: A Nine-Culture Sampling of University Student Opinions." *Journal of Comparative Family Studies* 4:197–214.

——. 1976. "Mormon Sexuality in Cross-cultural Perspective." *Dialogue* 10 (2): 62–75.

——. 1982. "The Persistence of Chastity: A Built-in Resistance within Mormon Culture to Secular Trends." *Sunstone* 7 (2): 7–14.

——. 1987. "Memoirs of a Marginal Man: Reflections of a Mormon Sociologist." *Dialogue* 20 (3): 115–28.

Christensen, Harold T., and Kenneth L. Cannon. 1964. "Temple vs. Non-temple Marriage in Utah: Some Demographic Considerations." *Social Science* 39 (1): 26–33.

——. 1978. "The Fundamentalist Emphasis at Brigham Young University, 1935–1973." *Journal for the Scientific Study of Religion* 17 (1): 53–57.

Christensen, Harold T., and G. R. Carpenter. 1962. "Value-Behavior Discrepancies regarding Pre-marital Coitus in Three Western Cultures." *American Sociological Review* 27 (1): 66–74.

Church Education System. 1980. *Old Testament Student Manual.* 2 vols. Salt Lake City: Church of Jesus Christ of Latter-day Saints.

——. 1981. *Book of Mormon Student Manual.* Salt Lake City: Church of Jesus Christ of Latter-day Saints.

——. 1992. *Zone Administrators' Coordinator* 13 (1): 1–2.

"Church Leader Decries Mormon Fraud." 1982. *Sunstone Review* 2 (9): 10.

Clark, J. Reuben. 1938. "The Charted Course of the Church in Education." *Improvement Era* 31 (Sept.).

——. 1954. "When Are the Writings or Sermons of Church Leaders Entitled to the Claim of Scripture?" *Church News*, July 31; reprinted in *Dialogue* 12, no. 2 (1979): 68–81.

——. 1956. *Why the King James Version.* Salt Lake City: Deseret Book.

Clark, James R. 1971. *Messages of the First Presidency.* Vol. 5. Salt Lake City: Bookcraft.

——. 1975. *Messages of the First Presidency.* Vol. 6. Salt Lake City: Bookcraft.

Clayton, James L. 1986. "On the Different World of Utah: The Mormon Church." *Vital Speeches of the Day* 52:186–92.

Cline, Victor B., and J. M. Richards, Jr. 1965. "A Factor-Analytic Study of Religious Belief and Behavior." *Journal of Personality and Social Psychology* 1 (6): 569–78.

Cornwall, Marie. 1987a. "The Social Bases of Religion: A Study of Factors Influencing Religious Belief and Commitment." *Review of Religious Research* 29 (1): 44–56.

——. 1987b. "What Do We Do about the Singles Problem?" *Sunstone* 11 (3): 5–6.

——. 1990. "The Paradox of Organizations." *Sunstone* 14 (5): 44–47.

——. 1994. "The Institutional Role of Mormon Women." In *Contemporary Mormonism: Social Science Perspectives*, ed. Marie Cornwall, Tim B. Heaton, and Lawrence A. Young. Urbana: University of Illinois Press.

Cornwall, Marie, and Perry H. Cunningham. 1989. "Surveying Latter-day Saints: A Review of Methodological Issues." *Review of Religious Research* 31 (2): 162–72.

Cornwall, Marie, S. L. Albrecht, P. H. Cunningham, and B. L. Pitcher. 1986. "The Dimensions of Religiosity: A Conceptual Model and an Empirical Test." *Review of Religious Research* 27 (3): 226–34.

Cowan, Richard O. 1993. "From Footholds to Strongholds: Spreading the Gospel Worldwide." *Ensign* 23 (6): 56–61.

Crapo, Richley H. 1987. "Grass-Roots Deviance from Official Doctrine: A Study of Latter-day Saint (Mormon) Folk-Beliefs." *Journal for the Scientific Study of Religion* 26 (4): 465–85.

Croft, Q. Michael. 1985. "The Influence of the LDS Church on Utah Politics, 1945–1984." Ph.D. diss., University of Utah.

Cross, Whitney R. 1950. *The Burned Over District: The Social and Intellectual History of Enthusiastic Religion in Western New York, 1800–1850.* Ithaca, N.Y.: Cornell University Press.

Cummings, Richard J. 1982. "Quintessential Mormonism: Literal Mindedness as a Way of Life." *Dialogue* 15 (4): 92–102.

——. 1986. "Out of the Crucible: The Testimony of a Liberal." *Dialogue* 19 (2): 119–26.

D'Arc, James V. 1989. "Darryl F. Zanuck's *Brigham Young:* A Film in Context." *BYU Studies* 29 (1): 5–33.

Davies, J. Kenneth. 1963. "The Mormon Church: Its Middle Class Propensities." *Review of Religious Research* 4 (1): 84–95.

——. 1968. "The Accommodation of Mormonism and Political-Economic Reality." *Dialogue* 3 (1): 42–54.

Davis, David B. 1960. "Some Themes of Counter-subversion: An Analysis of Anti-Masonic, Anti-Catholic, and Anti-Mormon Literature." *Mississippi Valley Historical Review* 47:205–24.

Davis, James A., and Tom W. Smith. 1990. *General Social Surveys, 1972–1990.* NORC ed. Chicago: National Opinion Research Corporation.

Day, Terence L. 1988. "A Parent's Guide: Sex Education or Erotophobia?" *Sunstone* 12 (2): 8–14.

Daynes, B. W., and R. Tatlovich. 1986. "Mormons and Abortion Politics in the United States." *International Review of History and Political Science* 23 (2): 1–13.

De Azevedo, Lex. 1982. *Pop Music and Morality.* North Hollywood, Calif.: Embryo Books; Salt Lake City: Publisher's Press.

DePillis, Mario S. 1991. "The Persistence of Mormon Community into the 1990s." *Sunstone* 15 (4): 28–49.

Derr, C. Brooklyn. 1988. "Messages from Two Cultures: Mormon Leaders in France, 1985." *Dialogue* 21 (2): 98–111.

Derr, Jill M., J. R. Cannon, and M. U. Beecher. 1992. *Women of the Covenant: The Story of the Relief Society.* Salt Lake City: Deseret Book.

Deseret News. 1984. *1985 Church Almanac.* Salt Lake City: Deseret News.

——. 1990. *1991–1992 Church Almanac.* Salt Lake City: Deseret News.

Duke, James T., and Barry L. Johnson. 1992. "Religious Affiliation and Congressional Representation." *Journal for the Scientific Study of Religion* 31 (3): 324–29.

Editors of *Dialogue.* 1977. "Image-Makers: Mormons and the Media." *Dialogue* 10 (3): 12–113.

——. 1986. "A 1945 Perspective." *Dialogue* 19 (1): 35–39.

Egerton, John. 1974. *The Americanization of Dixie: The Southernization of America.* New York: Harper and Row.

Elliott, D. W. 1991. "Women, the Mormon Family, and Class Mobility: Nineteenth Century Victorian Ideology in a Twentieth Century Church." *Sunstone* 15 (6): 19–26.

Emerson, Richard. 1976. "Social Exchange Theory." *Annual Review of Sociology* 2: 335–62.

England, Eugene. 1985. " 'Lamanites' and the Spirit of the Lord." *Dialogue* 18 (4): 25–32.

England, J. Lynn. 1990. "The Importance of Programs in Our Religious Community." *Sunstone* 14 (5): 41–43.

Epperson, Steven. 1992. *Mormons and Jews: Early Mormon Theologies of Israel.* Salt Lake City: Signature Books.

Ericksen, Ephraim E. [1922] 1975. *The Psychological and Ethical Aspects of Mormon Group Life.* Salt Lake City: University of Utah Press.

Esplin, Fred C. 1977. "The Church as Broadcaster." *Dialogue* 10 (3): 25–45.

Festinger, Leon. 1957. *A Theory of Cognitive Dissonance.* Palo Alto, Calif.: Stanford University Press.

Fife, Austin E. 1940. "The Legend of the Three Nephites among the Mormons." *Journal of American Folklore* 53 (1): 1–49.

——. 1948. "Folk Belief and Mormon Cultural Autonomy." *Journal of American Folklore* 61 (1): 19–30.

Fife, Austin, and Alta Fife. [1956] 1981. *Saints of Sage and Saddle: Folklore among the Mormons.* Salt Lake City: University of Utah Press.

Finke, Roger. 1989. "Demographics of Religious Participation: An Ecological Approach." *Journal for the Scientific Study of Religion* 28 (1): 45–58.

Finke, Roger, and Rodney Stark. 1988. "Religious Economies and Sacred Canopies: Religious Mobilization in American Cities, 1906." *American Sociological Review* 53 (1): 41–49.

——. 1989. "How the Upstart Sects Won America, 1776–1850." *Journal for the Scientific Study of Religion* 28 (1): 27–44.

——. 1992. *The Churching of America, 1776–1990: Winners and Losers in Our Religious Economy.* New Brunswick, N.J.: Rutgers University Press.

Firmage, Edwin B. 1983. "Allegiance and Stewardship: Holy War, Just War, and the Mormon Tradition in the Nuclear Age." *Dialogue* 16 (1): 47–61.

——. 1989. "Restoring the Church: Zion in the Nineteenth and Twenty-first Centuries." *Sunstone* 13 (1): 33–40.

Firmage, Edwin B., and R. Collin Mangrum. 1988. *Zion in the Courts: A Legal History of the Church of Jesus Christ of Latter-day Saints, 1830–1900.* Urbana: University of Illinois Press.

First Presidency of the Church of Jesus Christ of Latter-day Saints. 1982. Letter to all stake, mission, and district presidents; bishops; and branch presidents. Jan. 5.

——. 1991. "Statement on Symposia." Letter to all priesthood leaders in the United States and Canada. Nov. 5.

Fletcher, Peggy. 1982. "A Light unto the World: Issues in Mormon Imagemaking." *Sunstone* 7 (4): 17–23.

Foster, Lawrence. 1979. "From Frontier Activism to Neo-Victorian Domesticity:

Mormon Women in the Nineteenth and Twentieth Centuries." *Journal of Mormon History* 6:3–21.
——. 1981. *Religion and Sexuality: Three American Communal Experiments of the Nineteenth Century.* New York: Oxford University Press.
Frederickson, H. G., and A. J. Stevens. 1968. "The Mormon Congressman and the Line between Church and State." *Dialogue* 3 (2): 121–29.
Furman, Frida K. 1987. *Beyond Yiddishkeit: The Struggle for Jewish Identity in a Reform Synagogue.* Albany: State University of New York Press.
Geary, Edward A. 1977. "Mormondom's Lost Generation: The Novelists of the 1940s." *BYU Studies* 18 (1): 89–107.
Gerlach, Larry R. 1982. *Blazing Crosses in Zion: The Ku Klux Klan in Utah.* Logan: Utah State University Press.
Glass, Matthew. 1993. *Citizens against the MX: Public Languages in the Nuclear Age.* Urbana: University of Illinois Press.
Glazer, Nathan, and Daniel P. Moynihan. 1970. *Beyond the Melting Pot.* 2d ed. Cambridge, Mass.: MIT Press.
Glock, Charles Y., and Rodney Stark. 1964. *Codebook for "A Study of Religion in American Life."* Produced by the Survey Research Center, University of California, Berkeley.
——. 1966. *Christian Beliefs and Anti-Semitism.* New York: Harper and Row.
Goates, L. Brent. 1985. *Harold B. Lee: Prophet, Seer, and Revelator.* Salt Lake City: Bookcraft.
Goldscheider, Calvin, and Alan S. Zuckerman. 1986. *The Transformation of the Jews.* Chicago: University of Chicago Press.
Gordon, Milton M. 1964. *Assimilation in American Life.* New York: Oxford University Press.
Gottlieb, Robert, and Peter Wiley. 1984. *America's Saints: The Rise of Mormon Power.* New York: Putnam.
Grover, Mark L. 1984. "Religious Accommodation in the Land of Racial Democracy: Mormon Priesthood and Black Brazilians." *Dialogue* 17 (3): 23–34.
——. 1990. "The Mormon Priesthood Revelation and the Sao Paulo, Brazil, Temple." *Dialogue* 23 (1): 39–54.
Gunnell, K. S., and N. T. Hoffman. 1985. "'Train Up a Child in the Way He Should Go': What Are Little Laurels Made Of?" *Sunstone* 10 (3): 34–37.
Hampshire, A. P., and J. A. Beckford. 1983. "Religious Sects and the Concept of Deviance: The Mormons and the Moonies." *British Journal of Sociology* 34 (2): 208–29.
Hansen, Klaus. 1981. *Mormonism and the American Experience.* Chicago: University of Chicago Press.
Hardy, B. Carmon. 1992. *Solemn Covenant: The Mormon Polygamous Passage.* Urbana: University of Illinois Press.
Hardy, Kenneth R. 1974. "Social Origins of American Scientists and Scholars." *Science*, Aug. 9, 497–506.
Harper, Charles L., and Bryan F. Le Beau. 1993. "The Social Adaptation of Marginal Religious Movements in America." *Sociology of Religion* 54 (2): 171–92.

Haslam, G. M. 1984. *Clash of Cultures: The Norwegian Experience with Mormonism, 1842–1920.* New York: Peter Lang.

Heaton, Tim B. 1986. "How Does Religion Influence Fertility?: The Case of the Mormons." *Journal for the Scientific Study of Religion* 25 (2): 248–58.

——. 1987a. "Four Characteristics of the Mormon Family: Contemporary Research on Chastity, Conjugality, Children, and Chauvinism." *Dialogue* 20 (2): 101–14.

——. 1987b. "Role Remodeling in the Mormon Family." *Sunstone* 11 (6): 6.

——. 1989. "Religious Influence on Mormon Fertility: Cross-national Comparisons." *Review of Religious Research* 30 (4): 401–11.

——. 1992. "Demographics of the Contemporary Mormon Family." *Dialogue* 25 (3): 19–34.

Heaton, Tim B., and Sandra Calkins. 1983. "Family Size and Contraceptive Use among Mormons, 1965–1975." *Review of Religious Research* 25 (2): 102–13.

Heaton, Tim B., and Kristen L. Goodman. 1985. "Religion and Family Formation." *Review of Religious Research* 26 (4): 343–59.

Hefner, Loretta L. 1982. "This Decade Was Different: Relief Society's Social Services Department, 1919–1929." *Dialogue* 15 (3): 64–73.

Heilman, Samuel C. 1982. "The Sociology of American Jewry: The Last Ten Years." *Annual Review of Sociology* 8:135–60.

Hicks, Michael. 1989. *Mormonism and Music: A History.* Urbana: University of Illinois Press.

Hildreth, S. A. 1982. "The First Presidency Statement on MX in Perspective." *BYU Studies* 22 (2): 215–25.

Hill, D. G., Jr. 1981. "Abortion Politics and Policy: The Beginning of Actual Human Life." *Sunstone* 6 (4): 25–27.

Hill, Marvin S. 1989. *Quest for Refuge: The Mormon Flight from American Pluralism.* Salt Lake City: Signature Books.

——. 1993. "Positivism or Subjectivism: Some Reflections on a Mormon Historical Dilemma." Presidential Address, Mormon History Association, Lamoni, Iowa, May 22.

Hinckley, Gordon B. 1988. "Our Responsibility to Our Young Women." *Ensign* 18 (9): 8–11.

Hinton, Wayne K. 1985. "Some Historical Perspectives on Mormon Responses to the Great Depression." *Journal of the West* 24 (4): 19–26.

Hoge, Dean, and David Roozen, eds. 1979. *Understanding Church Growth and Decline, 1950–1978.* New York: Pilgrim Press.

Homans, George C. 1974. *Social Behavior: Its Elementary Forms.* 2d ed. New York: Harcourt Brace.

Howard, J. R., ed. 1970. *Awakening Minorities.* Chicago: Aldine.

Huefner, D. S. 1978. "Church and Politics at the Utah IWY Conference." *Dialogue* 11 (1): 58–75.

Hutchinson, Anthony A. 1982. "LDS Approaches to the Holy Bible." *Dialogue* 15 (1): 99–124.

Iannaccone, Laurence R. 1988. "A Formal Model of Church and Sect." *American Journal of Sociology* 94 (S): 241–68.

——. 1990. "Religious Practice: A Human Capital Approach." *Journal for the Scientific Study of Religion* 29 (3): 297–314.

——. 1992. "Sacrifice and Stigma: Reducing Free Riding in Cults, Communes, and Other Collectives." *Journal of Political Economy* 100 (2): 271–92.

Iannaccone, Laurence R., and Carrie Miles. 1990. "Dealing with Social Change: The Mormon Church's Response to Change in Women's Roles." *Social Forces* 68:1231–50.

Inglesby, S. B. 1985. "Priesthood Prescriptions for Women: Aaronic Priesthood Lesson Manuals on a Woman's Place." *Sunstone* 10 (3): 28–33.

Jacob, Jeffrey C. 1989. "Explorations in Mormon Social Character: Beyond the Liahona and Iron Rod." *Dialogue* 22 (2): 44–74.

Janosik, G. E. 1951. "Political Theory of the Mormon Church." Ph.D. diss., University of Pennsylvania.

Jarvis, John C. 1991. "Mormonism in France: A Study of Cultural Exchange and Institutional Adaptation." Ph.D. diss., Washington State University.

Jenkins, Philip. 1992. *Intimate Enemies: Moral Panics in Contemporary Britain.* Hawthorne, N.Y.: Aldine de Gruyter.

Johnson, Benton. 1957. "A Critical Appraisal of the Church-Sect Typology." *American Sociological Review* 22 (1): 88–92.

——. 1963. "On Church and Sect." *American Sociological Review* 28 (4): 539–49.

——. 1971. "Church and Sect Revisited." *Journal for the Scientific Study of Religion* 10 (2): 124–51.

Johnson, F. R. 1979. "The Mormon Church as a Central Command System." *Review of Social Economics* 37 (1): 79–94.

Johnson, Martin, and Phil Mullins. 1992. "Mormonism: Catholic, Protestant, Different?" *Review of Religious Research* 34 (1): 51–62.

Jonas, F. H. 1969. "Utah the Different State." In *Politics in the American West*, ed. F. H. Jonas, 327–89. Salt Lake City: University of Utah Press.

Jones, Garth N. 1980. "Expanding LDS Church Abroad: Old Realities Compounded." *Dialogue* 13 (1): 8–22.

——. 1982. "Spreading the Gospel in Indonesia: Organizational Obstacles and Opportunities." *Dialogue* 15 (4): 79–90.

——. 1987. "Spiritual Searchings: The Church on Its International Mission." *Dialogue* 20 (2): 58–74.

Jorde, L. B. 1982. "The Genetic Structure of Utah Mormons: A Migration Analysis." *Human Biology* 54 (3): 23–32.

Kanter, Rosabeth M. 1972. *Commitment and Community: Communes and Utopias in Sociological Perspective.* Cambridge, Mass.: Harvard University Press.

Keller, Jeffrey E. 1982. "Discussion Continued: The Sequel to the Roberts/Smith/Talmage Affair." *Dialogue* 15 (1): 79–98.

——. 1985. "When Does the Spirit Enter the Body?" *Sunstone* 10 (3): 42–44.

Kelley, Dean M. 1972. *Why Conservative Churches Are Growing.* New York: Harper and Row.

Kennedy, Eugene. 1988. *Tomorrow's Catholics, Yesterday's Church: The Two Cultures of American Catholicism.* New York: Harper and Row.

Kenney, Scott. 1978. "E. E. Ericksen: Loyal Heretic." *Sunstone* 3 (5): 16–27.

——, ed. 1987. *Memories and Reflections: The Autobiography of E. E. Ericksen.* Salt Lake City: Signature Books.

Keyes, C. E. 1976. "Toward a New Formulation of the Concept of Ethnic Group." *Ethnicity* 3:202–13.

Knowlton, David. 1988. "Sticks and Stones: A Monologue on Conversation." *Sunstone* 12 (6): 41–42.

——. 1989a. "Missionaries and Terror: The Assassination of Two Elders in Bolivia." *Sunstone* 13 (4): 10–15.

——. 1989b. "Missionary, Native, and General Authority Accounts of Bolivian Conversion." *Sunstone* 13 (1): 14–20.

——. 1991. "Belief, Metaphor, and Rhetoric: The Mormon Practice of Bearing Testimonies." *Sunstone* 15 (1): 20–27.

——. 1992. "Thoughts on Mormonism in Latin America." *Dialogue* 25 (2): 41–53.

Kowalewski, Mark R. 1993. "Firmness and Accommodation: Impression Management in Institutional Roman Catholicism." *Sociology of Religion* 54 (2): 207–17.

Kurokawa, Minako, ed. 1970. *Minority Responses: Comparative Views of Reactions to Subordination.* New York: Random House.

Lambert, F. 1985. "Early Morning Seminary in Europe." *Sunstone* 10 (2): 36–37.

Lamy, Philip. 1992. "Millenialism in the Mass Media: The Case of *Soldier of Fortune* Magazine." *Journal for the Scientific Study of Religion* 31 (4): 408–24.

Larson, G. O. 1971. *The "Americanization" of Utah for Statehood.* San Marino, Calif.: Huntington Library.

Leone, Mark. 1979. *The Roots of Modern Mormonism.* Cambridge, Mass.: Harvard University Press.

Levine, S., and N. O. Lurie, eds. 1970. *The American Indian Today.* Baltimore, Md.: Penguin Books.

Lineham, Peter. 1991. "The Mormon Message in the Context of Maori Culture." *Journal of Mormon History* 17:62–93.

Logue, Larry M. 1988. *A Sermon in the Desert: Belief and Behavior in Early St. George.* Urbana: University of Illinois Press.

Lokos, Lionel. 1971. *The New Racism: Reverse Discrimination in America.* New Rochelle, N.Y.: Arlington House.

Ludlow, Daniel H., ed. 1992. *Encyclopedia of Mormonism.* 5 vols. New York: Macmillan.

Lyman, E. Leo. 1985. "The Alienation of an Apostle from His Church: The Moses Thatcher Case." *Dialogue* 18 (2): 67–91.

——. 1986. *Political Deliverance: The Mormon Quest for Utah Statehood.* Urbana: University of Illinois Press.

Lythgoe, D. L. 1968. "The Changing Image of Mormonism." *Dialogue* 3 (4): 45–58.

——. 1982. *Let 'Em Holler: A Political Biography of J. Bracken Lee.* Salt Lake City: Utah State Historical Society.

Mabey, Rendell, and Gordon T. Allred. 1984. *Brother to Brother: The Story of the Latter-day Saint Missionaries Who Took the Gospel to Africa.* Salt Lake City: Bookcraft.

McConkie, Bruce R. 1966. *Mormon Doctrine.* 2d ed. Salt Lake City: Bookcraft.

——. 1982. "The Seven Deadly Heresies." *1980 Devotional Speeches of the Year*, 74–80. Provo, Utah: Brigham Young University Press.
——. 1984. "The Bible a Sealed Book." In *Supplement to a Symposium on the New Testament*, 1–7. Salt Lake City: Church Education System, Church of Jesus Christ of Latter-day Saints.
Mackelprang, R. W. 1992. " 'And They Shall Be One Flesh': Sexuality and Contemporary Mormonism." *Dialogue* 25 (1): 49–67.
Mackey, Randall L., S. L. Swenson, A. D. Roberts, and D. A. Eagle. 1985. "*The Godmakers* Examined." *Dialogue* 18 (2): 14–39.
McMurrin, Sterling M. 1959. *The Philosophical Foundations of Mormon Theology*. Salt Lake City: University of Utah Press.
——. 1969. *The Theological Foundations of the Mormon Religion*. Salt Lake City: University of Utah Press.
——. 1979a. "A Note on the 1963 Civil Rights Statement." *Dialogue* 12 (2): 60–63.
——. 1979b. "Problems in Universalizing Mormonism." *Sunstone* 4 (5–6): 9–17.
Mangum, G. L. 1968. "The Church and Collective Bargaining in American Society." *Dialogue* 3 (2): 106–11.
Mangum, Garth L., and Bruce D. Blumell. 1993. *The Mormons' War on Poverty: A History of LDS Warfare, 1830–1990*. Salt Lake City: University of Utah Press.
Mann, D. E. 1967. "Mormon Attitudes toward the Political Roles of Church Leaders." *Dialogue* 2 (2): 32–48.
Marsden, George. 1980. *Fundamentalism and American Culture*. New York: Oxford University Press.
Martin, Thomas K., Tim B. Heaton, and Stephen J. Bahr, eds. 1986. *Utah in Demographic Perspective: Regional and National Contrasts*. Salt Lake City: Signature Books.
Marty, Martin. 1987. "It Finally All Depends on God." *Sunstone* 11 (2): 42–48.
Matthews, Robert J. 1982. "The New Publications of the Standard Works—1979, 1981." *BYU Studies* 22 (4): 387–424.
Mauss, Armand L. 1966. "Mormonism and Secular Attitudes toward Negroes." *Pacific Sociological Review* 9 (2): 91–99.
——. 1968. "Mormon Semitism and Anti-Semitism." *Sociological Analysis* 29 (Spring): 11–27.
——. 1970. "Mormonism and Minorities." Ph.D. diss., University of California, Berkeley.
——. 1971. "On Being Strangled by the Stars and Stripes: The New Left, the Old Left, and the Natural History of American Radical Movements." *Journal of Social Issues* 27 (1): 183–202.
——. 1972a. "Moderation in All Things: Political and Social Outlooks of Modern Urban Mormons." *Dialogue* 7 (1): 57–69.
——. 1972b. "Saints, Cities, and Secularism: Religious Attitudes and Behavior of Modern Urban Mormons." *Dialogue* 7 (2): 8–27.
——. 1976. " 'Shall the Youth of Zion Falter?': Mormon Youth and Sex: A Two-City Comparison." *Dialogue* 10 (2): 82–84.
——. 1981. "The Fading of the Pharoahs' Curse: The Decline and Fall of the

Priesthood Ban against Blacks in the Mormon Church." *Dialogue* 14 (3): 10–45.

——. 1983. "The Angel and the Beehive: Our Quest for Peculiarity and Struggle with Secularization." *BYU Today* 37 (Aug.): 12–15.

——. 1987. "Culture, Charisma, and Change: Reflections on Mormon Temple Worship." *Dialogue* 20 (4): 77–83.

——. 1989. "Assimilation and Ambivalence: The Mormon Reaction to Americanization." *Dialogue* 22 (1): 30–67.

——. 1990. "Mormons as Ethnics: Variable Historical and International Implications of an Appealing Concept." In *The Mormon Presence in Canada*, ed. Brigham Y. Card, Herbert C. Northcott, John E. Foster, Howard Palmer, and George K. Jarvis, 332–52. Edmonton: University of Alberta Press.

——. 1993. "Social Movements and New Religious Movements: Bridging the Literature." In *Handbook of Cults and New Religious Movements*, ed. Jeffrey K. Hadden and David G. Bromley. Greenwood, Conn.: JAI Press.

Mauss, Armand L., and Philip L. Barlow. 1991. "Church, Sect, and Scripture: The Protestant Bible and Mormon Sectarian Retrenchment." *Sociological Analysis* 52 (4): 397–414.

Mauss, Armand L., and M. Gerald Bradford. 1988. "Mormon Politics and Assimilation: Toward a Theory of Mormon Church Involvement in National U.S. Politics." In *The Politics of Religion and Social Change*, ed. Anson Shupe and Jeffrey K. Hadden, 40–66. New York: Paragon House.

Mauss, Armand L., and Jeffrey R. Franks. 1984. "Comprehensive Bibliography of Social Science Literature on the Mormons." *Review of Religious Research* 26 (1): 73–115.

Mauss, Armand L., and Dynette Ivie Reynolds. n.d. "Comprehensive Bibliography of Twentieth-Century Social Science Literature on the Mormons." Ms.

Mauss, Armand L., John R. Tarjan, and Martha D. Esplin. 1987. "The Unfettered Faithful: An Analysis of the *Dialogue* Subscribers Survey." *Dialogue* 20 (1): 27–53.

May, Dean L. 1980. "Mormons." In *Harvard Encyclopedia of American Ethnic Groups*, ed. Stephen Thernstrom, 720–31. Cambridge, Mass.: Harvard University Press.

Meinig, Donald W. 1965. "The Mormon Culture Region: Strategies and Patterns in the Geography of the American West, 1847–1964." *Annals of the Association of American Geographers* 55 (June): 191–220.

Miles, A. O. 1978. "Mormon Voting Behavior and Political Attitudes." Ph.D. diss., University of Utah.

Miller, S. D. 1985. "Thought Reform and Totalism: The Psychology of the LDS Church Missionary Training Program." *Sunstone* 10 (8): 24–29.

Millett, Robert J., ed. 1987. *To Be Learned Is Good If* . . . Salt Lake City: Deseret Book.

Moore, R. Laurence. 1986. *Religious Outsiders and the Making of Americans*. New York: Oxford University Press.

Morgan, Dale L. 1958. "The Contemporary Scene." In *Among the Mormons*, ed. William A. Mulder and A. Russell Mortensen, 467–74. New York: Alfred A. Knopf.

Morrison, Alexander B. 1990. *The Dawning of a Brighter Day: The Church in Black Africa.* Salt Lake City: Bookcraft.

Mouritsen, Dale C. 1972. *A Defense and a Refuge: Priesthood Correlation and the Establishment of Zion.* Provo: Brigham Young University Publications.

Mouw, Richard J. 1991. "Evangelical Mormonism?" *Christianity Today,* Nov. 11, 30.

Nelson, R. A. 1977. "From Antagonism to Acceptance: Mormons and the Silver Screen." *Dialogue* 10 (3): 59–69.

Nelson, R. M. 1985. "Reverence for Life." *Ensign* 15 (5): 11–14.

Nelson, Lowry. 1952. *The Mormon Village: A Pattern and Technique of Land Settlement.* Salt Lake City: University of Utah Press.

——. 1985. *In the Direction of His Dreams: Memoirs of Lowry Nelson.* New York: Philosophical Library.

Newell, L. Jackson. 1986. "An Echo from the Foothills: To Marshal the Forces of Reason." *Dialogue* 19 (1): 26–34.

Newton, Marjorie. 1991. "Almost like Us: The American Socialization of Australian Converts." *Dialogue* 24 (3): 9–20.

Nibley, Hugh. 1983. "Leaders to Managers: The Fatal Shift." *Dialogue* 16 (4): 12–21.

Niebuhr, H. Richard. 1929. *The Social Sources of Denominationalism.* New York: Holt.

Novak, Michael. 1972. *The Rise of the Unmeltable Ethnics.* New York: Macmillan.

Numano, Jiro. 1980. "How International Is the Church in Japan?" *Dialogue* 13 (1): 85–91.

O'Dea, Thomas F. 1954. "Mormonism and the Avoidance of Sectarian Stagnation: A Study of Church, Sect, and Incipient Nationality." *American Journal of Sociology* 60:285–93.

——. 1957. *The Mormons.* Chicago: University of Chicago Press.

——. 1972. "Sources of Strain in Mormon History Reconsidered." In *Mormonism and American Culture,* ed. Marvin S. Hill and James B. Allen, 147–68. New York: Harper and Row.

Oliphant, L. C. 1981. "Is There an ERA-Abortion Connection?" *Dialogue* 14 (1): 65–72.

Olson, John K., and Ann C. Beck. 1990. "Religion and Political Realignment in the Rocky Mountain States." *Journal for the Scientific Study of Religion* 29 (2): 198–209.

Oswald, Delmont. 1990. "A Lone Man in the Garden." *Dialogue* 23 (1): 139–46.

Packer, Boyd K. 1990. "The Law and the Light." In *The Book of Mormon: Jacob through the Words of Mormon,* ed. M. S. Nyman and C. D. Tate, 1–31. Provo: BYU Religious Studies Center.

Palmer, Spencer J. 1970. *The Church Encounters Asia.* Salt Lake City: Deseret Book.

——. 1978. *The Expanding Church.* Salt Lake City: Deseret Book.

Parry, Keith. 1990. "Mormons as Ethnics: A Canadian Perspective." In *The Mormon Presence in Canada,* ed. Brigham Y. Card, Herbert C. Northcott, John E. Foster, Howard Palmer, and George K. Jarvis, 353–65. Edmonton: University of Alberta Press.

Paul, Erich Robert. 1992. *Science, Religion, and Mormon Cosmology*. Urbana: University of Illinois Press.

Pearson, Roger. 1985. *An Anthropological Glossary*. Malabar, Fla.: R. E. Krieger.

Perrin, Robin D. 1989. "American Religion in the Post-Aquarian Age: Values and Demographic Factors in Church Growth and Decline." *Journal for the Scientific Study of Religion* 28 (1): 75–89.

Perrin, Robin D., and Armand L. Mauss. 1991. "Saints and Seekers: Sources of Recruitment to the Vineyard Christian Fellowship." *Review of Religious Research* 33 (2): 97–111.

Petersen, Morris. 1987. "Fossils and Scripture." *Ensign* 9:28–29.

Petersen, William. 1980. "Concepts of Ethnicity." In *Harvard Encyclopedia of American Ethnic Groups*, ed. Stephen Thernstrom, 234–42. Cambridge, Mass.: Harvard University Press.

Poll, Richard D. 1967. "What the Church Means to People like Me." *Dialogue* 2 (4): 107–17.

——. 1983. "Liahona and Iron Rod Revisited." *Dialogue* 16 (2): 69–78.

——. 1985. "The Swearing Elders: Some Reflections." *Sunstone* 10 (9): 14–17.

Poloma, Margaret, and Brian F. Pendleton. 1989. "Religious Experiences, Evangelism, and Institutional Growth in the Assemblies of God." *Journal for the Scientific Study of Religion* 28 (4): 415–31.

Priddis, Ronald, and Gary J. Bergera. 1993. *The Lord's University: Inside BYU.* Salt Lake City: Signature Books.

Quinn, D. Michael. 1983. *J. Reuben Clark: The Church Years*. Provo: Brigham Young University Press.

——. 1984. "The Mormon Church and the Spanish-American War: An End to Selective Pacifism." *Dialogue* 17 (4): 11–30.

——. 1985. "Conscientious Objectors or Christian Soldiers?: The Latter-day Saint Position on Militarism." *Sunstone* 10 (3): 15–23.

——. 1992a. "On Being a Mormon Historian (and Its Aftermath)." In *Faithful History: Essays on Writing Mormon History*, ed. George D. Smith, 69–111. Salt Lake City: Signature Books.

——. 1992b. "One Hundred Fifty Years of Truth and Consequences about Mormon History." *Sunstone* 16 (1): 12–14.

——. 1993. "Ezra Taft Benson and Mormon Political Conflicts." *Dialogue* 26 (2): 1–87.

Ramseyer, A. A. 1908. "Who Wrote the Pentateuch?" *Improvement Era* 9 (6): 437–42.

Rees, Robert A. 1991. "Bearing Our Crosses Gracefully: Sex and the Single Mormon." *Dialogue* 24 (4): 98–111.

Richardson, J. T., and S. W. Fox. 1972. "Religious Affiliation as a Predictor of Voting Behavior in Abortion Reform Legislation." *Journal for the Scientific Study of Religion* 11 (4): 347–59.

——. 1975. "Religion and Voting on Abortion Reform: A Follow-up Study." *Journal for the Scientific Study of Religion* 14 (2): 159–64.

Richardson, James T. 1984. "The 'Old Right' in Action: Mormon and Catholic Involvement in an Equal Rights Amendment Referendum." In *New Christian*

Politics, ed. David G. Bromley and Anson D. Shupe, Jr., 213–33. Macon, Ga.: Mercer University Press.

Richardson, James T., Joel Best, and David G. Bromley, eds. 1991. *The Satanism Scare*. Hawthorne, N.Y.: Aldine de Gruyter.

Roberts, B. H. 1905. "Comments on Higher Criticism." *Improvement Era* 8 (4): 358–70.

——. 1911. "Higher Criticism and the Book of Mormon." *Improvement Era* 14 (8): 667–68.

——. 1929. "The Way, the Truth, and the Life." Ms. in the archives of the Church of Jesus Christ of Latter-day Saints.

Robertson, Richard, Jerry Kramer, Mark Trahant, Andy Hall, and John Doherty. 1991. "Mormon, Inc." *Arizona Republic*, June 30-July 3.

Robson, Kent. 1983. "Omnis on the Horizon: Are We Copying Protestant Theology?" *Sunstone* 8 (4): 20–23.

Roof, W. Clark, and William McKinney. 1987. *American Mainline Religion: Its Changing Shape and Future*. New Brunswick, N.J.: Rutgers University Press.

Seidler, John, and Catherine Meyer. 1989. *Conflict and Change in the Catholic Church*. New Brunswick, N.J.: Rutgers University Press.

Servin, M. P., ed. 1970. *The Mexican Americans: An Awakening Minority*. Beverly Hills, Calif.: Glencoe Press.

Seshachari, Candadai. 1980. "Revelation: The Cohesive Element in International Mormonism." *Dialogue* 13 (4): 38–46.

Shaffir, William. 1978. "Witnessing as Identity Consolidation: The Case of the Lubavitcher Chassidim." In *Identity and Religion*, ed. Hans Mol, 39–57. Beverly Hills, Calif.: Sage Publications.

Shepherd, Gordon, and Gary Shepherd. 1984. *A Kingdom Transformed: Themes in the Development of Mormonism*. Salt Lake City: University of Utah Press.

Sherlock, Richard. 1978. "A Turbulent Spectrum: Mormon Reactions to the Darwinist Legacy." *Journal of Mormon History* 5:33–59.

——. 1979. "Faith and History: The Snell Controversy." *Dialogue* 12 (1): 27–41.

——. 1980. " 'We Can See No Advantage to a Continuation of the Discussion': The Roberts/Smith/Talmage Affair." *Dialogue* 13 (3): 63–87.

——. 1981. "Abortion Politics and Policy: A Deafening Silence in the Church." *Sunstone* 6 (4): 17–19.

Shibley, Mark A. 1991. "The Southernization of American Religion: Testing a Hypothesis." *Sociological Analysis* 52 (2): 159–74.

Shields, Steven L. 1982. *Divergent Paths of the Restoration*. 3d ed. Bountiful, Utah: Restoration Research.

Shipps, Jan B. 1967. "Utah Comes of Age Politically: A Study of the State's Politics in the Early Years of the Twentieth Century." *Utah Historical Quarterly* 35 (2): 91–111.

——. 1985. *Mormonism: The Story of a New Religious Tradition*. Urbana: University of Illinois Press.

——. 1994. "Making Saints: In the Early Days and the Latter Days." In *Contemporary Mormonism: Social Science Perspectives*, ed. Marie Cornwall, Tim B. Heaton, and Lawrence A. Young. Urbana: University of Illinois Press.

Shupe, Anson D. 1991. *The Darker Side of Virtue: Corruption, Scandal, and the Mormon Empire.* Buffalo: Prometheus Books.

Shupe, A., and J. Heinerman. 1985. "Mormonism and the New Christian Right: An Emerging Coalition?" *Review of Religious Research* 27 (2): 146–57.

Sillito, John R. 1992. "The Making of an Insurgent: Parley P. Christensen and Utah Republicanism, 1900–1912." *Utah Historical Quarterly* 60 (4): 319–34.

Sillitoe, Linda. 1990. "Off the Record: Telling the Rest of the Truth." *Sunstone* 14 (6): 12–26.

Sillitoe, Linda, and Allen D. Roberts. 1988. *Salamander: The Story of the Mormon Forgery Murders.* Salt Lake City: Signature Books.

Silva, Erin R. 1992. "Ecclesiastical Implications of Grace." *Dialogue* 25 (1): 70–85.

Sjodahl, J. M. 1929. "Some Questions Considered." *Improvement Era* 32 (4): 287–90.

Smith, Joseph, Jr. [1902] 1980. *History of the Church of Jesus Christ of Latter-day Saints.* Salt Lake City: Deseret News Press.

Smith, Joseph Fielding. 1911. "Jonah and the Bible." *The Juvenile Instructor* (July): 400–411.

Smith, Timothy L. 1980. "The Book of Mormon in a Biblical Culture." *Journal of Mormon History* 7:3–21.

Smith, Tom W. 1986. "Classifying Protestant Denominations." GSS Technical Report No. 67. Chicago: National Opinion Research Corporation.

———. 1990. "Classifying Protestant Denominations." *Review of Religious Research* 31 (3): 225–45.

Smith, Wilford E. 1959. "The Urban Threat to Mormon Norms." *Rural Sociology* 24 (4): 355–61.

———. 1976. "'Mormon Sex Standards on College Campuses'; or, Deal Us Out of the Sexual Revolution." *Dialogue* 10 (2): 76–81.

Sorenson, John L. 1983. "Mormon Folk and Mormon Elite." *Horizons* 1:4–18.

Stark, Rodney. 1984. "The Rise of a New World Faith." *Review of Religious Research* 26 (1): 18–27.

———. 1987. "How New Religions Succeed: A Theoretical Model." *The Future of New Religious Movements*, ed. David G. Bromley and Phillip E. Hammond, 11–29. Macon, Ga.: Mercer University Press.

Stark, Rodney, and William S. Bainbridge. 1985. *The Future of Religion: Secularization, Revival, and Cult Formation.* Berkeley: University of California Press.

Stark, Rodney, and Charles Y. Glock. 1968. *American Piety: The Nature of Religious Commitment.* Berkeley: University of California Press.

Stark, Rodney, and Laurence R. Iannaccone. 1991. "Sociology of Religion." In *Encyclopedia of Sociology*, ed. Edgar F. Borgatta and Marie Borgatta, 2029–37. New York: Macmillan.

Stathis, Stephen W. 1981. "Mormonism and the Periodical Press: A Change Is Underway." *Dialogue* 14 (2): 48–73.

Stathis, Stephen W., and Dennis L. Lythgoe. 1977. "Mormonism in the Nineteen-Seventies: The Popular Perception." *Dialogue* 10 (3): 95–113.

Steiner, Stan. 1968. *The New Indians.* New York: Dell.

Stump, Roger. 1984. "Regional Migration and Religious Commitment in the United States." *Journal for the Scientific Study of Religion* 23 (3): 292–303.

Swatos, William H., Jr. 1979. *Into Denominationalism: The Anglican Metamorphosis.* West Lafayette, Ind.: Society for the Scientific Study of Religion.

Swensen, Russel B. 1972. "Mormons at the University of Chicago Divinity School." *Dialogue* 7 (2): 37–47.

Taber, Susan B. 1992. "Being Mormon: The Elkton Branch, 1926–1981." *Dialogue* 25 (3): 87–112.

——. 1993. *Mormon Lives: A Year in the Elkton Ward.* Urbana: University of Illinois Press.

Tarjan, John. 1990. "Goal Displacement in the Church; or, Why Did They Carpet the Gym?" *Sunstone* 14 (1): 20–25.

——. 1992. "Heavenly Father or Chairman of the Board?: How Organizational Metaphors Can Define and Confine Religious Experience." *Dialogue* 25 (3): 36–55.

Thernstrom, Stephen, ed. 1980. *The Harvard Encyclopedia of American Ethnic Groups.* Cambridge, Mass.: Harvard University Press.

Thomas, Darwin L. 1983. "Family in the Mormon Experience." In *Families and Religions*, ed. William V. D'Antonio and Joan Aldous, 267–88. Beverly Hills, Calif.: Sage Publications.

Thompson, Brent G. 1983. "Standing between Two Fires: Mormons and Prohibition, 1908–1917." *Journal of Mormon History* 10:35–52.

Thorndike, E. L. 1943. "The Origins of Superior Men." *Scientific Monthly* 56: 424–32.

Thornton, Arland. 1979. "Religion and Fertility: The Case of Mormonism." *Journal of Marriage and the Family* 41 (1): 131–42.

Thorp, Malcolm. 1988. "James E. Talmage and the Tradition of the Victorian Lives of Jesus." *Sunstone* 12 (1): 8–13.

Toscano, Paul J. 1988. "Beyond Tyranny, beyond Arrogance." *Dialogue* 21 (1): 58–61.

——. 1993. "A Plea to the Leadership of the Church: Choose Love Not Power." *Dialogue* 26 (1): 95–106.

Troeltsch, Ernst. 1931. *The Social Teaching of the Christian Churches.* Vol. 2. New York: Macmillan.

Tullis, F. Lamond, ed. 1978. *Mormonism: A Faith for All Cultures.* Provo: Brigham Young University Press.

——. 1987. *Mormons in Mexico: The Dynamics of Faith and Culture.* Logan: Utah State University Press.

Turley, Richard E., Jr. 1992. *Victims: The LDS Church and the Mark Hofmann Case.* Urbana: University of Illinois Press.

Turner, Rodney. 1972. *Woman and the Priesthood.* Salt Lake City: Deseret Book.

Underwood, Grant. 1986. "Revisioning Mormon History." *Pacific Historical Review* 55 (3): 403–26.

Van den Berghe, Pierre L. 1981. *The Ethnic Phenomenon.* New York: Elsevier.

Van Wagenen, Lola. 1991. "In Their Own Behalf: The Politicization of Mormon Women and the 1870 Franchise." *Dialogue* 24 (4): 31–43.

Van Wagoner, Richard S. 1986. *Mormon Polygamy.* Salt Lake City: Signature Books.

Vernon, Glenn M. 1955. "An Inquiry into the Scalability of Church Orthodoxy." *Sociology and Social Research* 39:324–27.

——. 1956. "Background Factors Related to Church Orthodoxy." *Social Forces* 34:252–54.

Victor, Jeffrey S. 1993. *Satanic Panic: The Creation of a Contemporary Legend.* Peru, Ill.: Open Court Publishing.

Vogt, Evon Z., and Ethel M. Albert. 1966. *The People of Rimrock: A Study of Values in Five Cultures.* Cambridge, Mass.: Harvard University Press.

Vogt, Evon Z., and Thomas F. O'Dea. 1955. "A Comparative Study of the Role of Values in Social Action in Two Southwest Communities." *American Sociological Review* 18 (6): 645–54.

Walker, Ronald W. 1982. "Sheaves, Bucklers, and the State: Mormon Leaders Respond to the Dilemmas of War." *Sunstone* 7 (4): 43–56.

——. 1993. "Seeking the 'Remnant': The Native American during the Joseph Smith Period." *Journal of Mormon History* 19 (1): 1–33.

Webb, Robert. 1916a. "Criticism of the 'Higher Critics.'" *Improvement Era* 19 (June): 706–13.

——. 1916b. "What Is the Higher Criticism?" *Improvement Era* 19 (May): 629–36.

Welter, Barbara. 1966. "The Cult of True Womanhood: 1820–1860." *American Quarterly* 18:151–74.

White, O. Kendall. 1983. "Overt and Covert Politics: The Mormon Church's Anti-ERA Campaign in Virginia." *Virginia Social Science Journal* 18 (Winter): 11–12.

——. 1986. "A Review and Commentary on the Prospects for a Mormon/New Christian Right Coalition." *Review of Religious Research* 28 (2): 180–88.

——. 1987. *Mormon Neo-orthodoxy: A Crisis Theology.* Salt Lake City: Signature Books.

——. 1989. "Mormonism and the Equal Rights Amendment." *Journal of Church and State* 31 (2): 249–67.

Wiley, Peter. 1984–85. "The Lee Revolution and the Rise of Correlation." *Sunstone* 10 (1): 18–22.

Williams, J. D. 1966. "Separation of Church and State in Mormon Theory and Practice." *Dialogue* 1 (2): 30–54.

——. 1981. "In a Democracy, Church Interference Is Dangerous." *Sunstone* 6 (4): 36, 40–44.

Wilson, Bryan R. 1987. "Factors in the Failure of New Religious Movements." In *The Future of New Religious Movements,* ed. David G. Bromley and Phillip E. Hammond, 30–35. Macon, Ga.: Mercer University Press.

——. 1990. *The Social Dimensions of Sectarianism: Sects and New Religious Movements in Contemporary Society.* New York: Oxford University Press.

Wilson, William A. 1988. "Freeways, Parking Lots, and Ice Cream Stands: The Three Nephites in Contemporary Society." *Dialogue* 21 (3): 13–26.

Winder, L. 1980. "LDS Position on the ERA: An Historical View." *Exponent II* 6 (Winter): 6–7.

Winick, Charles. 1969. *Dictionary of American Anthropology.* New York: Greenwood Press.

Wirthlin, Richard B., and Bruce D. Merrill. 1968. "The LDS Church as a Significant Political Reference Group in Utah: 'Right to Work.'" *Dialogue* 3 (2): 129–33.

Woodworth, Warner P. 1987. "Brave New Bureaucracy." *Dialogue* 20 (3): 25–36.

——. 1990. "Third World Strategies toward Zion." *Sunstone* 14 (5): 13–23.

Woolley, Robert J. 1990. "Hearkening unto Other Voices." *Dialogue* 23 (2): 170–73.

Wooton, Richard T. 1992. *Saints and Scientists.* Mesa, Ariz.: EduTech Corp.

Wright, Stuart A. 1992. "Satanic Cults, Kidnapping, and Ritual Sacrifice: A Study of Rumor-Panic in Rural Texas." Paper presented at the annual meeting of the Society for the Scientific Study of Religion, Washington, D.C., Nov.

Yancey, W. L., E. P. Ericksen, and R. Juliani. 1976. "Emergent Ethnicity: A Review and Reformulation." *American Sociological Review* 41 (June): 391–403.

Yinger, J. Milton. 1970. *The Scientific Study of Religion.* New York: Macmillan.

Young, Lawrence A. 1990. "Being Single, Mormon, and Male." *Dialogue* 23 (1): 146–51.

Index